NOV 2 1 1973

D1266324

CONFEDERATION AND CONSTITUTION,
1781-1789

CONFEDERATION AND CONSTITUTION,

1781-1789

Edited By

FORREST MCDONALD

and

ELLEN SHAPIRO MCDONALD

DISCARDED
UNIVERSITY OF TULSA LIBRARY

University of South Carolina Press
Columbia, S.C.

University of Tulsa
McFarlin Library
Tulsa, Okla.

CONFEDERATION AND CONSTITUTION,
1781–1789

Introduction, editorial notes, and compilation copyright ©
1968 by Forrest McDonald.

Printed in the United States of America.

All rights reserved.

First edition: HARPER TORCHBOOKS, Harper & Row, Pub-
lishers, Incorporated, 49 East 33rd Street, New York, N.Y.
10016.

This edition published by the University of South Carolina
Press, Columbia, S.C., 1968, by arrangement with Harper
Torchbooks, from whom a paperback edition is available
(TB/1396).

Library of Congress Catalog Card Number: 68-65042.

Standard Book Number: 87249-126-9.

E303. 3
.C66 3
1968

Contents

PART FOUR: THE CONSTITUTIONAL CONVENTION,
MAY–SEPTEMBER 1787

PART FIVE: THE CONTEST OVER RATIFICATION,
1787–1790

CONFEDERATION AND CONSTITUTION,
1781-1789

Introduction

From the surrender of Lord Cornwallis in 1781 to the inauguration of George Washington as President in 1789, one question dominated and gave unity to events in the United States: Would this be politically one nation or not? In 1781 most Americans assumed, however vaguely, that it would be, but they were far from agreed as to the principles upon which they should establish their national government.

Reaching such agreement would not be easy, though the practical limits of choice were fairly narrow. For one thing, having disowned their king and being without a hereditary aristocracy, Americans were, by default, committed to a republican form of government. For another, being committed—by virtue of colonial charters and revolutionary constitutions, by history and tradition—to organization into thirteen distinct political entities, it followed that any union they might effect must be some sort of federal system. Furthermore, it was essential that the system preserve both the traditional "rights of Englishmen" and the newly "discovered" natural rights of man.

There were neither examples nor theories to guide them in their search for a viable plan for creating a federal union on republican principles. Such hints as there were, in history and the writings of political theorists, were discouraging. For instance, the most respected political theorist of the time, the Frenchman Charles de Secondat, Baron de Montesquieu, had taught that republics could be successfully founded only in small homogeneous areas; the United States extended over a vast expanse of territory and its people were a heterogeneous lot.

Thus it was an intellectual and political feat of no mean order that three million cantankerous Americans managed to come together as one nation under the Constitution. Elsewhere I have tried to narrate and analyze the political and economic aspects of the way they did so;[1] the central aim of this book is to illustrate the thought processes that accompanied their achievement.

Before the student embarks on these notes and documents, however, it may be advantageous to have a brief narrative of the history of the period, a brief analysis of the political theory involved— with some suggestions about its relevance to current American life —and a note on the extant documents of the period.

1. The History

For practical purposes, the United States won its war for independence without a national government: the Continental Congress, which acted as the *de facto* central authority from 1774 to 1781, had no grant of authority to sanction its existence. A pact between the thirteen rebellious states establishing such authority, the Articles of Confederation, had been drawn in 1776, shelved by the Congress itself, then revised and submitted to the states for their approval in November 1777. But the smaller and weaker states in general, and Maryland in particular, held up ratification for a variety of reasons, mainly the hope that they could extort from the larger states a share of the vast expanse of rich and unoccupied lands that the United States would obtain if they succeeded in gaining their independence. In February 1781 Maryland, the thirteenth state, ratified the Articles, and they became formally operative on March 1, 1781. Six months later, on October 17, Cornwallis surrendered to Washington at Yorktown, and the war was all but over.

Even before the Articles were ratified, almost all Americans who thought about public affairs at all were convinced that the pact was inadequate for the needs of the country. The Articles were in fact a treaty between thirteen powers, which explicitly reserved their sovereignty and independence; and the national governing body—the unicameral Congress in which each state had one vote— had neither coercive power over individuals or states nor any power to raise money through taxation. In February 1781, even before the Articles became operative, Congress asked the states to ratify an

[1] Forrest McDonald, *We The People: The Economic Origins of the Constitution* (Chicago, 1958), and *E Pluribus Unum: The Formation of the American Republic, 1781–1790* (New York, 1965).

amendment giving it power to levy a 5 per cent impost—that is, a tax on imported goods. But under the Articles, amendments had to be ratified by all thirteen states before they became effective, and Rhode Island refused to ratify. When, in November of 1782, Virginia rescinded its earlier ratification, the amendment was dead.

That precipitated a crisis. Though the war was won and preliminary articles of peace were shortly to arrive from London, the Congress had problems in abundance. Without power to tax, devoid of money or credit, and pressed by creditors on all sides, Congress faced imminent financial collapse in the winter of 1782–83. The most dangerous creditor was the army: not having received full payment in years and eager to receive the various bonuses that had been promised them, faced with the prospect of returning home paupers if payment were not forthcoming, the soldiers (and the officers in particular) threatened to obtain "justice" by force of arms if Congress did not satisfy their claims.

At the time there were in Congress, as Alexander Hamilton put it, "two classes of men," one of which was "attached to State, the other to continental politics." Those in the first group, which drew its strength mainly from Virginia, North Carolina, and New England, were ideologically oriented, more concerned with establishing government on "proper" republican principles than with creating a nation as such; they trusted local authority above national authority, and local militias over regular armies. (For classic examples of republican thinking, see Documents 16, 39, and 41.) Those in the second group, which was based mainly in New York, Pennsylvania, and South Carolina, were practically oriented, more concerned with the nation than with forms of government, and trusted central authority over local. (For classic examples of the thinking of nationalists, see Documents 3C, 29, 30, and 40.) Early in 1783 the nationalists attempted to capitalize on the crisis in Congress, the discontents of the army, and the avarice of civilian creditors, and to use these as instruments to force the establishment of a strong national government. Their efforts failed, and by summer the army had disbanded, Congress had fallen into disgrace, and nationalism had become discredited. Out of the episode came a series of proposed amendments to the Articles of Confederation, dated April 18, 1783, which would, if ratified, give Congress means of obtaining revenues adequate to meet its responsibilities. On the fate of these amendments at the hands of the state legislatures hung the fate of the whole Confederation (for this entire affair, see Documents 3A, B, and C, and the accompanying comments).

Meantime, during the ensuing four years the states went about their business—trying to cope with their needs and seeking to fulfill their hopes—pretty much on their own, without interference or aid from Congress or from one another. In broad terms, state policy was focused upon two kinds of concerns, each a by-product of the Revolution. On the one hand, there were practical problems of adjusting to independence, principally the commercial and political dislocations that ensued from disrupting ties with the British Empire. On the other were less tangible but equally important problems of reconciling the ideals of the Revolution with the realities of American society.

On the practical level, problems and solutions were as diverse as the several states, and so was the measure of success the states achieved. Massachusetts, for example, finding its economy a shambles and its government crushed by a burden of war debts, adopted a wide-ranging but entirely futile program of attempted remedies, and experienced domestic insurrection during the winter of 1786–87. Virginia, on the other hand, devised a workable, if somewhat fraudulent, commercial system that gave its tobacco plantation economy a greater measure of prosperity than had been possible inside the Empire. Rhode Island disposed of its heavy burden of war debts by the simple expedient of printing virtually worthless paper money for the purpose, and thereafter the state thrived. Generally speaking, the New England states were least successful in their experiments in independence: Massachusetts and Connecticut were almost total failures, New Hampshire and Rhode Island were reasonably prosperous but unstable. Except for New Jersey, the states from North Carolina through New York generally thrived in their newly independent status, though Pennsylvania and Maryland were plagued by bitter political struggles and some attendant instability. South Carolina, for a complex of peculiar reasons, experienced severe depression until 1786 but was prospering again by 1787 and was politically and socially stable throughout. Georgia was booming throughout the postwar years but, as a frontier state, was endangered by a threat of Indian uprisings she was not strong enough to deal with.

On the level of ideals and ideas, the record was likewise mixed.

On the whole, as the Revolution began more Americans enjoyed the blessings of liberty than was the case for any other people on earth; and yet social and political reality in America far from measured up to the ideals proclaimed in the Declaration of Independence and the Revolutionary state constitutions. Americans proclaimed that all just governments rested on the consent of the governed, but fully half the adult males were unable to vote; that freedom of conscience was among the most sacred of natural rights, yet tax-supported established churches existed in more than half the states and non-Protestants were at least partially disfranchised in virtually every state. All men were declared to be born equal, yet nearly one American in five was a Negro slave.

All these injustices and inconsistencies could not be eliminated overnight, and indeed no small part of the rhetoric of the Revolution was nothing more than rhetoric, which no one expected would be transformed into reality. Even so, most of the promises of the Revolution were taken seriously—if only because they were so often reiterated—and many of the states introduced major reforms during the postwar years. In 1783 the Massachusetts Supreme Court declared that the state constitution of 1780 had abolished slavery, and before the end of the decade several other states, even some in the South, had taken steps in that direction. In 1786 Virginia passed its celebrated act for establishing religious freedom, and by 1790 established churches were gone or soon to go in all states except Connecticut and Massachusetts. On the other hand, there was no further liberalization of the franchise during the period. Indeed, because of the excesses of virtually unchecked legislatures, there were in many quarters attacks on personal and property rights and occasional curtailments of political liberty.

Despite the impotence of Congress and the spotty record of the state governments, there was no general discontent with the state of things—certainly not as much as partisan propaganda and long-cherished myth depicted. Ardent nationalists were, it is true, able to bring about a meeting of a constitutional convention in 1787, and subsequently to effect a revolutionary change in the federal system; but it was largely a coincidental chain of circumstances, not widespread dissatisfaction or general political instability, that gave them the opportunity to do so. In 1785, commissioners from Virginia and Maryland worked out an agreement for bi-state control of navigation on the Potomac and Pokomoke rivers and Chesapeake

Bay, and proposed another local conference, this one to include Pennsylvania and Delaware, to deal with other minor interstate commercial problems in the area. A handful of nationalists in the Virginia legislature succeeded in broadening the call to include all the states to meet in a general commercial conference at Annapolis in September 1786. Delegates from only five states showed up, but under the leadership of Alexander Hamilton, James Madison, and John Dickinson, they resolved that it was futile to try to put together a general commercial agreement, and decided instead to request Congress and the several states to call a full-fledged constitutional convention to meet in Philadelphia the following May. Congress promptly shelved the resolutions: it referred them to a committee which referred them to another committee which was never appointed. On their own, the legislatures of Virginia and New Jersey then elected delegates to the proposed convention (September 1786), and by the end of December Pennsylvania and North Carolina had followed suit; but otherwise the call from Annapolis was generally ignored.

Then circumstances intervened: Shays' Rebellion broke out in Massachusetts. That insurrection went through two phases. The first came in September 1786, when large but unorganized bands of malcontents gathered and closed the courts in the southeastern, central, and western counties of the state. Concurrently, groups of the discontented met in county conventions and drew up lists of grievances, protesting particularly the high cost of court proceedings and the heavy burden of taxes that had been levied to retire Massachusetts' war debts. (The latter was especially vexing, for most of the certificates of indebtedness in the state had passed out of the hands of the soldiers and other creditors who had originally earned them, being bought up by speculators at ten and fifteen cents on the dollar.)

The second phase was more nearly an armed insurrection. In November the insurgents were organized into military companies and upwards of 2,000 of them began regular drilling, though none of them seemed quite sure what they proposed to do except drill. Exaggerated rumors of the strength and intentions of the rebels began to circulate around the country. The most widely read version of what was happening was concocted by Henry Knox of Massachusetts—devout nationalist, Congress' Superintendent of War, and onetime artillery general under Washington—and sent to Washington in a letter that, in one form or another, found its way into most American newspapers. Deliberately falsifying the facts in a deliberate effort to shock Americans into strengthening their national government, Knox wrote that there were 12,000 to 15,000 well-disciplined men under arms in western Massachusetts. They proposed to march on Boston, he said, to secure a common division of all property in Massachusetts, and then to pick up reinforcements from elsewhere in New England and spread anarchy and bloodshed the length and breadth of the land.

Knox's letter, together with the other rumors, had its effect. The rebellion itself was easily put down, in one engagement on January 25, but Governor James Bowdoin of Massachusetts added to the general alarm outside New England by sending to Congress (and the newspapers) a declaration that a state of rebellion existed in his state. At just that moment, Congress received the news that New York had finally and irrevocably rejected the revenue amendments of April 1783, and thus that Congress' own future was limited. At its wits' end, Congress voted on February 21 to ask the states to send delegates to the proposed convention in Philadelphia. Three more states, on hearing the news from Massachusetts, had already decided to do so. Five other states heeded the call from Congress, which meant that twelve states—all but Rhode Island—would be represented in the convention.

The convention began its work on May 28, 1787, and completed it on September 17. Fifty-five delegates attended at one time or another, the average attendance being thirty-five to forty. More than half the delegates were men of modest abilities, of local influence only, who would have been forgotten by history had not attendance in the convention immortalized them. The remainder, however, were men of almost unbelievable ability; and taken as a whole, the convention comprised possibly the most able group of statesmen ever gathered under one roof. With few exceptions, they were not doctrinaire or theorist in outlook, but hard-nosed, practical merchants, planters, lawyers, and men of affairs, most of whom happened also to be extremely well versed in the principles of political theory and the history of governmental institutions. Some were unabashedly there to look out after their personal interests or those of their economic or social classes, and most kept a watchful eye on the interests of their states and sections. But the guiding figures in the convention were moved, first and foremost, by the ideal of

creating a strong, viable national government, and thus to demonstrate for the ages that a society of free men could, by reason and
consent, establish a great republic that would endure.

The central question faced by the convention was whether a national government would be created. In turn, this question, like the
various problems that Congress and the states had been dealing
with, had both practical and theoretical aspects. The practical problems were those that attend the work of most legislative bodies:
managing the proceedings and making the deals and effecting the
compromises necessary to reconcile the conflicting interests and
prejudices represented. The principal conflict requiring management
was that between states with valid claims to unoccupied lands and
those which had no such claims (what Madison and most historians
describe as the conflict between "large" and "small" states over the
issue of equal representation in Congress). Other important conflicts were those between slave states and free, between agricultural
and commercial interests, between republican ideologues and men
of more practical bent. The delegates most responsible for ensuring
the success of the convention in this political sense were Roger
Sherman and Oliver Ellsworth of Connecticut, John Rutledge of
South Carolina, and—because his stately presence in the presiding
chair ensured decorous debate even on strained occasions that otherwise might have degenerated into petty bickering or even a break-up
of the convention—George Washington.

The theoretical problems were those having to do with striking
an appropriate balance between the powers of national and state governments and between legislative, executive, and judicial branches
of the national government. In considerable measure the solutions
to these questions turned on the management of the practical problems facing the convention. Otherwise, the solutions arrived at were
largely the work of James Madison, James Wilson, Gouverneur
Morris, Charles Pinckney, and Benjamin Franklin.

The convention passed through four broad phases. In the first,
which lasted from May 28 to July 25, the delegates adopted as a
basic working plan the general resolutions presented by Edmund
Randolph of Virginia (providing a three-branch national government, with representation in both branches of its bicameral legislature based on population, but with only vague and unspecified
powers); rejected the alternate plan proposed by William Paterson
of New Jersey (a three-branch national government with a uni-

cameral legislature in which each state would continue to have one vote, and with broad but enumerated powers); haggled endlessly about the appropriate basis of representation as well as the proper form for the executive and judicial branches; and finally agreed on a compromise between the two plans, representation to be based on population in the House of Representatives and to be equal by states in the Senate. In the second phase, July 25 to August 6, the convention recessed and turned its labors over to a five-man Comittee of Detail, which reduced the convention's resolutions to some semblance of coherence, added a number of features worked out privately, and emerged with a 23-clause working draft of a constitution. In the third phase, August 6 to September 12, the delegates haggled and traded over special-interest features that various individuals proposed to incorporate into the document, and renewed an almost interminable debate over the means of electing the President—a debate that was finally settled on September 6 by the adoption of the ungainly institution of the electoral college. By September 12 the rough draft of the Constitution was complete; the fourth and final phase of the convention was the work of the Committee on Style, which reduced the Constitution to its final polished form (and, incidentally, slipped in a few last-minute changes of its own). On September 17 the finished document was signed by thirty-nine of the forty-two delegates who stayed until the end. The abstainers were three arch-republicans, Edmund Randolph and George Mason of Virginia and Elbridge Gerry of Massachusetts.[2]

The convention ignored the amending procedure prescribed by the Articles of Confederation, requiring approval by the legislatures of all thirteen states. Instead, the Constitution was sent to Congress, with a request that it be passed on to the state legislatures, who in turn would be asked to submit it to popularly elected special ratifying conventions. If the conventions of nine states ratified, the Constitution would become binding on those states and they could proceed to organize a government. The other states were at liberty to join the new compact or not, as they pleased.

[2] Actually only thirty-eight signed, though the document contains thirty-nine signatures; George Read of Delaware signed for John Dickinson, who had to be absent at the end. Four other delegates—John Lansing and Robert Yates of New York and Luther Martin and John Francis Mercer of Maryland—almost certainly would have refused to sign, for they walked out on the proceedings of the convention and subsequently opposed ratification. Randolph later changed his mind and supported ratification.

A number of factors governed the attitudes that Americans took toward the proposed Constitution. Perhaps the most important was habitual ways of thinking, based largely on accessibility to transportation and communication (which, given the existing technology, were the same thing). Simply by virtue of living in one place rather than another, Americans were less or more prone to think in national as opposed to state and local terms. Even the most enlightened inhabitants of the interior regions of New England—and of the piedmont plateau and mountain country of the states from Pennsylvania southward—normally encountered information, ideas, or people from the outside world only two or three times a year. Accordingly, they thought in local terms, trusted only local government if they trusted any government at all, and tended by virtue of all the force of inertia to oppose the creation of a strong national government. People in the busier places, those in or near seaport cities and towns, had regular contact with the other states and with Europe as well, and their horizons were thus inevitably broader. (Two other considerations reinforced the voting tendencies of seaboard residents. One was that their areas generally suffered the greatest damages from the war, and thus that they were most conscious of the military advantages of a strong national government. The other was that, though country-dwellers far outnumbered those in or near cities and towns, convenience of access to polling places gave the townsfolk somewhat disproportionate voting strength. In the several elections held for delegates to state ratifying conventions, some 480,000 of the roughly 640,000 free adult males in the country did not participate—some because of disfranchisement by law, most because it was simply too much trouble to get into the towns where the polling places were.)

Otherwise, attitudes turned largely on three pivots. One was the measure of success individual states had had in coping with the problems of political independence; hence New York and North Carolina, for example, which had succeeded quite well, were strongly opposed to ratification, and Connecticut and New Jersey, which had failed abysmally, enthusiastically favored ratification. Another was a matter of ideals, ideology, principles. The Constitution—as a product of compromise and as the handiwork of men who tended to put national interest and practical concerns above ideology—violated many of the accepted principles of republican political theory, and it contained no bill of rights; and for these reasons no small number of republican ideologues who favored the establishment of a national government, on what they regarded as proper principles, opposed ratification of the Constitution. Finally, there were vested interests: of some in the *status quo*, of others in investments or occupations that would be directly and immediately benefited by the establishment of the government under the Constitution.

Five states ratified the Constitution within four months after its completion, all of them by overwhelming majorities. Ratification in three of them—Delaware, New Jersey, and Connecticut—reflected the weakness of the states, the tangible benefits that could be expected to accrue to them under the Constitution, and the resulting enthusiasm of the electorates. Ratification in Pennsylvania was largely the product of skillful propaganda and political maneuvering by friends of the Constitution, based mainly in Philadelphia. Georgia's unanimous vote for ratification was, more than anything else, the product of an impending Indian uprising.

The conventions of Massachusetts and New Hampshire came up next, in January 1788 (the times of the elections and conventions and the apportionment of delegates had been left to the state legislatures). Opposition in Massachusetts—deriving from ignorance, distrust of central authority, Shaysism, and hostility to the features of the Constitution that sanctioned slavery—was strong and widespread. After a learned and sometimes brilliant defense of the Constitution by its proponents, and no small measure of political chicanery, the Massachusetts convention ratified by the narrow margin of 187 delegates to 168. New Hampshire's convention met, found that a large majority of the delegates opposed ratification (for essentially the same reasons that the Constitution was opposed in Massachusetts), and adjourned until June, to see what the other states did in the interim.

In the interim the opposition to ratification finally got organized. The Federalists, as the friends of ratification called themselves, got the jump on their opponents, organizing their campaigns and grinding out reams of persuasive, often brilliant, propaganda in support of the Constitution.[3] After some delay the anti-Federalists, as the

---

[3] The term "propaganda" is not used here in its pejorative sense, but merely in the sense of arguments designed to sell people on the merits of an idea and a proposed course of political action. Such propaganda can be true or false, sincere or hypocritical. In the contest over the Constitution the propaganda sometimes had both false and hypocritical elements, but in the main it was sincere and aimed at truth. The most celebrated, and possibly

Federalists called opponents of ratification, became organized, established headquarters in the customs house in New York City, and began circulating such anti-ratification propaganda as the shrill manifesto of the anti-Federalist minority in Pennsylvania, the carefully reasoned *Letters from the Federal Farmer* written by Richard Henry Lee, and large quantities of writings by New York dissenters.

They also planned a strategy to prevent the adoption of the Constitution: on the plea that the Constitution would be acceptable if only it had a bill of rights and incorporated a few structural changes, they sought to have a second constitutional convention called, ostensibly to alter but in fact to destroy the work of the first. To force the calling of a second convention, they proposed to hold up ratification in five states. This task appeared to be manageable, for New Hampshire had already postponed a vote, all available information indicated that North Carolina and Rhode Island would flatly refuse to ratify, anti-Federalists in New York had a solid majority, and opposition to the Constitution was strong, if not decisive, in Virginia.

In the spring of 1788 Maryland and South Carolina ratified, as was generally expected, bringing the Federalists within one state of their nine-state goal. The Federalists in Maryland, commanding an overwhelming majority in the ratifying convention, did not bother to defend the Constitution: they let the enemies talk themselves out, then voted, 63 to 11, in favor of ratification. The debate in South Carolina was considerably more interesting, though virtually all the intelligent discussion there was on the side of ratification. The vote was better than two to one in favor.

The contest came to a climax in June, when the conventions of New Hampshire, Virginia, and New York convened. New Hampshire became the ninth state to ratify; the contest was close and spirited but scarcely reasoned or enlightened, the increased votes for the Constitution being obtained by such means as spreading rumors in the back country that an Indian invasion was imminent, though in fact no hostile Indians had been seen in the area for twenty-five years. The debate in the Virginia convention, by contrast, was one

---

the most profound, defense of the Constitution was contained in *The Federalist* papers written by John Jay, Alexander Hamilton, and James Madison. It was not, however, the most successful, for the New York voters, at whom it was primarily aimed, opposed ratification by the overwhelming popular vote of 16,000 to 6,000.

of unparalleled brilliance. Edmund Randolph (who had changed his mind since September and decided to support the Constitution, after all), Edmund Pendleton, George Wythe, James Madison, and John Marshall defended the Constitution; George Mason, William Grayson, Theodorick Bland, James Monroe, and the incomparable Patrick Henry opposed it. Henry's arguments were generally lacking in substance, but few men since the days of the Roman republic could match him in appealing to the emotions and prejudices of a popular assembly, in virtually paralyzing reason with his hypnotic oratory. After three weeks of debate, however, the Federalists carried the issue by the narrow margin of 89 votes to 79. After another long and brilliant debate—though not on a par with that in Virginia— New York's convention also ratified, 30 to 27. The anti-Federalists there went into the convention with a 46 to 19 majority, but in the face of the news from New Hampshire and Virginia and New York City's threat to secede from the state and ratify the Constitution separately, they had little choice but to capitulate.

Opponents of the Constitution had only one hope left, and that was to use the agitation for a bill of rights—which by now was fairly widespread—as a lever for calling a second convention. Even that hope was soon dashed. The first national elections were held late in 1788, Washington being the unanimous choice for President and Federalists gaining a strong preponderance in both houses of Congress. The government was duly organized in the spring of 1789 and Federalists, under the leadership of new Congressman James Madison, proposed a series of amendments to the Constitution. That action defeated, once and for all time, the movement for a second convention. Two of the proposed amendments were rejected but the other ten, collectively known as the Bill of Rights, were ratified and declared in effect in December 1791.

2. The Theory: Why Bother?

When one hears talk of the Constitution today, it is likely to be concerned with rights and liberties, not with the distribution of power within the framework of a federal republic; the language is likely to be that of Richard Henry Lee and others who opposed the Constitution, not that of Hamilton or Madison and others who defended it. On one level it makes little difference what people understand or fail to understand about the Constitution, for in its organic sense the Constitution has a resilience that enables it to live, essentially unchanged, in spite of changes in everything else or even in spite of amendments to the instrument itself.

On another level it makes a great deal of difference. The current generation of college-age Americans—whether in college or not—tends to question everything and to be impatient for results. Now it is true that these attributes mark virtually every new generation as it comes of age, but the members of the present generation are different: they are considerably more informed and generally more intelligent than their predecessors, they ask more fundamental questions and are more insistent upon getting answers, and they are less patient in waiting for results and more willing to participate in direct group action to obtain them. Furthermore, their elders are poorly equipped with answers to their questions and, what is worse, are generally unable to offer satisfactory reasons for doing things the way they do. When a young person asks of society: Why can we not do so-and-so, why must we go through cumbersome procedures to obtain what is patently good, why can we not simply get together and do what everyone agrees is right, the older generation has no answer. "That's just the way things are" never satisfied any insistent questioner.

It is for these reasons that I believe that Americans—older and younger alike—can profitably study the lives and thoughts of the Founding Fathers. About the Fathers, let it be made clear at the outset that they were not, by any definition of the term, "squares." In the first place they were, for the most part, a young band of rebels, leading a nation of young people: half of the people in the United States were under sixteen years of age and almost three quarters were under twenty-five—as opposed to a median age in the 1960's of about twenty-seven or twenty-eight. At the time of the Declaration of Independence Charles Pinckney was nineteen, Alexander Hamilton and Rufus King were twenty-one, Edmund Randolph was twenty-three, Gouverneur Morris was twenty-four, James Madison twenty-six; at the Philadelphia Convention a decade later, fifteen of the thirty-nine signers of the Constitution were still in their twenties and thirties, and nine more were just in their early forties. By and large too they were a romantic, lusty, and robust lot; almost all, even the prissy and scholarly James Wilson, enjoyed a good drink and a not-so-good woman, and their capacity for consuming these delicacies was often prodigious.

Their speculations and observations about man and society, about the best means of ensuring social justice, about entrenched power "establishments," about riots, about military service, about Negroes in a white society, and about a host of other subjects may or may not coincide with what present Americans think, but Americans can profit from studying their reflections nonetheless. More important, perhaps, is what they did and saw and thought that led them to create a government in which ways of doing things are so cumbersome, in which corruption is so common, in which the will of the people can be so readily thwarted.

When they declared their independence from the British Empire, the founders-in-charge were distrustful of bureaucratized central power, confident in the wisdom and virtue of the people, impatient to bring about the millennium. Accordingly, they established virtually no central governing authority but rather state governments that were both responsive to the will of popular majorities and capable of unfettered action. In the few American cities that existed, government was in practice scarcely distinguishable from direct democracy. After a decade of living under such a system, the Founders—most of them, anyway—learned that there was more than one form of tyranny, more than one form of government in which no person could feel secure in life, liberty, and property, or in his own personal way of pursuing happiness. Tyranny, as they came to see it, was the unchecked expression of the will of the sovereign, whether sovereignty resided in kings, lords, bureaucrats, or popular majorities. Give all power to the few, said Hamilton, and they will oppress the many. Give all power to the many, he added, and they will oppress the few.

So they devised a system in which power was not quite anywhere. In drafting the Constitution, they did not specify what power could be legitimately exercised by government, but rather proclaimed a loose definition of the means by which governmental power could be exercised. They did provide strong and energetic government, for, as Madison pointed out, in the absence of such government the weaker members of society inevitably fell victim to the stronger. But on the other hand, the governmental system they devised was marvelously irrational and inefficient. The Constitution proclaimed itself and laws passed under it to be the supreme law of the land, which is to say sovereign, but the essential quality of the American system was that within it sovereignty resided no place in particular. A vaguely defined portion resided in the national government, but that portion was loosely distributed among three branches of government which were chosen for periods of time ranging from two years to life, and at various stages of removal from the direct voice of the electorate. The presidency theoretically represented the whole people but was elected indirectly by electors, the Senate represented the states and was elected by the legislature, members of the House represented and were elected by the people of local districts, and the judicial branch represented nobody at all. Then there were the states, each having authority, within its confines, at least equal to that of the national government in all its branches, and each having its powers distributed in similarly diverse fashion. Beyond these were a variety of local governments—counties, towns, municipalities, taxing districts—whose powers were often also divided into branches. All told, there were well over a thousand governments in the United States. Thus for purposes of government the people of the United States were a plural people—every man a plural person—and the supreme law of the land was a plural law, being the combined and often contradictory expression of the various parts.

This division of every citizen into many artificial parts of himself was one of the three aspects of the genius of the American constitutional system. The second stemmed from the fact that the division and definition of power was neither static nor precise. The lines between the authority of state and national governments were unclear; the executive and legislative branches of the national government, though separate, each had a foot in the door of the other; many powers were ambiguously stated; the court structure was only outlined, Congress being left to fill in the details, and even being permitted to incorporate state courts as part of the national court system or to deprive the Supreme Court of any but the most trivial cases. This very fact—that power was ill-defined and free to shift from one place to another, as time and circumstance should dictate —made the system viable. It could live through wars and revolutions and the most profound economic, social, and technological changes the world had ever seen, and still its essence would remain the same.

The third aspect concerned the actuating principle of the governmental system. Montesquieu had taught that the proper actuating principle of a republic was virtue, the classical meaning of which was not goodness but manliness. The framers of the Constitution, being skeptical of man's virtue, designed a republic whose actuating principle would rest upon man's baser attributes. So cumbersome and inefficient was the governmental system that the people as a whole, however virtuous or wicked, could not activate it. It could be moved only through deals and demagoguery, through bribery and deceit, through logrolling and lobbying and trickery and trading, tactics that go with man's greed, vanity, love of power. And yet, in the broad range and on the average, these private tactics and motivations could operate effectively only when they were compatible with the public good, for they were braked not only by one another but by the massive inertia of society as a whole.

That's the way things are, and why.

It will perhaps be argued that in erecting a government on such principles and, the while, declaring that they were doing so in the name of the people, the Founders were being more than a little hypocritical. To this charge I expect they would reply that civilization is founded upon hypocrisy, upon pretending to be what we are not, upon the noblest pretense of all, that man is not a mere animal.

It will also be argued, perhaps, that their lack of faith in the people might have been justified in the eighteenth century but has no merit in these enlightened times, though no one who has seriously studied the popular discussion of public issues in the United States of the 1780's would advance such an argument. The Founders believed that government must rest ultimately on popular consent, but that those portions of government that were closest to the people (however enlightened) were and always would be the most corrupt and the most tyrannical. So far, history has confirmed their judgment. As to corruption, the branch of government furthest removed from the people, the Supreme Court, has rendered many an unpopular decision but it has been almost entirely free of any hint of corruption; the next most removed branch, the presidency, has rarely been infested with corruption; the Senate and House have been a bit more so, the state governments far more so, and so on down to county commissioners, city councils, local schoolboards, and ward and precinct officials. As to tyranny, we have in recent years had abundant opportunity to observe the results of the unchecked will of the majority in various portions of the United

States: in a hundred rural counties in Mississippi and Alabama, and in all or parts of Little Rock, Bogalusa, Birmingham, Berkeley, Detroit. When the people speak as one man, he who would be different or think different thoughts or utter different words is safe in neither property, nor liberty, nor even life. His only options are to move, to drop out, or to be crushed.

3. The Documents

Primary source materials for the history of the period covered by this book are abundant and, thanks to modern techniques of reproduction, are becoming generally and cheaply available. A huge volume of state and local governmental records is preserved in the archives of the thirteen original states, and virtually all these records have been microfilmed by the Library of Congress, from which copies may be purchased. The records of the Continental Congress, from 1774 to 1789, have been published in a 34-volume collection, and have been supplemented by Edmund C. Burnett's 8-volume edition of all the known letters of members of the Congress. Records of the army and the various departments that Congress established from time to time are preserved in the National Archives.

The files of extant newspapers for the period are also copious, though they are not, of course, as voluminous as governmental records. The best collections of newspapers are in the American Antiquarian Society (Worcester, Mass.), the Library of Congress, the New York Public Library, the Pennsylvania Historical Society, and the Boston Public Library. Every known copy of every American newspaper printed before 1820 has been photographed and made available on microcards. All the known pamphlets and books published during the same period are in process of being so photographed. In the meantime, good collections exist in the institutions named above; the best such collection is probably that in the John Carter Brown Library, Providence, R.I.

The letters and other papers of two or three dozen of the Founding Fathers have been gathered and published, and those of Washington, Jefferson, Hamilton, Jay, John Adams, and Madison are currently being edited and published in more complete and more accurate editions. The personal and public papers of scores of lesser figures are preserved in manuscript form in the Library of Congress and in the state historical societies of the original states and of Maine, Vermont, West Virginia, and Wisconsin.

Of greatest interest and value to the general student and general reader are the records of the Philadelphia Convention and of the contest over ratification of the Constitution. The records of the convention, unfortunately, are limited. The convention's official secretary, Major William Jackson, kept a journal of the proceedings, and several delegates kept notes; but the convention resolved at the outset that everything said and done, except for the final product, should remain secret. The first major violations of the agreement came in 1819 and 1821, when the official journal and the notes kept by delegate Robert Yates of New York were published. These documents did not tell a great deal: the journal contained a record of the votes and formal proceedings but none of the debates; Yates's notes were reasonably full abridgments of the debates, but extended only until July 5, just before Yates left the convention. It was widely known that Madison had kept a fairly full account of the debates, but he refused to reveal their contents. He did, however, provide in his will that his notes should be published after all the delegates were dead. As it happened, Madison himself was the last to die, and his notes were published four years later, in 1840. Thereafter, fragmentary notes—kept by Hamilton, James Mc-Henry of Maryland, Rufus King of Massachusetts, William Paterson of New Jersey, and a few others—gradually came to light. All these were published by Congress in a 5-volume edition as *Documentary History of the Constitution of the United States of America* (Washington, D.C., 1894–1905).

The more or less definitive edition of the records was edited by Max Farrand and published in three volumes in 1911, and republished, with enough additional material to add a fourth volume, in 1937. Farrand's edition contained all the known journals and notes of the convention and all other records that throw any direct contemporary light on the subject. Only one important document has turned up since, a brief journal kept by the New York delegate John Lansing, edited by J. R. Strayer and published in New York in 1939 under the title, *The Delegate from New York.*

Of the voluminous debates on ratification, in the press and in the ratifying conventions, only a small portion have been gathered and published. The fullest available account of the debates in the ratifying conventions is the unreliable 5-volume collection edited by

Jonathan Elliott and published in several editions between the 1830's and 1890's. *The Federalist* papers, written in defense of the Constitution, are available in many editions, but relatively little of the other material written either for or against the Constitution is generally available. The principal exception to this generalization is that much of the public debate in Pennsylvania is reproduced in John Bach McMaster and Frederick Stone, eds., *Pennsylvania and the Federal Constitution* (Philadelphia, 1888). Forthcoming is a projected 12-volume documentary history of the contest over ratification, now being edited by Robert E. Cushman.

In selecting and arranging the documents for the present work, I have been guided by two principal criteria. The first is that the great majority of the documents, though not quite all, are relevant to what I regard as the central theme of the history of the period— the grand question, whether there would be a national government, and the subsidiary questions, how powers could best be arranged so as to protect the life, liberty, and property of all Americans. The second is that the documents are so arranged that, as far as possible, they flow from one another with some measure of continuity of narrative. To that end, the running headnotes are devised in a somewhat unconventional form: instead of merely identifying the document and explaining its background, they are intended to provide a narrative thread connecting all the documents.

F. McD.

PART ONE:

The American Confederation in War and Peace, 1781-1783

1. The Articles of Confederation, 1781

The first "constitution" of the United States was the Articles of Confederation, drafted in November 1777, ratified in February 1781, and officially instituted on March 1, 1781. Cast in the form of a treaty between sovereign powers, the Articles created an alliance and "league of friendship," not a national government. The document vested considerable responsibility—but virtually no power independent of the member states—in a unicameral Congress in which each state had one vote:

"Articles of Confederation and perpetual Union between the states of Newhampshire, Massachusetts-bay, Rhode-island and Providence Plantations, Connecticut, New-York, New-Jersey, Pennsylvania, Delaware, Maryland, Virginia, North-Carolina, South-Carolina and Georgia."

Article I. The Stile of this confederacy shall be "The United States of America."

Article II. Each state retains its sovereignty, freedom, and independence, and every Power, Jurisdiction and right, which is not by this confederation expressly delegated to the United States, in Congress assembled.

Article III. The said states hereby severally enter into a firm league of friendship with each other, for their common defence, the security of their Liberties, and their mutual and general welfare, binding themselves to assist each other, against all force offered to,

SOURCE: *Journals of the Continental Congress* (34 vols., Washington, D.C., 1904–1937), XIX, 214ff.

or attacks made upon them, on account of religion, sovereignty, trade, or any other pretence whatever.

Article IV. The better to secure and perpetuate mutual friendship and intercourse among the people of the different states in this union, the free inhabitants of each of these states, paupers, vagabonds and fugitives from justice excepted, shall be entitled to all privileges and immunities of free citizens in the several states; and the people of each state shall have free ingress and regress to and from any other state, and shall enjoy therein all the privileges of trade and commerce, subject to the same duties, impositions, and restrictions as the inhabitants thereof respectively, provided that such restriction shall not extend so far as to prevent the removal of property imported into any state, to any other state, of which the Owner is an inhabitant; provided also that no imposition, duties or restriction shall be laid by any state, on the property of the united states, or either of them.

If any Person guilty of, or charged with, treason, felony, or other high misdemeanor in any state, shall flee from Justice, and be found in any of the united states, he shall, upon demand of the Governor or executive power, of the state from which he fled, be delivered up and removed to the state having jurisdiction of his offence.

Full faith and credit shall be given in each of these states to the records, acts and judicial proceedings of the courts and magistrates of every other state.

Article V. For the more convenient management of the general interests of the united states, delegates shall be annually appointed, in such manner as the legislature of each state shall direct, to meet in Congress on the first Monday in November, in every year, with a power reserved to each state, to recal its delegates, or any of them, at any time within the year, and to send others in their stead, for the remainder of the Year.

No state shall be represented in Congress by less than two, nor by more than seven Members; and no person shall be capable of being a delegate for more than three years in any term of six years; nor shall any person, being a delegate, be capable of holding any office under the united states, for which he, or another for his benefit, receives any salary, fees or emolument of any kind.

Each state shall maintain its own delegates in a meeting of the states, and while they act as members of the committee of the states.

In determining questions in the united states in Congress assembled, each state shall have one vote.

Freedom of speech and debate in Congress shall not be impeached or questioned in any Court, or place out of Congress, and the members of congress shall be protected in their persons from arrests and imprisonments, during the time of their going to and from, and attendance on congress, except for treason, felony, or breach of the peace.

Article VI. No state, without the Consent of the united states in congress assembled, shall send any embassy to, or receive any embassy from, or enter into any conference, agreement, alliance or treaty with any King, prince, or state; nor shall any person holding any office of profit or trust under the united states, or any of them, accept of any present, emolument, office or title of any kind whatever from any king, prince or foreign state; nor shall the united states in congress assembled, or any of them, grant any title of nobility.

No two or more states shall enter into any treaty, confederation, or alliance whatever between them, without the consent of the united states in congress assembled, specifying accurately the purposes for which the same is to be entered into, and how long it shall continue.

No state shall lay any imposts or duties, which may interfere with any stipulations in treaties, entered into by the united states in congress assembled, with any king, prince or state, in pursuance of any treaties already proposed by congress, to the courts of France and Spain.

No vessels of war shall be kept up in time of peace by any state, except such number only, as shall be deemed necessary by the united states in congress assembled, for the defence of such state, or its trade; nor shall any body of forces be kept up by any state, in time of peace, except such number only, as in the judgment of the united states, in congress assembled, shall be deemed requisite to garrison the forts necessary for the defence of such state; but every state shall always keep up a well regulated and disciplined militia, sufficiently armed and accoutred, and shall provide and constantly have ready for use, in public stores, a due number of field pieces and tents, and a proper quantity of arms, ammunition and camp equipage.

No state shall engage in any war without the consent of the united states in congress assembled, unless such state be actually invaded by enemies, or shall have received certain advice of a resolution being formed by some nation of Indians to invade such state, and the danger is so imminent as not to admit of a delay till the united states in congress assembled can be consulted: nor shall any state grant commissions to any ships or vessels of war, nor letters of marque or reprisal, except it be after a declaration of war by the united states in congress assembled, and then only against the kingdom or state and the subjects thereof, against which war has been so declared, and under such regulations as shall be established by the united states in congress assembled, unless such state be infested by pirates, in which case vessels of war may be fitted out for that occasion, and kept so long as the danger shall continue, or until the united states in congress assembled, shall determine otherwise.

Article VII. When land-forces are raised by any state for the common defence, all officers of or under the rank of colonel, shall be appointed by the legislature of each state respectively, by whom such forces shall be raised, or in such manner as such state shall direct, and all vacancies shall be filled up by the State which first made the appointment.

Article VIII. All charges of war, and all other expences that shall be incurred for the common defence or general welfare, and allowed by the united states in congress assembled, shall be defrayed out of a common treasury, which shall be supplied by the several states in proportion to the value of all land within each state, granted to or surveyed for any Person, as such land and the buildings and improvements thereon shall be estimated according to such mode as the united states in congress assembled, shall from time to time direct and appoint. The taxes for paying that proportion shall be laid and levied by the authority and direction of the legislatures of the several states within the time agreed upon by the united states in congress assembled.

Article IX. The united states in congress assembled, shall have the sole and exclusive right and power of determining on peace and war, except in the cases mentioned in the sixth article—of sending and receiving ambassadors—entering into treaties and alliances, provided that no treaty of commerce shall be made whereby the legislative power of the respective states shall be restrained from imposing such imposts and duties on foreigners as their own people are subjected to, or from prohibiting the exportation or importation of any species of goods or commodities whatsoever—of establishing rules for deciding in all cases, what captures on land or water shall be legal, and in what manner prizes taken by land or naval forces in the service of the united states shall be divided or appropriated —of granting letters of marque and reprisal in times of peace—appointing courts for the trial of piracies and felonies committed on the high seas and establishing courts for receiving and determining finally appeals in all cases of captures, provided that no member of congress shall be appointed a judge of any of the said courts.

The united states in congress assembled shall also be the last resort on appeal in all disputes and differences now subsisting or that hereafter may arise between two or more states concerning boundary, jurisdiction or any other cause whatever; which authority shall always be exercised in the manner following. Whenever the legislative or executive authority or lawful agent of any state in controversy with another shall present a petition to congress stating the matter in question and praying for a hearing, notice thereof shall be given by order of congress to the legislative or executive authority of the other state in controversy, and a day assigned for the appearance of the parties by their lawful agents, who shall then be directed to appoint by joint consent, commissioners or judges to constitute a court for hearing and determining the matter in question; but if they cannot agree, congress shall name three persons out of each of the united states, and from the list of such persons each party shall alternately strike out one, the petitioners beginning, until the number shall be reduced to thirteen; and from that number not less than seven, nor more than nine names as congress shall direct, shall in the presence of congress be drawn out by lot, and the persons whose names shall be so drawn or any five of them, shall be commissioners or judges, to hear and finally determine the controversy, so always as a major part of the judges who shall hear the cause shall agree in the determination: and if either party shall neglect to attend at the day appointed, without showing reasons, which congress shall judge sufficient, or being present shall refuse to strike, the congress shall proceed to nominate three persons out of each state, and the secretary of congress shall strike in behalf of such party absent or refusing; and the judgment and sentence of the court to be appointed, in the manner before prescribed, shall be final and conclusive; and if any of the parties shall refuse to submit to the authority of such court, or to appear or defend their claim or cause, the court shall nevertheless proceed to pronounce sentence, or judgment, which shall in like manner be final and decisive, the judgment or sentence and other proceedings being in either case transmitted to congress, and lodged among the acts of congress for the security of the parties concerned: provided that every commissioner, before he sits in judgment, shall take an oath to be administered by one of the judges of the supreme or superior court of the state, where the cause shall be tried, "well and truly to hear and determine the matter in question, according to the best of his judgment, without favour, affection or hope of reward:" provided also, that no state shall be deprived of territory for the benefit of the united states.

All controversies concerning the private right of soil claimed under different grants of two or more states, whose jurisdictions as they may respect such lands, and the states which passed such grants are adjusted, the said grants or either of them being at the same time claimed to have originated antecedent to such settlement of jurisdiction, shall on the petition of either party to the congress of the united states, be finally determined as near as may be in the same manner as is before prescribed for deciding disputes respecting territorial jurisdiction between different states.

The united states in congress assembled shall also have the sole and exclusive right and power of regulating the alloy and value of coin struck by their own authority, or by that of the respective states —fixing the standard of weights and measures throughout the united states—regulating the trade and managing all affairs with the Indians, not members of any of the states, provided that the legislative right of any state within its own limits be not infringed or violated—establishing or regulating post-offices from one state to another, throughout all the united states, and exacting such postage on the papers passing thro' the same as may be requisite to defray the expences of the said office—appointing all officers of the land forces, in the service of the united states, excepting regimental officers—appointing all the officers of the naval forces, and commissioning all officers whatever in the service of the united states—making rules for the government and regulation of the said land and naval forces, and directing their operations.

The united states in congress assembled shall have authority to appoint a committee, to sit in the recess of congress, to be denominated "A Committee of the States," and to consist of one delegate from each state; and to appoint such other committees and civil officers as may be necessary for managing the general affairs of the united states under their direction—to appoint one of their number to preside, provided that no person be allowed to serve in the office of president more than one year in any term of three years; to ascertain the necessary sums of money to be raised for the service of the united states, and to appropriate and apply the same for defraying the public expences—to borrow money, or emit bills on the credit of the united states, transmitting every half year to the respective states an account of the sums of money so borrowed or emitted,—to build and equip a navy—to agree upon the number of land forces, and to make requisitions from each state for its quota, in proportion to the number of white inhabitants in such state; which requisition shall be binding, and thereupon the legislature of each state shall appoint the regimental officers, raise the men and cloath, arm and equip them in a soldier-like manner, at the expence of the united states; and the officers and men so cloathed, armed and equipped shall march to the place appointed, and within the time agreed on by the united states in congress assembled: But if the united states in congress assembled shall, on consideration of circumstances, judge proper that any state should not raise men, or should raise a smaller number than its quota, and that any other state should raise a greater number of men than the quota thereof, such extra number shall be raised, officered, cloathed, armed and equipped in the same manner as the quota of such state, unless the legislature of such state shall judge that such extra number cannot be safely spared out of the same, in which case they shall raise officer, cloath, arm and equip as many of such extra number as they judge can be safely spared. And the officers and men so cloathed, armed and equipped, shall march to the place appointed, and within the time agreed on by the united states in congress assembled.

The united states in congress assembled shall never engage in a war, nor grant letters of marque and reprisal in time of peace, nor enter into any treaties or alliances, nor coin money, nor regulate the value thereof, nor ascertain the sums and expences necessary for the defence and welfare of the united states, or any of them, nor emit bills, nor borrow money on the credit of the united states, nor appropriate money, nor agree upon the number of vessels of war, to be built or purchased, or the number of land or sea forces to be raised, nor appoint a commander in chief of the army or navy, unless nine states assent to the same: nor shall a question on any other point, except for adjourning from day to day be determined, unless by the votes of a majority of the united states in congress assembled.

The congress of the united states shall have power to adjourn to any time within the year, and to any place within the united states, so that no period of adjournment be for a longer duration than the space of six Months, and shall publish the Journal of their proceedings monthly, except such parts thereof relating to treaties, alliances or military operations, as in their judgment require secrecy; and the yeas and nays of the delegates of each state on any question shall be entered on the Journal, when it is desired by any delegate; and the delegates of a state, or any of them, at his or their request shall be furnished with a transcript of the said Journal, except such parts as are above excepted, to lay before the legislatures of the several states.

Article X. The committee of the states, or any nine of them, shall be authorized to execute, in the recess of congress, such of the powers of congress as the united states in congress assembled, by the consent of nine states, shall from time to time think expedient to vest them with; provided that no power be delegated to the said committee, for the exercise of which, by the articles of confederation, the voice of nine states in the congress of the united states assembled is requisite.

Article XI. Canada acceding to this confederation, and joining in the measures of the united states, shall be admitted into, and entitled to all the advantages of this union: but no other colony shall be admitted into the same, unless such admission be agreed to by nine states.

Article XII. All bills of credit emitted, monies borrowed and debts contracted by, or under the authority of congress, before the assembling of the united states, in pursuance of the present confederation, shall be deemed and considered as a charge against the united states, for payment and satisfaction whereof the said united states, and the public faith are hereby solemnly pledged.

Article XIII. Every state shall abide by the determinations of the united states in congress assembled, on all questions which by this confederation are submitted to them. And the Articles of this confederation shall be inviolably observed by every state, and the union shall be perpetual; nor shall any alteration at any time hereafter be made in any of them; unless such alteration be agreed to in a congress of the united states, and be afterwards confirmed by the legislatures of every state.

And Whereas it hath pleased the Great Governor of the World to incline the hearts of the legislatures we respectively represent in congress, to approve of, and to authorize us to ratify the said articles of confederation and perpetual union. Know Ye that we the undersigned delegates, by virtue of the power and authority to us given for that purpose, do by these presents, in the name and in behalf of our respective constituents, fully and entirely ratify and confirm each and every of the said articles of confederation and perpetual union, and all and singular the matters and things therein contained: And we do further solemnly plight and engage the faith of our respective constituents, that they shall abide by the determinations of the united states in congress assembled, on all questions, which by the said confederation are submitted to them. And that the articles thereof shall be inviolably observed by the states we respectively represent, and that the union shall be perpetual.

In Witness whereof we have hereunto set our hands in Congress. Done at Philadelphia in the state of Pennsylvania the ninth day of July, in the Year of our Lord one Thousand seven Hundred and Seventy-eight, and in the third year of the independence of America.

2. Treaty of Peace between the United States and Great Britain, 1782–1783

Even as the Articles were being ratified, they were found wanting, and the American cause almost collapsed for lack of government revenues. The states proved unable or unwilling to comply with the requisitions levied by Congress, and Congress was sorely pressed to keep the armies in the field. Indeed on January 1, 1781, soldiers of the Pennsylvania line mutinied and others threatened to do likewise. Congress responded by proposing an amendment to the Articles, authorizing Congress to levy a 5 per cent duty on imports. Most states quickly ratified, but Rhode Island stubbornly refused. Congress kept the army together, however,

SOURCE: Samuel F. Bemis, *The Diplomacy of the American Revolution* (New York, 1935), 259ff.

through promises of future benefits and through the financial wizardry of Superintendent of Finance Robert Morris, a Philadelphia merchant; and in October 1781, the British army under Cornwallis surrendered to General Washington at Yorktown. Thirteen months later (November 30, 1782) American and British negotiators signed preliminary articles of peace (finalized, without change, as the Definitive Articles of Peace, on September 3, 1783):

[Article 1 recognizes the independence of the United States.]

[Article 2 defines the boundaries of the United States: the Atlantic on the east, the Mississippi on the west, approximately the present boundary on the north, and the 31st parallel—which excluded Florida and New Orleans—on the south.]

ARTICLE 3

It is agreed that the People of the United States shall continue to enjoy unmolested the Right to take Fish of every kind on the Grand Bank and on all the other Banks of New-foundland, also in the Gulph of St. Lawrence, and at all other Places in the Sea where the Inhabitants of both Countries used at any time heretofore to fish. And also that the Inhabitants of the United States shall have Liberty to take Fish of every Kind on such Part of the Coast of New-foundland as British Fishermen shall use, (but not to dry or cure the same on that Island) And also on the Coasts Bays & Creeks of all other of his Britannic Majesty's Dominions in America, and that the American Fishermen shall have Liberty to dry and cure Fish in any of the unsettled Bays Harbours and Creeks of Nova Scotia, Magdalen Islands, and Labrador, so long as the same shall remain unsettled but so soon as the same or either of them shall be settled, it shall not be lawful for the said Fishermen to dry or cure Fish at such Settlement, without a previous Agreement for that purpose with the Inhabitants, Proprietors or Possessors of the Ground.

ARTICLE 4

It is agreed that Creditors on either Side shall meet with no lawful Impediment to the Recovery of the full Value in Sterling Money of all bona fide Debts heretofore contracted.

ARTICLE 5

It is agreed that the Congress shall earnestly recommend it to the Legislatures of the respective States to provide for the Restitution of all Estates, Rights and Properties which have been confiscated belonging to real British Subjects; and also of the Estates Rights and Properties of Persons resident in Districts in the Possession of his Majesty's Arms, and have not borne Arms against the said United States. And that Persons of any other Description shall have free Liberty to go to any Part or Parts of any of the thirteen United States and therein to remain twelve Months unmolested in their Endeavours to obtain the Restitution of such of their Estates Rights & Properties as may have been confiscated. And that Congress shall also earnestly recommend to the several States, a Reconsideration and Revision of all Acts or Laws regarding the Premises, so as to render the said Laws or Acts perfectly consistent, not only with Justice and Equity, but with that Spirit of Conciliation, which, on the Return of the Blessings of Peace should universally prevail. And that Congress shall also earnestly recommend to the several States, that the Estates, Rights and Properties of such last mentioned Persons shall be restored to them, they refunding to any Persons who may be now in Possession, the Bona fide Price (where any has been given) which such Persons may have paid on purchasing any of the said Lands, Rights or Properties, since the Confiscation.

And it is agreed that all Persons who have any Interest in confiscated Lands, either by Debts, Marriage Settlements, or otherwise, shall meet with no lawful Impediment in the Prosecution of their just Rights.

Article 6

That there shall be no future Confiscations made nor any Prosecutions commenc'd against any Person or Persons for or by Reason of the Part, which he or they may have taken in the present War, and that no Person shall on that Account suffer any future Loss or Damage, either in his Person Liberty or Property; and that those who may be in Confinement on such Charges at the Time of the Ratification of the Treaty in America shall be immediately set at Liberty, and the Prosecutions so commenced be discontinued.

Article 7

There shall be a firm and perpetual Peace between his Britannic Majesty and the said States and between the Subjects of the one, and the Citizens of the other, wherefore all Hostilities both by Sea and Land shall from henceforth cease: All Prisoners on both Sides shall be set at Liberty, and his Britannic Majesty shall with all convenient speed, and without causing any Destruction, or carrying away any Negroes or other Property of the American Inhabitants, withdraw all his Armies, Garrisons & Fleets from the said United States, and from every Port, Place and Harbour within the same; leaving in all Fortifications the American Artillery that may be therein: And shall also Order & cause all Archives, Records, Deeds & Papers belonging to any of the said States, or their Citizens, which in the Course of the War may have fallen into the Hands of his Officers, to be forthwith restored and deliver'd to the proper States and Persons to whom they belong.

ARTICLE 8

The Navigation of the River Mississippi, from its source to the Ocean shall for ever remain free and open to the Subjects of Great Britain and the Citizens of the United States.

ARTICLE 9

In Case it should so happen that any Place or Territory belonging to great Britain or to the United States should have been conquer'd by the Arms of either from the other before the Arrival of the said Provisional Articles in America it is agreed that the same shall be restored without Difficulty and without requiring any Compensation.

ARTICLE 10

The solemn Ratifications of the present Treaty expedited in good & due Form shall be exchanged between the contracting Parties in the Space of Six Months or sooner if possible to be computed from the Day of the Signature of the present Treaty. In Witness whereof we the undersigned their Ministers Plenipotentiary have in their Name and in Virtue of our Full Powers signed with our Hands the present Definitive Treaty, and caused the Seals of our Arms to be affix'd thereto.

3. The Crisis at Newburgh and Its Aftermath (1783)

The successful conclusion of the war did not end the problems of Congress. It had huge debts, and public creditors, civilian as well as military, were clamoring for payment. Rumblings of revolt were heard from the army. When hopes for an independent revenue through the impost amendment were dashed in November 1782—Rhode Island continued to hold out and Virginia rescinded its ratification—Congress faced a major crisis. In December the army, encamped at Newburgh, New York, sent a deputation to petition Congress for a satisfactory settlement of accounts with the officers. A group of dedicated nationalists in Congress attempted to employ "the terror of a mutinying army" to force Congress to adopt, and the states to ratify, amendments that would give Congress a taxing power—thus enabling it to meet immediate needs and, in time, to evolve into a genuine national government. The civilian creditors would see to the latter; as the brilliant New York aristocrat Gouverneur Morris (close associate but no kin of Robert Morris) wrote to General Henry Knox, outlining the scheme, "after you have carried the post the public creditors will garrison it for you."

A. Proceedings of Congress, January 25, 1783

For a time it appeared that the effort might succeed, as the following extract from the proceedings of Congress indicates:

By the United States in Congress assembled,
January 25, 1783

The grand committee consisting of a member from each State, report, "That they have considered the contents of a memorial presented by the army and find that they comprehend five different articles.

1st. Present pay.

2d. A settlement of accounts of the Arreareages of pay and security for what is due.

3d. A commutation of the half-pay allowed by different resolutions of Congress for an equivalent in gross.

SOURCE: John C. Fitzpatrick, ed., *The Writings of George Washington* (39 vols., Washington, D.C., 1931–1944), XXVI, 221–222.

4th. A settlement of the accounts of deficiencies of rations and compensation.

5th. A settlement of the accounts of deficiencies of clothing and compensation:"

Whereupon, Resolved, As to the first, that the Superintendant of finance be directed conformable to the measures already taken for that purpose, as soon as the state of the public finances will permit, to make such payment and in such manner as he shall think proper, till the further order of Congress.

Resolved, With respect to the second article, so far as relates to the settlement of accounts, that the several states be called upon to complete without delay, the settlements with their respective lines of the army, up to the first day of August, 1780, and that the Superintendant of finance be directed to take such measures as shall appear to him proper for effecting the settlement from that period.

As to what relates to the providing security for what shall be found due on such settlement.

Resolved, That the troops of the United States in common with all creditors of the same have an undoubted right to expect such security; and that Congress will make every effort in their power to obtain from the respective states substantial funds, adequate to the object of funding the whole debt of the United States, and will enter upon an immediate and full consideration of the nature of such funds, and the most likely mode of obtaining them.

Ordered that the remainder of the report be referred to a committee of five.

But the scheme could not succeed, for Congress could not act swiftly enough to suit the discontented officers. Early in March, stimulated by a pair of seditious addresses (written by Major John Armstrong, Jr., and circulated anonymously from the tent of General Horatio Gates), the officers proposed to join in armed defiance of Congress if their demands were not immediately satisfied. Washington was able to prevent the rebellion, but the narrowness of escape from mutiny, and the continued bad mood of the officers, dissuaded nationalists from any further attempts at employing the army for political purposes.

B. The Commutation of Half Pay (1783)

Congress, for its part, reacted to the news of the near mutiny with an action that would have vast repercussions, including the discrediting of

SOURCE: Journals of the Continental Congress, XXIV, 207ff.

both the army and the Congress itself. In 1780, to head off wholesale desertion by officers, Congress had promised a bonus of half pay for life for all officers who would serve until the end of the war. The officers' deputation of December 1782 had asked that that bonus be commuted to a lump-sum payment. The resolutions of January 25 had avoided the issue. Now, in the wake of the troubles at Newburgh, Congress adopted the following resolution (March 22, 1783):

Whereas the officers of the several lines under the immediate command of His Excellency General Washington did, by their late memorial transmitted by their committee, represent to Congress that the half pay granted by sundry resolutions was regarded in an unfavourable light by the citizens of some of these states, who would prefer a compensation for a limited term of years, or by a sum in gross, to an establishment for life; and did on that account solicit a commutation of their half pay for an equivalent in one of the two modes above-mentioned, in order to remove all subject of dissatisfaction from the minds of their fellow citizens:

And Whereas Congress are desirous as well of gratifying the reasonable expectations of the officers of the army as of removing all objections which may exist in any part of The United States to the principle of the half-pay establishment, for which the faith of The United States hath been pledged; persuaded that those objections can only arise from the nature of the compensation, not from any indisposition to compensate those whose services sacrifices and sufferings have so just a title to the approbation and rewards of their country:

Therefore Resolved That such officers as are now in service and shall continue therein to the end of the war shall be intitled to receive the amount of five years full pay in money or securities on interest at six per cent as congress shall find most convenient, instead of the half pay promised for life by the resolution of the 21 of October 1780, the said securities to be such as shall be given to other creditors of The United States. . . .

That resolution set off a storm of protest across the new nation (see Document 6, below). The protest was scarcely abated when, in May, the officers formed a permanent fraternal organization called the Society of the Cincinnati, with hereditary membership; the organization aroused suspicions that the officers proposed to become a hereditary aristocracy as well as a group of pensioners.

C. Correspondence between Washington and Hamilton, April 4, April 8, 1783

Meantime, Congress continued to work on a plan for handling its obligations, and the army remained encamped at Newburgh. Gradually, Washington became aware that there had been a conspiracy between certain nationalists, public creditors, and officers, and he mentioned the matter in a letter to his former aide-de-camp Alexander Hamilton, now in Congress:

April 4, 1783

. . . I will now, in strict confidence, mention a matter which may be useful for you to be informed of. It is that some men (& leading ones too) in this Army, are beginning to entertain suspicions that Congress, or some members of it, regardless of the past sufferings & present distress, maugre the justice which is due to them, & the returns which a grateful people should make to men who certainly have contributed more than any other class to the establishment of Independency, are to be made use of as mere Puppits to establish Continental funds; & that rather than not succeed in this measure, or weaken their ground, they would make a sacrafice of the Army and all its interests.

I have two reasons for mentioning this matter to you: the one is, that the Army (considering the irritable state it is in, its sufferings & composition) is a dangerous instrument to play with. The other, that every possible means consistant with their own views (which certainly are moderate) should be essayed to get it disbanded without delay. I might add a third: it is, that the Financier [Robert Morris] is suspected to be at the bottom of this scheme. If sentiments of this sort should become general their operation will be opposed to this plan; at the same time that it would encrease the present discontents. Upon the whole, disband the Army, as soon as possible; but consult the wishes of it; which really are moderate, in the mode, & perfectly compatible with the honor, dignity, and justice which is due from the Country to it.

Hamilton, who had in fact been one of the leading conspirators, answered with a classic statement of the nationalist point of view:

SOURCE: Harold C. Syrett and Jacob E. Cooke, eds., *The Papers of Alexander Hamilton* (13 vols. to date, New York, 1961—), III, 315–321.

April 8, 1783

. . . I thank your Excellency for the hints you are so obliging as to give me in your private letter. I do not wonder at the suspicions that have been infused, nor should I be surprised to hear that I have been pointed out as one of the persons concerned in playing the game described. But facts must speak for themselves. . . .

There are two classes of men Sir in Congress of very Different views—one attached to state, the other to Continental politics. The last have been strenuous advocates for funding the public debt upon solid securities, the former have given every opposition in their power and have only been dragged into the measures which are now near being adopted by the clamours of the army and other public creditors. The advocates for Continental funds have blended the interests of the army with other Creditors from a conviction, that no funds for partial purposes will go through those states to whose citizens the United States are largely indebted—or if they should be carried through from impressions of the moment would have the necessary stability; for the influence of those unprovided for would always militate against a provision for others, in exclusion of them. It is in vain to tell men who have parted with a large part of their property on the public faith that the services of the army are intitled to a preference. . . .

But the question was not merely how to do justice to the creditors, but how to restore public credit. Taxation in this Country, it was found, could not supply a sixth part of the public necessities. The loans in Europe were far short of the ballance and the prospect every day diminishing. The Court of France telling us in plain terms she could not even do as much as she had done—Individuals in Holland & every where else refusing to part with their money on the precarious tenure of the mere faith of this country, without any pledge for the payment either of principal or interest.

In this situation what was to be done? It was essential to our cause that vigorous efforts should be made to restore public credit —it was necessary to combine all the motives to this end, that could operate upon different descriptions of persons in the different states. The necessity and discontents of the army presented themselves as a powerful engine. . . .

As to Mr. Morris, I will give Your Excellency a true explanation of his conduct. He had been for some time pressing Congress to endeavour to obtain funds, and had found a great backwardness in the business. He found the taxes unproductive in the different states—he found the loans in Europe making a very slow progress —he found himself pressed on all hands for supplies; he found himself in short reduced to this alternative either of making engagements which he could not fulfill or declaring his resignation in case funds were not established by a given time. Had he followed the first course the bubble must soon have burst—he must have sacrificed his credit & his character, and public credit already in a ruinous condition would have lost its last support. He wisely judged it better to resign; this might increase the embarrassments of the moment, but the necessity of the case it was to be hoped would produce the proper measures; and he might then resume the direction of the machine with advantage and success.

. . . The matter with respect to the army which has occasioned most altercation in Congress and most dissatisfaction in the army has been the half pay. The opinions on this head have been two. One party was for referring the several lines to their states to make such commutation as they should think proper—the other for making the commutation by Congress and funding it on continental security. I was of this last opinion and so were all those who will be represented as having made use of the army as puppets. . . .

I have gone into these details to give You a just idea of the parties in Congress. I assure you upon my honor Sir I have given you a candid state of facts to the best of my judgment. The men against whom the suspicions you mention must be directed are in general the most sensible the most liberal, the most independent and the most respectable characters in our body as well as the most unequivocal friends to the army. In a word they are the men who think continentally.

But the men who "thought continentally" did not entirely prevail. In the idiom of the day, the mountain labored and gave birth to a mouse: after endless wrangling, Congress adopted a diluted version of a broad revenue plan that Robert Morris had requested. In resolutions adopted on April 18, it asked for authority to collect specific duties on certain imported goods and 5 per cent duties on other imports, the authority to extend only for twenty-five years and the proceeds to be applicable only to paying principal and interest on the public debt; requested that the states establish effective revenues for the same twenty-five years, to yield, by quotas, $1.5 million to Congress annually; and requested that Article 8 of the Confederation be amended to change the basis of requisition quotas from land to population, with slaves (in a historic compromise that later found its way into the Constitution) to count as three fifths of a person. The proposals were not to become effective until all states had agreed to them. Upon their fate rested the fate of the Confederation.

4. Washington's Circular Letter to the Governors, 1783

By summer the army had been disbanded—or, more properly, in a comedy of errors it simply dissolved. As one of his last acts as commander in chief, General Washington drafted a letter to the governors of the several states, lending his great prestige to a plea for a firmer Union and a strengthened Congress:

[June 8, 1783]

. . . There are four things, which I humbly conceive, are essential to the well being, I may even venture to say, to the existence of the United States as an Independent Power:

1st. An indissoluble Union of the States under one Federal Head.

2dly. A Sacred regard to Public Justice.

3dly. The adoption of a proper Peace Establishment, and

4thly. The prevalence of that pacific and friendly Disposition, among the People of the United States, which will induce them to forget their local prejudices and policies, to make those mutual concessions which are requisite to the general prosperity, and in some instances, to sacrifice their individual advantages to the interest of the Community.

These are the Pillars on which the glorious Fabrick of our Independency and National Character must be supported; Liberty is the Basis, and whoever would dare to sap the foundation, or overturn the Structure, under whatever specious pretexts he may attempt it, will merit the bitterest execration, and the severest punishment which can be inflicted by his injured Country.

On the three first Articles I will make a few observations, leaving the last to the good sense and serious consideration of those immediately concerned.

Under the first head, altho' it may not be necessary or proper for

SOURCE: Fitzpatrick, ed., The Writings of George Washington, XXVI, 483–496.

me in this place to enter into a particular disquisition of the principles of the Union, and to take up the great question which has been frequently agitated, whether it be expedient and requisite for the States to delegate a larger proportion of Power to Congress, or not, Yet it will be a part of my duty, and that of every true Patriot, to assert without reserve, and to insist upon the following positions, That unless the States will suffer Congress to exercise those prerogatives, they are undoubtedly invested with by the Constitution, every thing must very rapidly tend to Anarchy and confusion, That it is indispensable to the happiness of the individual States, that there should be lodged somewhere, a Supreme Power to regulate and govern the general concerns of the Confederated Republic, without which the Union cannot be of long duration. That there must be a faithfull and pointed compliance on the part of every State, with the late proposals and demands of Congress, or the most fatal consequences will ensue, That whatever measures have a tendency to dissolve the Union, or contribute to violate or lessen the Sovereign Authority, ought to be considered as hostile to the Liberty and Independency of America, and the Authors of them treated accordingly, and lastly, that unless we can be enabled by the concurrence of the States, to participate of the fruits of the Revolution, and enjoy the essential benefits of Civil Society, under a form of Government so free and uncorrupted, so happily guarded against the danger of oppression, as has been devised and adopted by the Articles of Confederation, it will be a subject of regret, that so much blood and treasure have been lavished for no purpose, that so many sufferings have been encountered without a compensation, and that so many sacrifices have been made in vain. Many other considerations might here be adduced to prove, that without an entire conformity to the Spirit of the Union, we cannot exist as an Independent Power; it will be sufficient for my purpose to mention but one or two which seem to me of the greatest importance. It is only in our united Character as an Empire, that our Independence is acknowledged, that our power can be regarded, or our Credit supported among Foreign Nations. The Treaties of the European Powers with the United States of America, will have no validity on a dissolution of the Union. We shall be left nearly in a state of Nature, or we may find by our own unhappy experience, that there is a natural and necessary progression, from the extreme of anarchy to the extreme of Tyranny; and that arbitrary power is most easily established on the ruins of Liberty abused to licentiousness.

5. Mutiny of the Pennsylvania Line, 1783

"Liberty abused to licentiousness," in Washington's phrase, soon followed. Eleven days after Washington dispatched his letter to the governors, several hundred soldiers of the Pennsylvania line mutinied, became drunk and disorderly, and surrounded the State House in Philadelphia, where both Congress and the Pennsylvania Executive Council were sitting. Terrified, congressmen and councilmen exchanged insults and charges of responsibility, but no violence or further rioting ensued. Congress, however, discreetly decided to abandon Philadelphia and to hold its future meetings in the village of Princeton, New Jersey—a humiliating fate for the governing body of the newest member of the family of nations.

In the wake of the episode, an anonymous Philadelphian made some interesting—and still pertinent—comments upon riots, which he regarded as an inevitable feature of life in republican countries. It was to be remarked, he said (July 9, 1783):

That the most dangerous and fatal of all riots, are those which have in the beginning, a peaceable appearance, and can be supported at first by a fair pretence. Was not the city of London about three years ago, thrown into the utmost consternation and confusion, hundreds of lives lost, all the shops and courts of justice shut up for seven or eight days, both Houses of Parliament obliged to adjourn, and their King to withdraw himself to Windsor Castle, and all this occasioned by a meeting in St. George's Fields, under the peaceable name of religion.

There always are in every populous city and country a number of loose disorderly characters ready to join any tumult, or to make one, where they may have an opportunity of laying their hands on what is not their own; and had any thing of an actual riot began here, numbers of such characters would have joined it, under the pretence of being soldiers, who never were, in the least, connected with any part of the army; and thus, not only the city might have

SOURCE: *Connecticut Courant*, July 21, 1783.

been exposed to plunder, but the real and deserving soldier to un-merited censure. . . .

6. Resolutions of the Town Meeting of Torrington, Connecticut, July 15, 1783

Some Americans shared the anonymous Philadelphian's concern about the mutiny, but it was much more common to share the attitude of the mutineers. After eight years of war, most Americans were simply fed up —with Congress, with the Continental army and its officers, with any-thing that smacked of national causes. Typical of the postwar mood— and portentous for the fate of Congress and the nation—was the action of the town meeting in Torrington, Connecticut, which was but one of several dozen towns to adopt resolutions in opposition to Congress' commutation of the officers' bonus (Document 3B, above) and, by im-plication, in opposition to any increase in the powers of Congress:

. . . Eight years past, the inhabitants of America, alarmed at the number of placemen and pensioners supported by the British gov-ernment; at the vast revenues annually expended; and at the enor-mous debt in which the nation was involved, and jealous of the power assumed by Parliament, boldly revolted. Since which we have suffered an eight years bloody and expensive war.—Our armies in the field, and citizens, both in the field and at home, have haz-arded their lives and risqued their fortunes. . . . Decrepid old men, and feeble matrons, were obliged to venture out, in winter's cold and summer's sun, and undergo the fatigues of farming labour, to preserve a little food for themselves and families. . . . Our cities have been burnt, towns plundered, and houses robbed; many opu-lent families been reduced to poverty, and thousands and thousands of individuals been obliged to receive their bread at the hand of charity.

But while we dwell on the patience, perseverance, and calamities of the citizens, we cannot with justice, omit the hardships, patience and perseverance of a barefoot army, whose very footsteps stained the ground with blood. An army void of almost every necessary, which by patience of fatigue and alacrity in discipline, have sud-

SOURCE: *Connecticut Courant*, July 29, 1783.

denly rose to a pitch of valour, sufficient to vie with veteran troops. We have the highest opinion of those brave heroes, whose exertions have been vigorous, their conquests various, and their achievements glorious. . . . Shall any class of men who have been so eminently serviceable to an oppressed country be treated with neglect?

Justice requires a careful examination of the matter. Let the patience, and perseverance of the citizens; their heavy taxes; the debt, that still remains unpaid; their amazing sufferings and losses, be balanced by the hardships, patience, and perseverance of the army. If the payment of the army has not been compleated, let it be done. If depreciation, has not been made as good to the army, as to the citizen, let that be done. . . . Let every contract made with the army, at it's first establishment, be compleatly fulfilled. Let a just computation be made and ample satisfaction given, both to officer and soldier. Let the army, in every particular, be on an equal footing with the citizen. Let them be as well rewarded, for all services, and no better.

Why the sufferings of citizen and soldier should be neglected, and all the revenues of the country, be heaped on the officers, is, indeed, a problem, difficult to be solved. The officers it is generally agreed, in point of property, at the commencement of the war, was scarcely equal to the citizen. And who has made the greatest addition? Let their circumstances at the commencement and conclusion of the war be contrasted. The officer has lost lucrative employments, it is urged: Many of them indeed were employed in commerce whose business was lucrative, but the war totally obstructed their business, and a generous country gave them employ: They have suffered losses from depreciated notes, which the poor officer was obliged to sell much below par. As to them; the only citizens, who have made their fortunes by the war, are speculators; they in confederacy with speculators of the army, have robbed, we grant, some officers and many soldiers of large sums. As to those note speculators, it is credibly reported, there has been, in proportion to the number, ten officers to one citizen; and the officer, being continually in the army, has had ten times the chance of the citizen; so that, if reports be true, where one pound has been made by the citizen in that way, a hundred pounds have been made by the officer. Finally, it is an incontestible truth, that some officers left home in low, indigent circumstances; and it is a truth as incontestible that all who return, return in affluence. That the officers esteemed the service of the army a priviledge, is apparent from the complaints of those, who were mustered supernumerary and deranged.

As to the engagements of Congress, respecting half pay, the commutation, etc. . . . In our opinions, no such power was ever expressly delegated to Congress, therefore Congress, in that case, could only act as a committee, and their resolves can be considered, only as recommenditory; the States, therefore, are at their own election, whether to adopt them, or not. All charges of the war and other expences that are incurred for the common defence and general welfare are to be defrayed from a common treasury by direction of Congress. The five years pay every body knows is not a charge of the war: And whether it is for the common welfare is left to the scrutiny of a candid public. . . . Congress have the same power, and can, with as much justice, at the expiration of the present five years, grant another five years pay, and then, perhaps, half-pay during life. And is it likely, the evil will stop here! Is it not highly probable that Congress, at present, are feasting their imaginations on the prospects of future pensions?

Pensions are always as agreeable to men in office, as they are destructive to the community. Are there not individuals, in every State, who are endeavouring to saddle the people with pensions? Are there not many in the legislature of this State, who would see, with rapture, the establishment of pensions? . . . We have paid taxes upon taxes, to a very considerable amount, and where is the money? Our debts are increasing with amazing rapidity. . . . Congress gives no account to Assembly. Assembly gives no account to the people of the expenditure of money.—We know not half so much, neither of the debts, nor of the expenditure of money, nor of the debates, nor of the transactions, nor of the principles of the individuals, in the legislatures of America, as of Old England!

. . . We intreat the citizens of America, once more, to remember, they are free! . . to remember the constitution; whether our governments be monarchical, aristocratical, or Democratical; whether the power, of those in office, be hereditary, or delegated; if it be delegated, let them remember, by whom it is delegated. . . . Congress are delegated by the people, therefore Congress must be responsible to the people, in all cases whatever. . . . It is the unanimous opinion of this town, that no power was ever delegated to Congress, by confederation, to grant half pay, etc. and that those resolves are unconstitutional, unjust and oppressive. . . .

PART TWO:

A Nearly Impotent Congress, 1784-1787

From the summer of 1783 onward, Congress was in a completely untenable situation: lacking public confidence and lacking constitutional power to do much of anything, it was nonetheless burdened, at least theoretically, with large responsibilities. In the broadest of terms, these responsibilities lay in three general areas—1) the servicing of the huge public debt owed to foreign governments and investors as well as to American citizens, 2) the management of the vast public domain of unoccupied lands, and 3) the conduct of relations with foreign powers.

I. The Problem of Revenues

In 1783 the United States in Congress Assembled owed American citizens something over $25 million and foreigners something under $10 million. The annual bill for interest on such a debt, together with the modest costs of Congress' peacetime military and civilian establishments, amounted to a "fixed" expenditure of around $2.5 million a year. Unless and until the state legislatures approved the Revenue Plan of April 18, 1783, Congress had only two potential sources of income: requisitions upon the states and new loans from abroad. For a year or two a few states complied, at least in part, with congressional requisitions, and for a year or two modest loans were forthcoming from private investors in Holland. Congress defaulted on its debts to France, ignored the domestic creditors (who received some payment from state governments), and used its slender resources only to meet current and administrative costs. By the end of 1785 meeting even these costs was proving difficult, and by the summer of 1786 Congress seemed about to go out of business entirely, for want of funds—as the following letter between two Massachusetts congressmen attests:

7. Rufus King to Elbridge Gerry, New York, June 18, 1786

. . . Connecticut and New Jersey have finished their Sessions without attending to the situation of the confederacy; the former took into consideration the Requisition of last year, and refused a compliance with it—the latter in their late Session did not even treat the subject with the attention it received in Connecticut.

You my dear friend, must know our Situation, as fully as I do, who am a daily witness of the humiliating condition of the Union. You may depend on it, that the Treasury now is literally without a penny. By anticipations, and the collections from Virginia, Maryland and this State, the Board of Treasury have made provision for the Dutch interest, which fell due this month—but there is no Prospect of their being able to provide for the payments which will be due in January. The posts on the Ohio are not well supplied with military stores, the Secretary at War applied a few days since for *1000 Dollars* for the transportation of the necessary Ammunition to these Posts. The Board of Treasury, urgent as the occasion of this application is allowed to be, explicitly declare their utter inability to make this pitiful advance. What are we to expect? . . .

8. Report of the Congressional Committee on New York's Ratification of the Impost Amendment, August 22, 1786

Soon after King wrote his despairing letter, however, it suddenly appeared that Congress might be financially revived after all. By the end of the 1786 sessions of the state legislatures, it had developed that every state had, in one form or another, ratified that part of the April 18, 1783,

SOURCE (Selection 7): E. C. Burnett, ed., *Letters of Members of the Continental Congress* (8 vols., Washington, D.C., 1921–1936), VIII, 392–393.
SOURCE (Selection 8): *Journals of the Continental Congress*, XXXI, 532–534.

Revenue Plan that would vest Congress with power to levy import duties. Several states had hedged their ratifications with qualifications that might prove difficult, but Congress took the position that the conditions imposed by only one state—New York—were entirely incompatible with those imposed by the others. A committee, consisting of William Samuel Johnson of Connecticut, Rufus King of Massachusetts, Charles Pinckney of South Carolina, and James Monroe and William Grayson of Virginia, studied the subject and made the following report:

The Committee . . . Report:

That they have examined an act passed by the state of New-York, on the 4th day of May last, entitled "An act for giving and granting to the United States in Congress assembled, certain imposts and duties on foreign goods imported into that state, for the special purpose of paying the principal and interest of the debt contracted in the prosecution of the late war with Great-Britain:" That by the act of Congress of the 18th April, 1783, it is recommended to the several states, as indispensably necessary to the restoration of public credit, and to the punctual and honorable discharge of the public debts, to invest the United States in Congress assembled, with a power to levy certain duties upon goods imported into the United States; provided that the collectors of the said duties should be appointed by the states within which their offices are to be respectively exercised; but when so appointed, to be amenable to and removable by the United States in Congress assembled alone. The committee conceive that the investing the United States in Congress assembled with this power, which includes that of forming the necessary regulations, or revenue laws, with suitable penalties, of declaring the money in which the said duties shall be received, of establishing the number of revenue officers, and ascertaining their duties, has been and must be considered as an essential part of the plan submitted to the several states for their adoption: The exercise of this power by thirteen separate authorities, would introduce different laws upon the same subject, ordain various penalties for the same offence, destroy the equality of the tax, and might, in a great measure, defeat the revenue. All the states, except New-York, having in pursuance of the recommendation of the 18th April, 1783, granted the imposts by acts vesting this power, with certain qualifications, exclusively in the United States in Congress assembled; the long continued embarrassments of the public finances, and the indispensable demands on the federal government, dictate the necessity of an immediate and unanimous adoption of this measure: Impressed with these opinions, the committee have carefully examined the act of the state of New-York, and submit the following remarks:

1st. That several of the states which have passed acts, investing the United States in Congress assembled, under certain restrictions, with power to levy the duties on goods imported into the United States, agreeably to the recommendation of the 18th of April, 1783, have inserted in their acts, express conditions that the same shall not be in force, or begin to operate, until all the states in the confederacy have passed acts vesting the United States in Congress assembled, with power to levy in the several states like duties.

2d. That the act of the state of New-York, does not invest the United States in Congress assembled, with power to levy in that state the duties therein mentioned, but reserves to the state of New-York, the sole power of levying and collecting the same in the manner directed in and by an act of that state, entitled "An act imposing duties on certain goods, wares and merchandise imported into the said state," passed the 18th day of November, 1784, and consequently prevents the operation of the impost in those states which have made the exercise of this power, by the United States in Congress assembled, an indispensable and express condition of their grants.

3d. That the said act does not make the collectors of the said duties amenable to and removable by the United States in Congress assembled; but ordains, that upon conviction before the supreme court of judicature, or in the court of exchequer of the state of New-York, for any default or neglect in the execution of the duties required of them by the said act, or by an act of that state, entitled "An act imposing duties on certain goods, wares and merchandise imported into the said state," they shall be removed from office, and others appointed instead of the persons so convicted; which is a material departure from the plan recommended by Congress.

4th. That by an act of the state of New-York, entitled "An act for emitting the sum of 200,000*l.* in bills of credit, for the purposes therein mentioned," passed the 18th April, 1786, it is among other things enacted, "That gold and silver, and the bills of credit emitted by virtue of the said act, shall be received by the collector for duties arising on goods, wares and merchandise imported into the said state after the passing the said act;" in consequence whereof, admitting that the system of a general impost could be put in operation, it would remain optional with the importer to pay the duties on goods imported into the state of New-York, in specie or bills of credit, emitted by virtue of the aforesaid act.

5th. If bills of credit of the state of New-York should be received from the importer in that state, upon the principles of equal justice, bills of credit emitted by any other state, must be received from the importer of goods in such state, and thereby instead of the system yielding a sum in actual money, nothing but paper would be brought into the federal treasury, which would be wholly inapplicable to the payment of any part of the interest or principal of the foreign debt of the United States. Whereupon the committee submit the following resolutions:

1st. *Resolved,* That the act of the state of New-York, entitled "An act for giving and granting to the United States in Congress assembled, certain imposts and duties on foreign goods imported into that state, for the special purpose of paying the principal and interest of the debts contracted in the prosecution of the late war with Great-Britain," so essentially varies from the system of impost recommended by the United States in Congress assembled, on the 18th day of April, 1783, that the said act is not, and cannot be considered as a compliance with the same.

2d. *Resolved,* That the present critical and embarrassed situation of the finances of the United States is such, as to require, that the system of impost should be carried into immediate effect. That New-York being the only state which has not yet adopted the same, the United States in Congress assembled, deem this an occasion sufficiently important and extraordinary, to request, that the legislature of the said state be convened, for the purpose of taking the said system into their immediate and serious consideration, and granting the same, in the manner recommended by the resolution of the 18th April, 1783.

3d. *Resolved,* That it be earnestly recommended to the executive of the state of New-York, immediately to convene the legislature of the said state, to take into their consideration, the recommendation of the 18th April, 1783, for the purpose of granting the system of impost in such conformity with the acts and grants of the other states, as on their part to enable the United States in Congress assembled, to carry the same into effect.

The committee's report was not immediately approved, but in time Congress did act upon the proposal to recommend to Governor George Clinton of New York that he call the legislature into special session to approve the impost amendment. Clinton flatly refused, ostensibly on constitutional grounds. When the legislature met in regular session Clinton offered the following explanation—after which the legislature refused to change the form of its approval of the amendment. That refusal, in the words of one historian, was "the death knell of the Confederation."

9. Address of Governor George Clinton to the New York Legislature, January 13, 1787

. . . The Resolutions of the United States in Congress Assembled, of the 11th and 23d of August last, expressing their sense of our Act of last Session, for granting to them an Impost, and requesting on that occasion an immediate call of the Legislature, will again present to your view the Revenue System, recommended by that Honorable Body, on the 18th of April, 1783.

I shall forbear making any remarks on a subject which hath been so repeatedly submitted to the consideration of the Legislature, and must be well understood.—You will receive with these Resolutions the correspondence they produced; and I have only to add that a regard to our excellent Constitution, and an anxiety to preserve unimpaired the right of free deliberation on matters not stipulated by the Confederation, restrained me from convening you at an earlier period.

II. The Problem of the Public Domain

Lethal as the final rejection of the 1783 impost amendment was, no small number of members of Congress continued to believe that, in time, Congress would be able to fulfill its obligations. That faith rested upon the prospects for favorable disposition of the public domain. Before the Revolution several states had had claims, derived from colonial charters, to the unoccupied area west of the Appalachian Mountains.

SOURCE: New York Assembly Journal, 1787, p. 6.

After independence, through a long and complex process, the states ceded their claims to lands north and west of the Ohio River to Congress, thus creating the first national domain. In 1784 Congress passed an ordinance for governing the territory, once it was settled, and in 1785 it passed an ordinance providing for the survey and sale of the land. No one knew just how large or how rich the land was, but as Richard Henry Lee wrote from Congress (to James Madison, May 30, 1785), "We have, after much debate indeed and great waste of time, at last pass'd an Ordinance for disposing of such part of the Lands N.W. of the Ohio as belongs to the U.S. and have been purchased of the Indians. If this proves agreeable to the public, it will extinguish about 10 Millions of the pub. debt. And the remaining lands, going southward to the Mississippi, will nearly discharge all the domestic debt—Besides the probable prospect that we have of considerable cessions from N. and S. Carolina and Georgia. This source does indeed deserve our warmest cultivation as it seems to be almost the only one that we have for discharging our oppressive debt. . . ." The Land Ordinance of 1785 follows.

10. The Land Ordinance of 1785

This ordinance provided the basic survey and sale system that was used throughout American history for the disposition of the national domain. As long as it was in force, most sales were made in large blocks by special contracts. In the nineteenth century, however, the law was amended several times to facilitate sales to smaller purchasers.

May 20, 1785

AN ORDINANCE FOR ASCERTAINING THE MODE OF DISPOSING OF
LANDS IN THE WESTERN TERRITORY

Be it ordained by the United States in Congress assembled That the territory ceded by individual States to the United States which has been purchased of the Indian inhabitants shall be disposed of in the following manner

A Surveyor from each State shall be appointed by Congress or a committee of the States, who shall take an oath for the faithful discharge of his duty before the Geographer of the United States, who is hereby empowered and directed to administer the same; and the

SOURCE: *Journals of the Continental Congress*, XVIII, 375–381.

like oath shall be administered to each chain carrier by the surveyor under whom he acts.

The Surveyors as they are respectively qualified shall proceed to divide the said territory into townships of six miles square, by lines running due north and south and others crossing these at right angles as near as may be, unless where the boundaries of the late Indian purchases may render the same impracticable. . . .

The first line running north and south as aforesaid shall begin on the river Ohio at a point that shall be found to be due north from the western termination of a line which has been run as the southern boundary of the state of Pennsylvania and the first line running east and west shall begin at the same point and shall extend throughout the whole territory Provided that nothing herein shall be construed as fixing the western boundary of the State of Pennsylvania. The geographer shall designate the townships or fractional parts of townships by numbers progressively from south to North, always beginning each range with number one; and the ranges shall be distinguished by their progressive numbers to the westward. The first range extending from the Ohio to the lake Erie being marked number one. The Geographer shall personally attend to the running of the first east and west line and shall take the latitude of the extremes of the first north and south line and of the mouths of the principal rivers.

The lines shall be measured with a chain; shall be plainly marked by chaps on the trees and exactly described on a plat, whereon shall be noted by the Surveyor, at their proper distances, all mines, salt springs, salt licks and mill seats, that shall come to his knowledge, and all water courses mountains and other remarkable and permanent things over or near which such lines shall pass and also the quality of the lands.

The plats of the townships respectively shall be marked by subdivisions into lots of one mile square of 640 acres, in the same direction as the external lines and numbered from 1 to 36, always beginning the succeeding range of the lots with the number next to that with which the preceding one concluded. . . .

The geographer and surveyors shall pay the utmost attention to the variation of the magnetic needle, and shall run and note all lines by the true meridian, certifying with every plat what was the variation at the times of running the lines thereon noted.

As soon as seven ranges of townships & fractional parts of townships in the direction from south to north shall have been surveyed, the geographer shall transmit plats thereof to the board of treasury. . . . And the geographer shall make similar returns from time to time of every seven ranges as they may be surveyed. The secretary at war shall have recourse thereto, and shall take by lot therefrom a number of townships . . . as will be equal to one seventh part of the whole of such seven ranges as nearly as may be, for the use of the late continental army. . . .

The board of treasury shall transmit a copy of the original plats previously noting thereon the townships & fractional parts of townships, which shall have fallen to the several states by the distribution aforesaid to the Commissioners of the loan office of the several states, who after giving notice . . . shall proceed to sell the townships or fractional parts of townships at public vendue, in the following manner, viz. The township or fractional part of a township N 1. in the first range shall be sold entire, and N. 2 in the same range by lots, and thus in alternate order through the whole of the first range . . . provided that none of the lands within the said territory be sold under the price of one dollar the acre to be paid in specie or loan office certificates reduced to specie value by the scale of depreciation or certificates of liquidated debts of the United States including interest, besides the expence of the survey and other charges thereon, which are hereby rated at thirty six dollars the township . . . on failure of which payment the said lands shall again be offered for sale.

There shall be reserved for the United States out of every township the four lots being numbered, 8. 11. 26. 29 and out of every fractional part of a township so many lots of the same numbers as shall be found thereon for future sale: There shall be reserved the lot N 16 of every township for the maintenance of public schools within the said township; also one third part of all gold, silver, lead and copper mines, to be sold or otherwise disposed of as Congress shall hereafter direct. . . .

And whereas Congress . . . stipulated grants of land to certain officers and soldiers of the late continental army . . . for complying therefore with such engagements Be it ordained that the secretary at war determine who are the objects of the above resolutions and engagements and the quantity of land to which such persons or their representatives are respectively entitled and cause the townships or fractional parts of townships herein before reserved for the use of the late continental army to be drawn for in such manner as he shall deem expedient. . . .

11. The Northwest Ordinance, 1787

The basic territorial government act of the period, the Ordinance of 1787, is celebrated for its liberal principles, particularly its contributions on slavery, popular education, and the development of democratic political institutions. It was, in fact, considerably less liberal in most respects than an Ordinance of 1784 that it replaced, the changes being made largely in the interests of speculators who proposed to buy and recruit settlers for large blocks of land in the territory. The ordinance was, nonetheless, one of the great achievements of the period, and it provided the pattern for the government of newly occupied territories throughout most of American history.

AN ORDINANCE FOR THE GOVERNMENT OF THE TERRITORY OF THE
UNITED STATES NORTHWEST OF THE RIVER OHIO

Section 1. *Be it ordained by the United States in Congress assembled,* That the said Territory, for the purpose of temporary government, be one district, subject, however, to be divided into two districts, as future circumstances may, in the opinion of Congress, make it expedient.

Sec. 2. *Be it ordained by the authority aforesaid,* That the estates both of resident and non-resident proprietors in the said territory, dying intestate, shall descend to, and be distributed among, their children and the descendants of a deceased child in equal parts, the descendants of a deceased child or grandchild to take the share of their deceased parent in equal parts among them; and where there shall be no children or descendants, then in equal parts to the next of kin, in equal degree; and among collaterals, the children of a deceased brother or sister of the intestate shall have, in equal parts among them, their deceased parent's share; and there shall, in no case, be a distinction between kindred of the whole and half blood; saving in all cases to the widow of the intestate, her third part of the real estate for life, and one-third part of the personal estate; and this

SOURCE: *Journals of Congress, 1774–88* (Washington, D.C., 1823), pp. 754–756.

law relative to descents and dower, shall remain in full force until altered by the legislature of the district. And until the governor and judges shall adopt laws as hereinafter mentioned, estates in the said territory may be devised or bequeathed by wills in writing, signed and sealed by him or her in whom the estate may be, (being of full age,) and attested by three witnesses; and real estates may be conveyed by lease and release, or bargain and sale, signed, sealed, and delivered by the person, being of full age, in whom the estate may be, and attested by two witnesses, provided such wills be duly proved, and such conveyances be acknowledged, or the execution thereof duly proved, and be recorded within one year after proper magistrates, courts, and registers, shall be appointed for that purpose; and personal property may be transferred by delivery, saving, however, to the French and Canadian inhabitants, and other settlers of the Kaskaskies, Saint Vincents, and the neighboring villages, who have heretofore professed themselves citizens of Virginia, their laws and customs now in force among them, relative to the descent and conveyance of property.

Sec. 3. *Be it ordained by the authority aforesaid,* That there shall be appointed, from time to time, by Congress, a governor, whose commission shall continue in force for the term of three years, unless sooner revoked by Congress; he shall reside in the district, and have a freehold estate therein, in one thousand acres of land, while in the exercise of his office.

Sec. 4. There shall be appointed from time to time, by Congress, a secretary, whose commission shall continue in force for four years, unless sooner revoked; he shall reside in the district, and have a freehold estate therein, in five hundred acres of land, while in the exercise of his office. It shall be his duty to keep and preserve the acts and laws passed by the legislature, and the public records of the district, and the proceedings of the governor in his executive department, and transmit authentic copies of such acts and proceedings every six months to the Secretary of Congress. There shall also be appointed a court, to consist of three judges, any two of whom to form a court, who shall have a common-law jurisdiction and reside in the district, and have each therein a freehold estate, in five hundred acres of land, while in the exercise of their offices; and their commissions shall continue in force during good behavior.

Sec. 5. The governor and judges, or a majority of them, shall adopt and publish in the district such laws of the original States, criminal and civil, as may be necessary, and best suited to the circumstances of the district, and report them to Congress from time to time, which laws shall be in force in the district until the organization of the general assembly therein, unless disapproved of by Congress; but afterwards the legislature shall have authority to alter them as they shall think fit.

Sec. 6. The governor, for the time being, shall be commander-in-chief of the militia, appoint and commission all officers in the same below the rank of general officers; all general officers shall be appointed and commissioned by Congress.

Sec. 7. Previous to the organization of the general assembly the governor shall appoint such magistrates, and other civil officers, in each county or township, as he shall find necessary for the preservation of the peace and good order in the same. After the general assembly shall be organized the powers and duties of magistrates and other civil officers shall be regulated and defined by the said assembly; but all magistrates and other civil officers, not herein otherwise directed, shall, during the continuance of this temporary government, be appointed by the governor.

Sec. 8. For the prevention of crimes, and injuries, the laws to be adopted or made shall have force in all parts of the district, and for the execution of process, criminal and civil, the governor shall make proper divisions thereof; and he shall proceed, from time to time, as circumstances may require, to lay out the parts of the district in which the Indian titles shall have been extinguished, into counties and townships, subject, however, to such alterations as may thereafter be made by the legislature.

Sec. 9. So soon as there shall be five thousand free male inhabitants, of full age, in the district, upon giving proof thereof to the governor, they shall receive authority, with time and place, to elect representatives from their counties or townships, to represent them in the general assembly: Provided, That for every five hundred free male inhabitants there shall be one representative, and so on, progressively, with the number of free male inhabitants, shall the right of representation increase, until the number of representatives shall amount to twenty-five; after which the number and proportion of representatives shall be regulated by the legislature: Provided, That no person be eligible or qualified to act as a representative, unless he shall have been a citizen of one of the United States three years, and be a resident in the district, or unless he shall have resided in the district three years; and, in either case, shall likewise hold in his own right, in fee-simple, two hundred acres of land within the same: *Provided also,* That a freehold in fifty acres of land in the district, having been a citizen of one of the States, and being resident in the district, or the like freehold and two years' residence in the district, shall be necessary to qualify a man as an elector of a representative.

Sec. 10. The representatives thus elected shall serve for the term of two years; and in case of the death of a representative, or removal from office, the governor shall issue a writ to the county or township, for which he was a member, to elect another in his stead, to serve for the residue of the term.

Sec. 11. The general assembly, or legislature, shall consist of the governor, legislative council, and a house of representatives. The legislative council shall consist of five members, to continue in office five years, unless sooner removed by Congress; any three of whom to be a quorum; and the members of the council shall be nominated and appointed in the following manner, to wit: As soon as representatives shall be elected the governor shall appoint a time and place for them to meet together, and when met they shall nominate ten persons, resident in the district, and each possessed of a freehold in five hundred acres of land, and return their names to Congress, five of whom Congress shall appoint and commission to serve as aforesaid; and whenever a vacancy shall happen in the Council, by death or removal from office, the house of representatives shall nominate two persons, qualified as aforesaid, for each vacancy, and return their names to Congress, one of whom Congress shall appoint and commission for the residue of the term; and every five years, four months at least before the expiration of the time of service of the members of the council, the said house shall nominate ten persons, qualified as aforesaid, and return their names to Congress, five of whom Congress shall appoint and commission to serve as members of the council five years, unless sooner removed. And the governor, legislative council, and house of representatives shall have authority to make laws in all cases for the good government of the district, not repugnant to the principles and articles in this ordinance established and declared. And all bills, having passed by a majority in the house, and by a majority in the council, shall be referred to the governor for his assent; but no bill, or legislative act whatever, shall be of any force without his assent. The governor shall have power to convene, prorogue, and dissolve the general assembly when, in his opinion, it shall be expedient.

Sec. 12. The governor, judges, legislative council, secretary, and such other officers as Congress shall appoint in the district, shall take an oath or affirmation of fidelity, and of office; the governor before the President of Congress, and all other officers before the governor. As soon as a legislature shall be formed in the district, the council and house assembled, in one room, shall have authority, by joint ballot, to elect a delegate to Congress, who shall have a seat in Congress, with a right of debating, but not of voting, during this temporary government.

Sec. 13. And for extending the fundamental principles of civil and religious liberty, which form the basis whereon these republics, their laws and constitutions, are erected; to fix and establish those principles as the basis of all laws, constitutions, and governments, which forever hereafter shall be formed in the said territory; to provide, also, for the establishment of States, and permanent government therein, and for their admission to a share in the Federal councils on an equal footing with the original States, at as early periods as may be consistent with the general interest:

Sec. 14. It is hereby ordained and declared, by the authority aforesaid, that the following articles shall be considered as articles of compact, between the original States and the people and States in the said territory, and forever remain unalterable, unless by common consent, to wit:

ARTICLE I

No person, demeaning himself in a peaceable and orderly manner, shall ever be molested on account of his mode of worship, or religious sentiments, in the said territory.

ARTICLE II

The inhabitants of the said territory shall always be entitled to the benefits of the writs of *habeas corpus*, and of the trial by jury; of a proportionate representation of the people in the legislature, and of judicial proceedings according to the course of the common law. All persons shall be bailable, unless for capital offences, where the proof shall be evident, or the presumption great. All fines shall be moderate; and no cruel or unusual punishment shall be inflicted. No man shall be deprived of his liberty or property, but by the judgment of his peers, or the law of the land, and should the public exigencies make it necessary, for the common preservation, to take any person's property, or to demand his particular services, full compensation shall be made for the same. And, in the just preservation of rights and property, it is understood and declared, that no law ought ever to be made or have force in the said territory, that shall, in any manner whatever, interfere with or affect private contracts, or engagements, *bona fide*, and without fraud previously formed.

Article III

Religion, morality, and knowledge being necessary to good government and the happiness of mankind, schools and the means of education shall forever be encouraged. The utmost good faith shall always be observed towards the Indians; their lands and property shall never be taken from them without their consent; and in their property, rights, and liberty they never shall be invaded or disturbed unless in just and lawful wars authorized by Congress; but laws founded in justice and humanity shall, from time to time, be made, for preventing wrongs being done to them, and for preserving peace and friendship with them.

Article IV

The said territory, and the States which may be formed therein, shall forever remain a part of this confederacy of the United States of America, subject to the articles of Confederation, and to such alterations therein as shall be constitutionally made; and to all the acts and ordinances of the United States in Congress assembled, conformable thereto. The inhabitants and settlers in the said territory shall be subject to pay a part of the Federal debts, contracted, or to be contracted, and a proportional part of the expenses of government to be apportioned on them by Congress, according to the same common rule and measure by which apportionments thereof shall be made on the other States, and the taxes for paying their proportion shall be laid and levied by the authority and direction of the legislatures of the district, or districts, or new States, as in the original States, within the time agreed upon by the United

States in Congress assembled. The legislatures of those districts, or new States, shall never interfere with the primary disposal of the soil by the United States in Congress assembled, nor with any regulations Congress may find necessary for securing the title in such soil to the bona-fide purchasers. No tax shall be imposed on lands the property of the United States; and in no case shall non-resident proprietors be taxed higher than residents. The navigable waters leading into the Mississippi and Saint Lawrence, and the carrying places between the same, shall be common highways, and forever free, as well to the inhabitants of the said territory as to the citizens of the United States, and those of any other States that may be admitted into the confederacy, without any tax, impost, or duty therefor.

ARTICLE V

There shall be formed in the said territory not less than three nor more than five States; and the boundaries of the States, as soon as Virginia shall alter her act of cession and consent to the same, shall become fixed and established as follows, to wit: The western State, in the said territory, shall be bounded by the Mississippi, the Ohio, and the Wabash Rivers; a direct line drawn from the Wabash and Post Vincents, due north, to the territorial line between the United States and Canada; and by the said territorial line to the Lake of the Woods and Mississippi. The middle State shall be bounded by the said direct line, the Wabash from Post Vincents to the Ohio, by the Ohio, by a direct line drawn due north from the mouth of the Great Miami to the said territorial line, and by the said territorial line. The eastern State shall be bounded by the last-mentioned direct line, the Ohio, Pennsylvania, and the said territorial line: Provided, however, And it is further understood and declared, that the boundaries of these three States shall be subject so far to be altered, that, if Congress shall hereafter find it expedient, they shall have authority to form one or two States in that part of the said territory which lies north of an east and west line drawn through the southerly bend or extreme of Lake Michigan. And whenever any of the said States shall have sixty thousand free inhabitants therein, such States shall be admitted by its delegates, into the Congress of the United States, on an equal footing with the original States, in all respects whatever; and shall be at liberty to form a permanent constitution and State government: *Provided,* The constitution and government, so to be formed, shall be republican, and in conformity to the principles contained in these articles, and, so far as it can be consistent with the general interest of the confederacy, such admission shall be allowed at an earlier period, and when there may be a less number of free inhabitants in the State than sixty thousand.

ARTICLE VI

There shall be neither slavery nor involuntary servitude in the said territory, otherwise than in the punishment of crimes, whereof the party shall have been duly convicted: *Provided always,* That any person escaping into the same, from whom labor or service is lawfully claimed in any one of the original States, such fugitive may be lawfully reclaimed, and conveyed to the person claiming his or her labor or service as aforesaid.

Be it ordained by the authority aforesaid, That the resolutions of the 23d of April, 1784, relative to the subject of this ordinance, be, and the same are hereby, repealed, and declared null and void.

Done by the United States, in Congress assembled, the 13th day of July, in the year of our Lord 1787, and of their sovereignty and independence the twelfth.

III. The Problem of Foreign Relations

At the peace negotiations in 1782 the United States had fared admirably, partly because it was represented by extremely able negotiators (John Jay, John Adams, and Benjamin Franklin) and partly because it was dealing from strength. Through the remainder of the Confederation period it was far less successful in dealing with foreign powers. Though it continued to be represented by skilled diplomats—principally Secretary for Foreign Affairs John Jay, and John Adams and Thomas Jefferson, ministers to Paris and London—it was now dealing from weakness, from disunity, from virtual disintegration.

12. Adams and England: John Adams's Report to
John Jay, August 25, 1785

Despite the treaty of peace, friction between the United States and Great Britain continued to exist in several areas. One such area concerned wartime confiscations. British civilians and military forces had confiscated some 50,000 to 75,000 American-owned slaves during the war, and American state governments had confiscated the property, amounting to several millions of pounds sterling, of Loyalists and British subjects. The peace treaty recommended restitutions on both sides, but no slaves were returned and the value of unreturned Loyalist property in at least three states—New York, Maryland, and Virginia—was enormous. Again, in direct violation of the treaty, Britain refused to abandon several military outposts in western New York State and in the Northwest Territory—thus forming something of a barrier to western settlement and depriving Americans of a share in the lucrative fur trade with Indians. Once again, there were private debts, owed and owing on both sides. Most were debts due from American citizens to British subjects, the lion's share being the approximately £2 million sterling (about $10 million) that tobacco planters in Virginia and Maryland owed to British and Scottish merchants before the war. Virginia had sequestered those debts during the war and permitted local planters to cancel them by paying depreciated paper money into the state treasury; after the war it refused to open state courts to British subjects attempting to collect. In other states the treatment of British creditors was less extreme, but all held that American debtors were not liable for interest accrued during the war. Finally, there were commercial problems. By Orders in Council issued on several occasions in 1783 and confirmed by an Act of Parliament dated April 20, 1784, the British West Indies were closed to American shipping (though not to American goods), a prohibitive duty was placed on American whale oil imported into London, and the importation of tobacco into the British Isles was heavily taxed and strictly regulated. John Adams's efforts in regard to all these matters are summarized in his account to John Jay of his discussions with Prime Minister William Pitt:

DEAR SIR,—Yesterday, I had a long conference with Mr. Pitt for the first time. He never had proposed any interview with me, and I had delayed to request him to appoint any time, after the first ceremonial visit, for two reasons,—because, while parliament was

SOURCE: Charles Francis Adams, ed., *The Works of John Adams* (10 vols., Boston, 1853–1856), 8:302ff.

sitting, his time and mind were so engaged, that it was impossible he should attend in earnest to the affairs of the United States; and because I expected that a little time would bring, both from America and Ireland, intelligence which would somewhat lessen that confidence with which the ministry and the nation were elated. Such intelligence has now arrived. The twenty resolutions have been in effect given up, that they might not be rejected by the Irish parliament; and the Massachusetts act of navigation has appeared, together with advices from Virginia, Philadelphia, New York, and various other parts of the United States, which have excited a serious apprehension that all have the same principles and views.

I shall not attempt to give you the conversation in detail, yet it is necessary to give some particulars, from which you may judge how much or how little may result from the whole. He asked me what were the principal points to be discussed between us? I answered, that I presumed the Marquis of Carmarthen had laid before the King's servants some papers which I had done myself the honor to write to him. He said he had. I replied, that those letters related to the evacuation of the forts upon the frontier; to the construction of the armistice; and to a treaty of commerce; and that, besides these, there were the negroes carried off contrary to the treaty, and some other points which I had particularly explained to Lord Carmarthen. He said that the carrying off the negroes was so clearly against the treaty, that they must take measures to satisfy that demand, if we could prove how many were carried off. I told him that Sir Guy Carleton could easily ascertain the number, and that Colonel Smith, who negotiated with Sir Guy, could do the same, and that I had the evidence of their proceedings ready to produce, whenever it was wanted. He entered, then, into the subject of the armistice, and we were longer on this point that we needed to have been. [Finally] Mr. Pitt said he thought that was clear, and that this point might be easily settled; but, as to the posts, says he, that is a point connected with some others, that I think must be settled at the same time. I asked him, what these points were. He said, the debts. Several of the States had interfered, against the treaty, and, by acts of their legislatures, had interposed impediments to the recovery of debts, against which there were great complaints in this country. I replied to this, that I had explained this at great length to the Marquis of Carmarthen; but that I might now add, that congress had,

University of Tulsa
McFarlin Library
Tulsa, Okla.

very early after the peace, proposed an explanation of the article, as far as it respected the interest of debts contracted before the war. They had instructed their ministers at Paris to propose such an explanation to this Court; that we had proposed it through Mr. Hartley first, and the Duke of Dorset afterwards, and that I had renewed the proposition to my Lord Carmarthen, upon my first conference with him; but that we had never received an answer. I thought it was best there should be an explanation; for I was persuaded that an American jury would never give any interest for the time which ran during the war. Mr. Pitt said, that would surprise the people here; for that wars never interrupted the interest nor principal of debts, and that he did not see a difference between this war and any other, and the lawyers here made none. I begged his pardon here, and said, that the American lawyers made a wide difference; they contended that the late war was a total dissolution of all laws and government, and, consequently, of all contracts made under those laws; and that it was a maxim of law, that a personal right or obligation, once dissolved or suspended, was lost forever; that the intervention of the treaty and the new laws was necessary for the revival of those ancient rights and obligations; that these rights were in a state of non-existence during the war, and no interest during that period could grow out of them. These being the opinions in America, it was not probable that any jury would be found, from Georgia to New Hampshire, who would give, by their verdict, interest to a creditor; and, therefore, it was most fair and equitable, that an explanation should be made, that the same rule of law might be observed on both sides. This observation appeared to strike him. He said, if there was any danger of this, it would be best that an explanation should be made, but that the balance of debts was much in favor of this country, which I did not deny; but, he said, the government would not dare to make it, without previously feeling out the dispositions of the persons chiefly interested, and knowing how it would be taken by them. We had a much longer conversation concerning these debts, and the difficulty of paying them, arising from the restrictions on our trade, in which I repeated to him what I had before said to Lord Carmarthen and to the deputies of the Scotch creditors; but, as I have transmitted that to you before, it is unnecessary to repeat it here.

He then began upon the treaty of commerce, and asked what were the lowest terms that would be satisfactory to America. I answered, that I might not think myself competent to determine that question. Articles might be proposed to me that I should not think myself qualified to decide upon without writing to congress; but I would venture so far as to say, that I thought the project I had communicated to Lord Carmarthen would give satisfaction to America, and secure the friendship of the United States, and the essence of their trade to this country. But that, in proportion as a plan less liberal was adopted, that friendship would be precarious, and that trade would be scattered. I added, that the most judicious men in America had been long balancing in their minds the advantages and the disadvantages of a commerce perfectly free on one side, and of a navigation act on the other; that the present time was a critical one; the late intelligence from all parts of America concurred with the navigation act of Massachusetts, in proving which way the balance began to incline, and, in my opinion, it would be decided by the conduct of this country; it was now in his, Mr. Pitt's power, to decide it; but the more Americans reflected upon the great advantages which they might derive from a navigation act, the more they would become attached to that system. I had heard there were five hundred foreign ships employed the last year in the commerce of the United States. How easy would it be to have all these ships the property of American citizens, and the navigators of them, American seamen! There was once a statute in England (that of 5 Ric. II. c. 3), "That none of the King's liege people should ship any merchandise out of, or into the realm, but only in ships of the King's liegeance, on pain of forfeiture." I asked him what physical or political impediment there was to prevent the United States from adopting that very act in all its rigor. The right of every nation to govern its own commerce, its own exports and imports, would not be denied nor questioned by any nation. To this he agreed. Our ability to build the ships, and our abundance of materials, could not be doubted. This he assented to. Nobody would pretend that our produce would not find a market in Europe in our own ships, or that Europeans would not sell us their manufactures to carry home in them. Even England, if she should make ever so strict laws to prevent exports and imports in our bottoms, would still be glad to receive and consume considerable quantities of our produce, though she imported them through France or Holland; and to send us as many of her manufactures as we could pay for, through the same channels.

He more than smiled assent to this, for he added that there were American articles of much importance to them; but, he said, that Englishmen were much attached to their navigation. And Americans, too, said I, to theirs. But, said he, the United States having now become a foreign nation, our navigation act would not answer its end, if we should dispense with it towards you. Here I begged his pardon again; for I thought their navigation act would completely defeat its own end, as far as it respected us; for the end of the navigation act, as expressed in its own preamble, was to confine the commerce of the Colonies to the mother country; but, now we were become independent States, if carried into execution against us, instead of confining our trade to Great Britain, it would drive it to other countries. This he did not deny; but, said he, you allow we have a right. Certainly I do; and you, sir, will allow we have a right, too. Yes, I do; but you cannot blame Englishmen for being attached to their ships and seamen which are so essential to them. Indeed, I do not, sir; nor can you blame Americans for being attached to theirs, which are so much fewer and so much more essential to them. No, I do not blame them.

As this was a very sprightly dialogue, and in very good humor, I thought I might push it a little. I will be very frank with you, sir, said I, and I think it will be best for us to go to the bottom of these subjects. The Americans think that their exclusion from your West India Islands, the refusal of their ships and oil and other things, and their exclusion from your Colonies on the continent and Newfoundland, discover a jealousy of their little naval power, and a fixed system of policy to prevent the growth of it; and this is an idea that they cannot bear. No, said he, if we endeavored to lessen your shipping and seamen, without benefiting or increasing our own, it would be hard and unreasonable, and would be a just ground of uneasiness; but when we only aim at making the most of our own means and nurseries, you cannot justly complain. I am happy, sir, to hear you avow this principle, and agree with you perfectly in it; let us apply it. Both parties having the right and the power to confine their exports and imports to their own ships and seamen, if both exercise the right and exert the power in its full extent, what is the effect? The commerce must cease between them. Is this eligible for either? To be sure, said he, we should well consider the advantages and the disadvantages in such a case. If it is not found to be eligible for either, said I, after having well considered, what remains,

but that we should agree upon a liberal plan, and allow equal freedom to each other's ships and seamen? especially if it should be
found that this alone can preserve friendship and good humor. For
I fully believe that this plan alone can ever put this nation in good
humor with America, or America with this country. He then mentioned ships and oil. He said we could not think hard of them for
encouraging their own shipwrights, their manufactures of ships, and
their own whale fishery. I answered, by no means; but it appeared
unaccountable to the people of America, that this country should
sacrifice the general interest of the nation to the private interest of
a few individuals interested in the manufacture of ships and in the
whale fishery, so far as to refuse these remittances from America, in
payment of debts, and for manufactures which would employ so
many more people, augment the revenue so considerably, as well
as the national wealth, which would, even in other ways, so much
augment the shipping and seamen of the nation. It was looked upon
in America as reconciling themselves to a diminution of their own
shipping and seamen, in a great degree, for the sake of diminishing
ours in a small one, besides keeping many of their manufacturers
out of employ, who would otherwise have enough to do; and besides
greatly diminishing the revenue, and, consequently, contrary to the
maxim which he had just acknowledged, that one nation should
not hurt itself for the sake of hurting another, nor take measures
to deprive another of any advantage, without benefiting itself.

He then asked me, if we could grant to England, by a treaty, any
advantages which would not immediately become the right of
France. I answered, we could not. If the advantage was stipulated
to England, without a compensation, France would be entitled to
it without a compensation; but, if it was stipulated for an equivalent
or reciprocal privilege, France must allow us the same equivalent
or reciprocal privilege. But, I added, France would not be a very
successful rival to Great Britain in the American commerce, upon
so free a footing as that of the mutual liberty of natural-born subjects and citizens; upon the footing of the most favored nation,
France would stand a good chance in many things. In case of mutual navigation acts between Britain and America, France would
have more of our commerce than Britain. In short, Britain would
lose and France gain, not only in our commerce, but our affections,
in proportion as Britain departed from the most liberal system.
Upon this he asked me a question which I did not expect. "What

do you really think, sir, that Britain ought to do?" That question, sir, may be beyond my capacity to answer, and my answer may be suspected; but, if it is, I will answer it to the best of my judgment, and with perfect sincerity. I think this country ought to prescribe to herself no other rule, but to take from America every thing she can send as a remittance; nay, to take off every duty, and give every bounty that should be necessary to enable her to send any thing as a remittance. In this case, America would prescribe to herself no other rule than to take of British productions as much as she could pay for. He might think this no proof of our republican frugality, but such was the disposition of our people, and, how much soever I might lament it, I would not disguise it. He then led me into a long, rambling conversation about our whale fishery and the English, and the French whale fishery that M. de Calonne is essaying to introduce, too little interesting to be repeated. Yet I should mention that he asked me a sudden question, whether we had taken any measures to find a market for our oil anywhere but in France. This question must have been suggested to him, I think, either by information that our oil is wanted in some countries upon the continent, or by a suspicion that we have been trying to introduce our oil into Ireland. I answered, that I believed we had, and I have been told, that some of our oil had found a good market at Bremen; but there could not be a doubt that spermaceti oil might find a market in most of the great cities in Europe which were illuminated in the night, as it is so much better and cheaper than the vegetable oil that is commonly used. The fat of the spermaceti whale gives the clearest and most beautiful flame of any substance that is known in nature, and we are all surprised that you prefer darkness, and consequent robberies, burglaries, and murders in your streets, to the receiving, as a remittance, our spermaceti oil. The lamps around Grosvenor Square, I know, and in Downing Street, too, I suppose, are dim by midnight, and extinguished by two o'clock; whereas our oil would burn bright till nine o'clock in the morning, and chase away, before the watch-men, all the villains, and save you the trouble and danger of introducing a new police into the city.

He said, he owned he was for taking advantage of the present short time of leisure, to mature some plan about these things. I told him, I rejoiced to find that was his opinion, and that I would be at all times ready to attend him, or any other minister, whenever any explanation should be wanted from me; that I was anxious for an answer concerning the posts, as I was in duty bound to insist on their evacuation. He said he thought that connected with several other points, and should be for settling all these together, so that he must reserve himself at entire liberty concerning them.

I am sorry that, in representing all these conversations, I am obliged to make myself the principal speaker; but I cannot get them to talk. The reason is, they dare not. All must be determined in the cabinet, and no single minister chooses to commit himself, by giving any opinion which may be ever quoted to his disadvantage by any party.

This is not only the state of mind of every minister, but of every ministry. They have an unconquerable reluctance to deciding upon any thing, or giving any answer; and although Mr. Pitt and Lord Carmarthen have hazarded opinions upon some points to me, I do not believe I shall get any answer officially from the cabinet or the minister of foreign affairs. I wish for an answer, be it ever so rough or unwise. Mr. Pitt, I confess, was much more open than I expected. He was explicit in my favor, relative to the negroes and the armistice, and for digesting the whole in the present leisure, and giving me an answer. I should rejoice in a cabinet answer to all my letters, and especially in a counter-project of a treaty; but I will be so free as to say I do not expect any answer at all before next spring, nor then, unless intelligence should arrive of all the States adopting the navigation act, or authorizing congress to do it; and, even in that case, I am inclined to think they will try the experiment, and let our navigation acts operate, to satisfy themselves which people will first roar out with pain. They deceive themselves yet in many points, which I may enumerate in a future letter.

13. Jefferson and France: Jefferson's Report to Jay, May 27, 1786

Relations with France, America's "perpetual" friend and ally by virtue of a treaty of 1778, were not as strained as those with England, but they were far from perfectly harmonious. For one thing, Americans never

SOURCE: Julian P. Boyd, ed., *The Papers of Thomas Jefferson* (17 vols. to date, Princeton, N.J., 1950—), XII, 583–586.

seemed quite able to get anything settled with France; it took seven years, for example, attended by innumerable tangles, to work out so simple a matter as a consular convention with France. More seriously, there was the matter of American default upon France's wartime loans; and just as serious was the abrupt closing, in September 1785, of the French West Indies as a market for American fish. But the problem to which Jefferson most earnestly addressed himself concerned a monopoly of the marketing of American tobacco in France, established between Robert Morris and the Farmers-General, a private, crown-chartered French monopoly. A disastrous break in tobacco prices in Virginia had begun in the fall of 1784, and though Morris's contract with the Farmers-General was not signed until April 1785, Jefferson (along with most other Virginians) attributed the price collapse to the monopoly contract. Jefferson, as the following report to Jay indicates, worked assiduously but vainly to have the contract abolished.

. . . As to the article of tobacco, which had become an important branch of remittance to almost all the states, I had the honour of communicating to you my proposition to the Court to abolish the monopoly of it in their farm; that the Ct. de Vergennes was, I thought, thoroughly sensible of the expediency of this proposition, and disposed to befriend it, that the renewal of the lease of the farms had been consequently suspended six months and was still in suspence; but that so powerful were the Farmers general, [and so tottering the tenure of the Minister of finance in his office,] that I despaired of preventing the renewal of the farm at that time. Things were in this state when the M. de la Fayette returned from Berlin. On communicating to him what was on the carpet, he proposed to me a conference with some persons well acquainted with the commercial system of this country. We met. They proposed the endeavoring to have a committee appointed to enquire into the subject. The proposition was made to the Ct. de Vergennes, who befriended it, and had the M. de la Fayette named a member of the committee. He became of course the active and truly zealous member for the liberty of commerce, others tho' well disposed, not chusing to oppose the farm openly. This committee has met from time to time. It shewed an early and decisive conviction that the measure taken by the farm to put the purchase of their tobaccoes into monopoly on that side the water, as the sale of them was on this, tended to the annihilation of commerce between the two countries. Various palliatives were proposed from time to time. I confess that I met them all with indifference, my object being a radical cure of the evil by discontinuing the farm, and not a mere arrangement of it for the present moment which, rendering it more bearable, might lessen the necessity of removing it totally, and perhaps prevent that removal. In the mean time the other branches of the farm rendered the renewal of the lease necessary; and it being said to be too far advanced to have the article of tobacco separated from it and suspended, it was signed in the month of March, while I was in England, with a clause, which is usual, that the king may discontinue when he pleases on certain conditions. When I returned, I found here a Memorial from the merchants of l'Orient complaining of their having 6000 hogsheads of tobacco on hand, and of the distresses they were under from the loss of this medium of remittance. I inclosed it to the Count de Vergennes and asked his interference. I saw him on the 23d. inst. and spoke to him on the subject. He told me there was to be a committee held the next day at Berni, the seat of the Comptroller general, and that he would attend it himself to have something done. I asked him if I was to consider the expunging that article from the farm as desperate. He said that the difficulty of changing so antient an institution was immense, that the king draws from it a revenue of 29 millions of livres, that an interruption of this revenue, at least, if not a diminution, would attend a change, that their finances were not in a condition to bear even an interruption, and in short that no minister could venture to take upon himself so hazardous an operation. [This was only saying explicitly, what I had long been sensible of, that the Comptroller general's continuance in office was too much on a poise to permit him to shift this weight out of his own scale into that of his adversaries; and that we must be contented to await the completion of the public expectation that there will be a change in this office, which change may give us another chance for effecting this desirable reformation.] Incidents enough will arise to keep this object in our view, and to direct the attention to it as the only point on which the interests and harmony of the two countries (so far as this article of their commerce may influence) will ultimately find repose. The Committee met the next day. The only question agitated was how best to relieve the trade under it's double monopoly. The committee found themselves supported by the presence and sentiments of the Count de Vergennes. They therefore resolved that the contract with Mr. Morris, if executed on his part ought not to be annulled here, but that no similar one should ever be made hereafter; that, so long as it continued, the farmers should be obliged to purchase from twelve to 15,000 hogsheads of tobacco a year, over and above what they should receive from Mr. Morris, from such merchants as should bring it in French or American vessels, on the same conditions contracted with Mr. Morris; providing however that where the cargo shall not be assorted, the prices shall be 38^{lt} 36^{lt} and 34^{lt} for the 1st. 2d and 3d qualities of whichsoever the cargo may consist.[1] In case of dispute about the quality, specimens are to be sent to the council, who will appoint persons to examine and decide on it.

This is indeed the least bad of all the palliatives which have been proposed; but it contains the seeds of perpetual trouble. It is easy to foresee that the farmers will multiply difficulties and vexations on those who shall propose to sell to them by force, and that these will be making perpetual complaints, so that both parties will be kept on the fret. If, without fatiguing the friendly dispositions of the ministry, this should give them just so much trouble as may induce them to look to the demolition of the monopoly as a desireable point of rest, it may produce a permanent as well as temporary good. This determination of the committee needs the king's order to be carried into effect. I have been in hourly expectation of receiving official information that it is ultimately confirmed by him. But as yet it is not come, and the post will set out to-day. Should it arrive in time, I will inclose it. Should it not arrive, as I do not apprehend any danger of it's being rejected, or even altered materially (seeing that M. de Vergennes approved of it, and M. de Calonnes acquiesced) I have supposed you would wish to be apprized of it's substance, for a communication of which I am indebted to the M. de la Fayette. Tho' you cannot publish it formally till you know it is confirmed by the king yet an unauthoritative kind of notice may be given to the merchants to put them on their guard. Otherwise the merchants here, having first knowledge of it, may by their agents purchase up all the tobaccoes they have on hand, at a low price, and thus engross to themselves all the benefit. . . .

---

[1] The symbol lt stands for livres turnois, a French unit of currency then worth about nineteen cents.—Ed.

14. The Quest for Power to Regulate Commerce: Letters from Congressmen, August–September 1785

The efforts of Adams and Jefferson were not entirely futile; for example, between them and their assistants they worked out maritime treaties with Prussia and Morocco, the second of which reduced but did not end depredations on American shipping by Barbary Coast pirates. But in larger matters the diplomats were unsuccessful. One primary reason was that Congress had no power to regulate interstate or international commerce, and thus that any commercial agreements it might make would be worthless without the sanction of every state legislature. Accordingly, various congressmen grew excited from time to time about seeking an amendment to the Articles of Confederation so as to provide Congress with adequate regulatory power. The following three letters relate to such efforts made in the summer of 1785.

A. Congressman David Howell of Rhode Island to Governor William Greene of Rhode Island, August 23, 1785

. . . Another object of Mr. Adams' mission which is of principal importance is to obtain a commercial Treaty with the British nation founded on principles of reciprocal advantage. One great obstruction in his way, it is apprehended, will be the incompetence of the powers of Congress to make specific and effective Stipulation for reciprocating commercial advantages with the other party. It seems to be the opinion even of Congress, or of a great majority thereof that they ought to be vested with power to regulate commerce generally. Many propositions and plans have been suggested. One is an alteration of the confederation so as to vest Congress with the power of regulating trade without limitation of time. Others propose a limitation of 25, 15, or 10 years. Others have proposed that a navigation act be framed and laid before the Legislatures of the several States for their adoption for a term of years. Others there are, who are of opinion that we can go on very well in the present way. They say that the produce of the Southern States, being delivered from British monopoly and admitting to the ports the competition of all the World, fetches as good a price and frequently

SOURCE: Burnette, ed., *Letters of Members of the Continental Congress*, VIII, 199–200.

more and better pay than it did before the revolution. And they fear that the consequences of a navigation act, or of power to regulate trade in the hands of Congress might eventually be throwing a monopoly of the carrying trade into the hands of a few States, who would set their own price also on the produce to be exported, whereby they apprehend a very great injury to the Southern planters. Amidst this division of Sentiments and clashing of interests little is to be expected from the deliberations of the present Congress on this Subject. The voice of the people must come forward and give birth to some System.

B. James McHenry to George Washington, August 14, 1785

James McHenry, delegate to Congress from Maryland, former aide-de-camp of Washington, and dedicated nationalist, made the South's fear of congressional power over commerce more explicit, but he also attempted to take a longer-range national view of the problem:

. . . Congress have had it under consideration to recommend to the several States to vest them with the power of regulating the trade of the States as well with each other as with foreign nations. This power to constitute a part of the Confederation and to be exercised by nine states in congress assembled. Its object to enable Congress to lay as heavy duties and restrictions upon the trade of foreign nations, as foreign nations lay upon the trade of the united States. I apprehend that both the genius and interest of the Southern States will be found to be opposed to granting this power. I believe the eastern States, New York and Pennsylvania are exceedingly anxious for it; but I do not wonder at their anxiety to obtain a monopoly of the carrying trade of the union. What would be the consequence to the Southern States in particular, were foreign vessels to be prevented from exporting their products. They would for example, having only American vessels to carry off their commodities of export, have fewer purchasers for them, hence their prices would be unavoidably lowered. They would also have less foreign goods imported, which would oblige the consumers to pay dearer for what they must buy. It would seem therefore to be good policy in the Southern States to encourage the number of buyers for what they have to sell, and the number of importers of those articles they must buy, till they become as well peopled as the Eastern

SOURCE: *Ibid.,* 182–183.

States, when a naval defence will be easily established, or come of itself without the aid of restrictions. In the mean while however it may be said, that we ought to lay the foundation for a marine, and therefore ought to begin by discouraging foreign shipping and encouraging our own, for that the riches arising from buying what we want cheap and selling what we raise dear will avail us nothing without a navy to protect them. But is it true that a navy is at present necessary; and if necessary is it true that our people could go to the expence of supporting it? Would it be right to add to our present burthens; can we pay our present debts? Are we in a situation to enter into a war of imposts and prohibitions to force Great Britain or France to open to our shipping their West India possessions? Have we shipping enough to carry on our exports and imports? When Great Britain passed the navigation act she had in her harbours more than a sufficient number of vessels for her own trade. Great Britain too, was well peopled at that period and the capital of her traders equal to the exportation and purchase of her products. But our situation is different in both respects, and yet it is said we ought to force a navy—that we ought to prohibit British ships from exporting our products.

Perhaps the point of true policy lays between forcing the growth of our shipping and doing nothing that may forward their increase. Perhaps the Southern States should give up something, and the other States should not ask every thing. Were Congress, under the latter idea to frame a navigation act, the operation of which would gradually and slowly tend to augment the seamen and shipping of the states without sensibly wounding in its progress the interests of any state, and recommend the same to their adoption, is it not highly probable in such a case that the good sense of the States would readily induce them to come into the measure. Upon this plan they would see what they were to give—that it could not hurt them, and that it might work a general benefit. They could repeal it too, if it was found to hurt them, which alone would be a great inducement with some states to pass it.

C. Massachusetts Congressional Delegates to Governor James Bowdoin of Massachusetts, September 3, 1785

The state most damaged by the commercial restrictions imposed by Britain and France, and the one most energetic in its efforts to retaliate,
SOURCE: *Ibid.*, 206–209.

was Massachusetts. In 1785 the Massachusetts legislature enacted a series of measures discriminating against British shipping and commercial interests, sent out a plea to the other states to do the same, and instructed its delegates in Congress to seek a general convention to revise the commercial powers of Congress. All these efforts were ineffectual; only one state (New Hampshire) followed with a similar legislative program; and Massachusetts' congressional delegates refused to seek a general commercial convention, out of fear that such a convention would exceed its powers and attempt a general overhaul of the Confederation. The delegates cited three lesser reasons for their refusal, then proceeded to the heart of the matter:

. . . Fourthly. If an Alteration, either temporary or perpetual, of the commercial powers of Congress, is to be considered by a Convention, shall the latter be authorized to revise the Confederation generally, or only for express purposes?—the great object of the Revolution, was the Establishment of good Government, and each of the States, in forming their own, as well as the federal Constitution, have adopted republican principles. notwithstanding this, plans have been artfully laid, and vigorously pursued, which had they been successful, We think would inevitably have changed our republican Governments, into baleful Aristocracies. Those plans are frustrated, but the same Spirit remains in their abettors: And the Institution of the Cincinnati, honourable and beneficent as the Views may have been of the Officers who compose it, We fear, if not totally abolished, will have the same fatal Tendency. What the Effect then may be, of calling a Convention to revise the Confederation generally, We leave with your Excellency and the honorable Legislature to determine. We are apprehensive and it is our Duty to declare it, that such a Measure would produce thro'out the Union, an Exertion of the Friends of an Aristocracy, to send Members who would promote a Change of Government: and We can form some Judgment of the plan, which such members would report to Congress.—but Should the Members be altogether republican, such have been the Declamations of designing Men against the Confederation generally: against the Rotation of Members, which perhaps is the best Check to Corruption And against the Mode of altering the Confederation by the unanimous Consent of the Legislatures, which effectually prevents Innovations in the Articles, by Intrigue or Surprise, that we think there is great Danger of a Report which would invest Congress with powers, that the honorable Legislature have not the most distant Intention to delegate. . . .

Massachusetts has great Weight, and is considered as one of the most republican States in the Union; and when it is known, that the Legislature have proposed a general Revision, there can be no Doubt, that they will be represented as being convinced of the Necessity of increasing generally, the powers of Congress, and the Opinion of the State will be urged with such Art, as to convince Numbers that the Articles of the Confederation are altogether exceptionable. thus, whilst Measures are taken to guard against the Evils arising from the Want in one or two particulars, of power in Congress, we are in great danger of incurring the other Extreme— "more power in Congress" has been the Cry from all quarters; but especially of those whose Views, not being confined to a Government that will best promote the Happiness of the people, are extended to one that will afford lucrative Employments, civil and military. such a government is an Aristocracy, which would require a standing Army, and a numerous Train of pensioners and placemen to prop and support its exalted Administration. to recommend ones self to such an Administration, would be to secure an Establishment for Life and at the same Time to provide for his posterity. these are pleasing prospects, which republican Governments do not afford, And it is not to be wondered at, that many persons of elevated Views and idle Habits in these States are desirous of the Change. We are for increasing the power of Congress, as far as it will promote the Happiness of the people; but at the same Time are clearly of Opinion that every Measure should be avoided which would strengthen the Hands of the Enemies to a free Government: And that an Administration of the present Confederation with all its Inconveniences, is preferable to the Risque of general Dissentions and Animosities, which may approach to Anarchy and prepare the Way to a ruinous System of Government.

15. The Jay-Gardoqui Negotiations: Debate in
Congress, August 16, 1786

State and personal interests and the republican spirit were undermining Congress, but it was a conflict of sectional interests that came closest

SOURCE: *Ibid.,* 427–430.

to tearing the body (and the Union) asunder. The conflict arose over a proposed treaty with Spain. After the peace of 1783, Spain looked with alarm at the new nation she had helped create and, fearing that the United States' expansionist tendencies might jeopardize her own empire, promptly closed all her American possessions to trade with the United States and blocked navigation of the Mississippi through her control of the port of New Orleans. Tentative negotiations between Spain and the United States proved fruitless, and in the summer of 1785 Spain sent Don Diego de Gardoqui as minister plenipotentiary to treat with Secretary of Foreign Affairs John Jay. Congress instructed Jay not to make any agreement to surrender American claims to rights to navigate the Mississippi, for without such rights development of the western country was virtually impossible. But Gardoqui offered considerable advantages in exchange for the surrender of such rights: commercial concessions that would perhaps solve New England's commercial problems by opening vast markets for New England fish, and would bolster the economy of the Middle States by opening insatiable new markets for American wheat. In addition, such trade would be of great value to the entire American economy, for it would yield large quantities of badly needed gold and silver. But congressmen from the South, where speculation in western lands was widespread, united to defeat Jay's request for an alteration of his instructions, in a strictly sectional vote. The following is an extract of the debates on the issue.

Thursday Aug 16, 1786
Congress went into a Committee of the whole
Mr. Grayson [of Virginia] opened the debate with an extemporary speech. He followed the train of Mr. P[inckney of South Carolina] Laboured to depreciate the advantages to be derived from a commercial treaty with Spain and argued that nothing was offered by the treaty but what might be enjoyed without it. That the sacrifice to be made to obtain this treaty was great and far more than an equivalent, that the occlusion of the river would destroy the hopes of the principal men in the S[outhern] States in establishing the future fortunes of their families, that it would render the western country of no value and thereby deprive the U S of the fund on which they depended to discharge the domestic debt, that it would separate the interest of the western Inhabitants, from that of the rest of the Union and render them hostile to it, that it would weaken if not destroy the union by disaffecting the S[outhern] States when they saw their dearest interests sacrificed and given up to obtain a trivial commercial advantage for their brethren in the East. That Spain knew her own weakness and would not dare to go

to war to secure her unreasonable demands. That if she did, she would not be supported by any of the commercial nations in Europe, that it was their interest and wish that the trade of [South America] should be open, that although France was connected with Spain by the family compact and policy, yet in case of a rupture between the U S and Spain she would only mediate between them but not join the latter. But in case she did Great Britain would join the U.S. That she in particular wished to see Spain divested of her South American colonies and to participate in that trade. The interest and policy of the Dutch would lead them to the same measures. That the U S had nothing to fear from a war with Spain. That [Colonel Daniel] Morgan [a famed revolutionary soldier] with 1000 men could penetrate into the heart of Mexico and emancipate all the Spanish provinces—that the inhabitants there were ripe for a revolt and only waited for such an event to shake off the yoke of Spain. That the true policy of the U S was to stand firm to cement and strengthen the Union among themselves and to assert their right to the navigation of the Mississippi and he had no doubt but that Spain would finally agree to it.

Mr. King [of Massachusetts] spoke next. Having in behalf of the delegates for Massachusetts moved new Instructions to Mr. Jay and observed that this subject was forced upon us, and not to be put off at our pleasure. He proceeded to point out the distressed state of the Eastern States—that they had an ungrateful soil and no staple but what they drew from the Sea. That the fishery depended on a market, the best market was Spain, and this could not be secured but by treaty. Therefore a treaty with Spain was of the utmost consequence to the Eastern States in particular, but the terms which were then moved were beneficial to all the states. That the equivalent to be offered was of no great consequence. It was only an Agreement to forbear the use of that which we could not at present enjoy. That the Mouth of the river was in the possession of Spain. That she now excluded us until we were able to assert our right by arms. That if the value of the western lands depended upon the free navigation of the river Mississippi the forcible occlusion by Spain operated as strongly to that effect as a voluntary forbearance for a term of years. That however some gentlemen might depreciate the power of Spain she was by no means a contemptible enemy. That France must favour if not join her—that our hopes of assistance from any of the Maritime power of Europe were visionary and ill founded, and though they wished us to be independent they never wished us to be powerful. That refusing to treat on the terms proposed is sacrificing the interest and happiness of a Million to promote the views of speculating landjobbers. That entering into a treaty on conditions to forbear the use of the Navigation will give time to the U.S. to acquire strength, arrange their affairs, and strengthen the Union, so that at the end of the term they may be prepared to assert their right, whereas by breaking off the treaty, Spain will be disgusted and will strengthen her post to exclude us from the use of the river, the settlers in the Western country buoyed up with the hopes of assistance will attempt to force a passage and the U S will be precipitated into a war before they are prepared. That in case of such an event the existence of the Confederation will be endangered. For the States whose interests are now neglected if not sacrificed will not be willing to incur the expence and danger of a war brought upon them as they will think unnecessarily and prematurely, more especially when they considered that by this precipitate step they are deprived of the only advantages which they could expect from the Union. In such a case would there be found a man east of—where to draw the line he did not know—but would say east of Delaware who would give his vote for war.

PART THREE:

The Tree of Liberty:
Its Fruits and Its Flavor,
1783-1787

In the absence of a viable central authority, the management of American affairs devolved temporarily upon the people—which meant, for practical purposes, upon the several state governments, for during the Revolution the people of all but two of the states approved or acquiesced in the establishment of constitutions that created permanent state governments. (The two exceptions were Connecticut and Rhode Island, both of which continued to operate under colonial charters that had made them essentially self-governing.) Judging by these constitutions as well as by the reams of political theory that were published during the period, the people of the United States were strongly committed to the propositions that life, liberty, and property were natural, God-given rights of man, and that these rights were best secured under a republican form of government—by which they meant one that blended the principles of the three ancient forms of government: monarchy, aristocracy, and democracy. A few distinguished Americans, notably Alexander Hamilton and John Dickinson, held to the belief that natural rights were better guaranteed under a limited monarchy, but the overwhelming majority embraced republicanism.

Such concern with rights and republicanism could, in practice, yield pettiness in words and deeds—as was illustrated by the resolutions of the town meeting in Torrington, Connecticut (Document 6, above), or when the legislature of Georgia passed a law revoking the citizenship of any Georgian who spent more than three years being educated abroad, or when the inhabitants of Fairfax County, Virginia, instructed its state representatives to oppose sending American ambassadors to the courts of Europe, lest America become corrupted by association with monarchists. Yet there was a grand side to the concern as well. On November 11, 1786, for example, the Providence Gazette proudly reprinted the following quotation from a London newspaper: "There are 775,300,000 people in the World. Of these, arbitrary governments command 741,800,000, and the free ones (including 10 million Indians) only 33½ million. Of these few, 12½ million are subjects or descendants of the British Empire—1/3 of the freemen of the world. On the whole, slaves are three and twenty times more numerous than men enjoying, in any tolerable degree, the rights of human nature."

16. Richard Henry Lee on Republican Government in America (1787)

A number of writers, perhaps the most able being John Adams (in his Defence of the Constitutions of Government of the United States of America, 1787), attempted to explain and justify American republicanism to the world. Such efforts were hampered, however, by the fact that the United States was the first modern republic to extend over a large geographical area, and republican theorists were almost unanimously agreed that republics could succeed only in small countries. Possibly the best expression of the American answer to this theoretical problem—federal republicanism—was Richard Henry Lee's description of republicanism in the United States (December 25, 1787):

. . . Our territories are far too extensive for a limited monarchy, in which the representatives must frequently assemble, and the laws operate mildly and systematically. The most eligible system is a federal republic, that is, a system in which national concerns may be transacted in the center, and local affairs in state or district governments. . . .

In a federal system we must not only balance the parts of the same government, as that of the state, or that of the union; but we must find a balancing influence between the general and local governments—the latter is what men or writers have but very little or imperfectly considered.

A free and mild government is that in which no laws can be made without the formal and free consent of the people, or of their constitutional representatives; that is, of a substantial representative branch. Liberty, in its genuine sense, is security to enjoy the effects of our honest industry and labors, in a free and mild government, and personal security from all illegal restraints.

SOURCE: Richard Henry Lee, Letters from the Federal Farmer (New York, 1788), Letter VI.

Of rights, some are natural and inalienable, of which even the people cannot deprive individuals: Some are constitutional or fundamental; these cannot be altered or abolished by the ordinary laws; but the people, by express acts, may alter or abolish them—These, such as the trial by jury, the benefits of the writ of habeas corpus, etc. individuals claim under the solemn compacts of the people, as constitutions, or at least under laws so strengthened by long usage as not to be repealable by the ordinary legislature—and some are common or mere legal rights, that is, such as individuals claim under laws which the ordinary legislature may alter or abolish at pleasure.

The confederation is a league of friendship among the states or sovereignties for the common defense and mutual welfare—Each state expressly retains its sovereignty, and all powers not expressly given to congress—All federal powers are lodged in a congress of delegates annually elected by the state legislatures, except in Connecticut and Rhode Island, where they are chosen by the people— Each state has a vote in congress, pays its delegates, and may instruct or recall them; no delegate can hold any office of profit, or serve more than three years in any six years—Each state may be represented by not less than two, or more than seven delegates.

[Lee summarizes the powers of Congress under the Articles of Confederation, then continues]

The following, I think, will be allowed to be inalienable or fundamental rights in the United States:—

No man, demeaning himself peaceably, shall be molested on account of his religion or mode of worship—The people have a right to hold and enjoy their property according to known standing laws, and which cannot be taken from them without their consent, or the consent of their representatives; and whenever taken in the pressing urgencies of government, they are to receive a reasonable compensation for it—Individual security consists in having free recourse to the laws—The people are subject to no laws or taxes not assented to by their representatives constitutionally assembled—They are at all times entitled to the benefits of the writ of habeas corpus, the trial by jury in criminal and civil causes—They have a right, when charged, to a speedy trial in the vicinage; to be heard by themselves or counsel, not to be compelled to furnish evidence against themselves, to have witnesses face to face, and to confront their adversaries before the judge—No man is held to answer a crime charged upon him till it be substantially described to him; and he is subject to no unreasonable searches or seizures of his person, papers or effects—The people have a right to assemble in an orderly manner, and petition the government for a redress of wrongs—The freedom of the press ought not to be restrained—No emoluments, except for actual service—No hereditary honors, or orders of nobility, ought to be allowed—The military ought to be subordinate to the civil authority, and no soldier be quartered on the citizens without their consent—The militia ought always to be armed and disciplined, and the usual defense of the country—The supreme power is in the people, and power delegated ought to return to them at stated periods, and frequently—The legislative, executive, and judicial powers, ought always to be kept distinct—others perhaps might be added.

The organization of the state governments—Each state has a legislature, an executive, and a judicial branch—In general legislators are excluded from the important executive and judicial offices—Except in the Carolinas there is no constitutional distinction among Christian sects—The constitutions of New York, Delaware, and Virginia, exclude the clergy from offices civil and military—the other states do nearly the same in practice.

Each state has a democratic branch elected twice a year in Rhode Island and Connecticut, biennially in South Carolina, and annually in the other states—There are about 1500 representatives in all the states, or one to each 1700 inhabitants, reckoning five blacks for three whites—The states do not differ as to the age or moral characters of the electors or elected, nor materially as to their property.

Pennsylvania has lodged all her legislative powers in a single branch, and Georgia has done the same; the other eleven states have each in their legislatures a second or senatorial branch. In forming this they have combined various principles, and aimed at several checks and balances. It is amazing to see how ingenuity has worked in the several states to fix a barrier against popular instability. In Massachusetts the senators are apportioned to districts according to the taxes they pay, nearly according to property. In Connecticut the freemen, in September, vote for twenty counsellers, and return the names of those voted for in the several towns; the legislature takes the twenty who have the most votes, and give them to the people, who, in April, choose twelve of them, who, with the governor and deputy governor, form the senatorial branch. In Maryland the senators are chosen by two electors from each county; these electors are chosen by the freemen, and qualified as the members in the democratic branch are: In these two cases checks are aimed at in the mode of election. Several states hade taken into view the periods of service, age, property, etc. In South Carolina a senator is elected for two years, in Delaware three, and in New York and Virginia four, in Maryland five, and in the other states for one. In New York and Virginia one-fourth part go out yearly. In Virginia a senator must be twenty-five years old, in South Carolina thirty. In New York the electors must each have a freehold worth 250 dollars, in North Carolina a freehold of fifty acres of land; in the other states the electors of senators are qualified as electors of representatives are. In Massachusetts a senator must have a freehold in his own right worth 1000 dollars, or any estate worth 2000, in New Jersey any estate worth 2666, in South Carolina worth 1300 dollars, in North Carolina 300 acres of land in fee, etc. The numbers of senators in each state are from ten to thirty-one, about 160 in the eleven states, about one to 14000 inhabitants.

Two states, Massachusetts and New York, have each introduced into their legislatures a third, but incomplete branch. In the former, the governor may negative any law not supported by two-thirds of the senators, and two-thirds of the representatives: in the latter, the governor, chancellor, and judges of the supreme court may do the same.

Each state has a single executive branch. In the five eastern states the people at large elect their governors; in the other states the legislatures elect them. In South Carolina the governor is elected once in two years; in New York and Delaware once in three, and in the other states annually. The governor of New York has no executive council, the other governors have. In several states the governor has a vote in the senatorial branch—the governors have similar powers in some instances, and quite dissimilar ones in others. The number of executive counsellors in the states are from five to twelve. In the four eastern states, New Jersey, Pennsylvania, and Georgia, they are of the men returned legislators by the people. In Pennsylvania the counsellers are chosen triennially, in Delaware every fourth year, in Virginia every three years, in South Carolina biennially, and in the other states yearly.

Each state has a judicial branch; each common law courts, superior and inferior; some chancery and admiralty courts: The courts in general sit in different places, in order to accommodate the citizens. The trial by jury is had in all the common law courts, and in some of the admiralty courts. The democratic free men principally form the juries; men destitute of property, of character, or under age, are excluded as in elections. Some of the judges are during good behavior, and some appointed for a year, and some for years; and all are dependant on the legislatures for their salaries—Particulars respecting this department are too many to be noticed here.

17. Virginia Act for Establishing Religious Freedom, January 16, 1786

One of the most cherished of republican principles was that of the separation of church and state. Transforming the principle into practice was no simple matter, for established, state-supported churches of one sect or another were the rule in virtually all parts of the western world, and Anglo-Saxon America was no exception. Among those that led the way toward disestablishment was the state of Virginia, which early in 1786 enacted its celebrated Act for Establishing Religious Freedom:

WHEREAS Almighty God hath created the mind free; that all attempts to influence it by temporal punishments or burthens, or by civil incapacitations, tend only to beget habits of hypocrisy and meanness, and are a departure from the plan of the Holy Author of our religion, Who . . . chose not to propagate it by coercions . . . that the impious presumption of legislators and rulers . . . who being themselves but fallible and uninspired men, have assumed dominion over the faith of others, setting up their own opinions and modes of thinking as the only true and infallible, and as such endeavoring to impose them on others, hath established and maintained false religions over the greatest part of the world, and through all time; that to compel a man to furnish contributions of money for the propagation of opinions which he disbelieves, is sinful and tyrannical; that even the forcing him to support this or that teacher of his own religious persuasion, is depriving him of the comfortable liberty of giving his contributions to the particular pastor,

SOURCE: W. W. Hening, ed., *Statutes At Large of Virginia* (Richmond, Va., 1823), XII, 84–86.

whose morals he would make his pattern, and whose powers he feels most persuasive to righteousness, and is withdrawing from the ministry those temporary rewards, which proceeding from an approbation of their personal conduct, are an additional incitement to earnest and unremitting labors for the instruction of mankind; that our civil rights have no dependence on our religious opinions . . . that therefore the proscribing any citizen as unworthy the public confidence by laying upon him an incapacity of being called to offices of trust and emolument, unless he profess or renounce this or that religious opinion, is depriving him injuriously of those privileges and advantages to which in common with his fellow-citizens he has a natural right; that it tends only to corrupt the principles of that religion it is meant to encourage, by bribing with a monopoly of worldly honors and emoluments, those who will externally profess and conform to it . . . that to suffer the civil magistrate to intrude his powers into the field of opinion, and to restrain the profession or propagation of principles . . . is a dangerous fallacy, which at once destroys all religious liberty, because he . . . will make his opinions the rule of judgment, and approve or condemn the sentiments of others only as they shall square with or differ from his own; that it is time enough for the rightful purposes of civil government, for its officers to interfere when principles break out into overt acts against peace and good order; and finally that truth is great and will prevail if left to herself, that she is the proper and sufficient antagonist to error, and has nothing to fear from the conflict, unless by human interposition disarmed of her natural weapons, free argument and debate. . . .

Be it enacted by the General Assembly. That no man shall be compelled to frequent or support any religious worship, place, or ministry whatsoever, nor shall be enforced, restrained, molested, or burthened in his body or goods, nor shall otherwise suffer on account of his religious opinions or belief; but that all men shall be free to profess, and by argument to maintain, their opinion in matters of religion, and that the same shall in no wise diminish, enlarge, or affect their civil capacities.

And though we well know that this assembly elected by the people for the ordinary purposes of legislation only, have no power to restrain the acts of succeeding assemblies, constituted with powers equal to our own, and that therefore to declare this act to be irrevocable would be of no effect in law; yet we are free to declare, and do declare, that the rights hereby asserted are of the natural rights of mankind, and that if any act shall be hereafter passed to repeal the present, or to narrow its operation, such act will be an infringement of natural right.

18. The Problem of Slavery

One aspect of American society made most sincere republicans squirm in discomfort: for all the declarations on liberty and equality, almost a fifth of the three and a half million Americans were Negro slaves. To rectify this evil, anti-slavery societies were formed in every state except the Carolinas and Georgia, and laws providing for manumission or gradual abolition were passed in a few states, but with one exception (Massachusetts) slavery continued to exist in every state until the 1790's.

A. Quock Walker v. Nathaniel Jennison (1783)

One Nathaniel Jennison of Massachusetts, arrested for beating a Negro named Quock Walker, defended himself on the ground that Walker was his slave. Walker contended that slavery had been abolished by the first article of the Massachusetts constitution of 1780, which declared that all men were born free and equal. The Massachusetts Supreme Court, Chief Justice Caleb Cushing presiding, ruled in favor of Walker:

As to the doctrine of slavery and the right of Christians to hold Africans in perpetual servitude, and sell and treat them as we do our horses and cattle, that (it is true) has been heretofore countenanced by the Province Laws formerly, but nowhere is it expressly enacted or established. It has been a usage—a usage which took its origin from the practice of some of the European nations, and the regulations of British government respecting the then Colonies, for the benefit of trade and wealth. But whatever sentiments have formerly prevailed in this particular or slid in upon us by the example of others, a different idea has taken place with the people of America, more favorable to the natural rights of mankind, and to that natural, innate desire of Liberty, which with Heaven (without regard to color, complexion, or shape of noses—features) has inspired all the

SOURCE: Albert B. Hart, ed., *Commonwealth History of Massachusetts* (5 vols., New York, 1927–1930), IV, 37–38.

human race. And upon this ground our Constitution of Government, by which the people of this Commonwealth have solemnly bound themselves, sets out with declaring that all men are born free and equal—and that every subject is entitled to liberty, and to have it guarded by the laws, as well as life and property—and in short is totally repugnant to the idea of being born slaves. This being the case, I think the idea of slavery is inconsistent with our own conduct and Constitution; and there can be no such thing as perpetual servitude of a rational creature, unless his liberty is forfeited by some criminal conduct or given up by personal consent or contract. . . . *Verdict Guilty.*

B. *John Brown to Moses Brown, November 27, 1786*

Others took a more callous view. In 1786 Moses Brown of Rhode Island, a Quaker and abolitionist, heard that his brother John, a wealthy Providence merchant, was contemplating a venture in the slave trade. Moses sent a note on the subject to John. The latter, pretending that he was having business difficulties, gave the following cynical reply:

Providence Novem 27th. 1786

D[r]. Brother

Your Esteemed Favour was this Day at Diner handed me by your Son. I have not yet had time to peruse the Treeteice you was so kind as to Accompany with the Letter but will do it Soone, by begining it this Evening. You mention that you had heard, as Last Evening, I had it in Contemplation the Sending an Other Vessell to Affrica in the Slave Trade. Its true that I have not onley had an Other Voyage in Contemplation but have been prepairing the Cargo for this 4 Months past & this Day before I Received yours began taking in the Ballis having before Shipt the Captin & Mate. I have no Doubt of your Sinserity, in Your Exurtions to Discorage the Slave Trade, and did I Consider it as You do I would by no means be Concernd in it, but from the best Information I can Git & that has beene from Grait Numbers the Slaves are possitively better off, that is brought from the Coast then those who are Left behind or then those would be was they not brought away—More aspetially those who are Caried Among the French, as I propose this Vessill as Well as the One Allredy Gone will Land them on High spanolia, where all Accounts Agree they are better Treeted

SOURCE: Peck Collection, Rhode Island Historical Society. Minor changes in punctuation and spelling have been made in the interest of clarity.

then in Aney part of the English West Indies. This Trade has beene permitted by the Supreame Govenour of all things for time Immemmoriel, and whenever I am Convinced, as you are, that its Rong in the Sight of God, I will Immediately Deasist, but while its not only allowd by the Supreeme Govenour of all States but by all the Nations of Europe, and perhaps the most of Any by that Very Government which has beene & is Still So Much Esteemed & Incoraged by those Very people who Appears the Most Active in Writing and Clammering Against the Trade I cannot thinke this State ought to Decline the Trade. I fulley Agree with You that no past Proffit that I have purtooke in the trade Can be My Inducement having Lost & that Very Graitly in allmost Every Voyage to Guiney I have beene Concernd in but You are Sencible much property has beene Acquired by this Trade from Newport. I Lately heard Severil of their principle people Say that the Merchants of Newport Very Scarsly Ever Cleard any property in Aney other Trade & that all the Estates that had Ever beene Acquired in that Town had beene Got in the Guiney Trades. It may be as you Suppose Determind by that power which presides over all Events that no Inhabitant of this Town Shall Ever Prosper in the Slave Trade. You Mention that the Melasses Trade may be Caried on without Extending it to the Guiney Trade. I agree it may be in a Limmited Degree. The Neufoundlands as well as all other British ports you are Sencible is Shet up from this Commerce which Used to be Very Grait

I owe an Enormus Sum of Money in Europe & am Striving in Every Trade Which Appears Lawfull & Right to me, to pay as Much of the Debt as possable Dureing My Life time as I Wish Most Ardently to Leave My Famely Less Involved In Debt then is Now the Case. You are Sencible I have Tryd the Tobacco Trade, have a Ship Now Gone to Verginnia for a Load, have Tryd the Fishery having fifteen Schooners in the Buissiness, but have not yet beene So Fortunate as to Lessen the Debt. Should the Brigg I am now Fitting to Guiney & the Snow Captain Cooke who Saild in July Last the Ship Captain Sheldon now Gone to Virginnia & bound to France together with the Fisherman, which I propose Shall all Sail Very Early in the Spring in order to Make up a Cargo of the best & Earlyest Spring Fish for Billbo [Bilbao, Spain]; I Say Should all these Succeede but Tollorably Well I hope to Discharge a Very Large propotion of My Debts, and I do Assure You I have not nor never had one Feeling in my Mind but that the Guiney Trade, or the Slave Trade as you More Explissetly Call it, was and is as Just & Right as as Aney Trade I am or Ever Was Concernd in & Vastly More So then to Send a Vessill to Jamacia with a Two Fold or Double Intention nay Three Fold Contrediction to the professions of Some Owners of Vessills. First, if the Slave Trade is Rong why will the Men Who thinkes So Incorage it by Sending for the produce Raised & made by those Slaves So Rongfully & unritchously Imported from their own Native Countery. Are they Not doing as bad as tho they was to Undertake to Incorage A Theif by purchessing his Goods tho they knew they was Stole from an Honest Man?

Secondly, to thus Incorage the Trade of Carying Slaves to the West Indies have they Not Coverd their property with Fals papers & by this Means Indeverd to Disseive the people they was bound Among, by bringing their produce to this Countery Directly Conterary to their Laws?

& Thirdly, to Intreduce the produce of the English Islands In to this State Under Different Cullers & Different papers their others being Conseal'd, & all this Done by Owners & a Captin who are So Consheus bound as to use None but the plain Langwige & the better to Cover their Wickedness they Appear Among the Foremust to write & Taulke against the Guiney Trade & The Lord deliver me from Such Wolves in Sheeps Cloathing.

If you Incline to have a Law passed in this State to Stop the Guiney Trade, I once told you & I now Repeete it that I Shall be happy to Step out of the Seet Whenever it Can be So much better Fild as it will be when you Accept.[1] I am Fulley Sencible that you Can Searve the Town & State at Large all better as a Legislater than I Can and wish with all My hart you woud once more Concent to Searve the publick in that Way. Our Different Sentiments Respecting the Guiney Trade will Weigh Nothing in My Mind against your taking my place in the House

I will not Detain you aney Longer. I am Exceeding Sorry to Differ So much from you in this Buissiness, but I have Charrity for You that you thinke you are doing Gods Service when you go According to the Lite of Your Contience. I only wish for the Same Charritable Dispossition towards me that will I go According to

---

[1] By custom, one of the seats in the Rhode Island legislature went to a member of the Brown family, though the state had annual popular elections. In 1786 John Brown occupied the seat—Ed.

the Dicketates of my Contious I may have mercey Extended to me tho I am not Endowd with that Devine Light to See the Guiney Trade with the Same Eyes as you do. I Respect you as a Brother & a Friend. I Respect your Childron and Sincearly wish they mought be Indulged to be More Furmillior with mine. I am Shure my Childron has a perticular Regard for Yours—

C. Thomas Jefferson, Notes on Virginia (1782)

Among Southerners, who owned about 90 per cent of the slaves, attitudes were mixed. In Maryland, Virginia, and much of North Carolina, where slave labor was employed at marginal profits and often at a loss in the cultivation of tobacco and wheat, and where republicanism was strongest, opposition to slavery was widespread. Quite apart from the economic aspects of the matter, however, the problem of emancipation was a complicated one, as is indicated by this prejudiced but carefully reasoned analysis by Thomas Jefferson (Jefferson is discussing a series of proposed revisions to the Virginia laws):

. . . To emancipate all slaves born after the passing the act. The bill reported by the revisers does not itself contain this proposition; but an amendment containing it was prepared, to be offered to the legislature whenever the bill should be taken up, and farther directing, that they should continue with their parents to a certain age, then to be brought up, at the public expense, to tillage, arts, or sciences, according to their geniuses, till the females should be eighteen, and the males twenty-one years of age, when they should be colonized to such place as the circumstances of the time should render most proper, sending them out with arms, implements of household and of the handicraft arts, seeds, pairs of the useful domestic animals, etc., to declare them a free and independent people, and extend to them our alliance and protection, till they have acquired strength; and to send vessels at the same time to other parts of the world for an equal number of white inhabitants; to induce them to migrate hither, proper encouragements were to be proposed. It will probably be asked, Why not retain and incorporate the blacks into the State, and thus save the expense of supplying by importation of white settlers, the vacancies they will leave? Deep-rooted prejudices entertained by the whites; ten thousand recollec-

SOURCE: Thomas Jefferson, *Notes on Virginia* (Harper Torchbook edition, New York, 1964), pp. 132–139.

tions, by the blacks, of the injuries they have sustained; new provocations; the real distinctions which nature has made; and many other circumstances, will divide us into parties, and produce convulsions, which will probably never end but in the extermination of the one or the other race. To these objections, which are political, may be added others, which are physical and moral. The first difference which strikes us is that of color. . . . And is this difference of no importance? Is it not the foundation of a greater or less share of beauty in the two races? Are not the fine mixtures of red and white, the expressions of every passion by greater or less suffusions of color in the one, preferable to that eternal monotony, which reigns in the countenances, that immovable veil of black which covers the emotions of the other race? Add to these, flowing hair, a more elegant symmetry of form, their own judgment in favor of the whites, declared by their preference of them, as uniformly as is the preference of the Oranootan for the black woman over those of his own species. The circumstance of superior beauty, is thought worthy attention in the propagation of our horses, dogs, and other domestic animals; why not in that of man? Besides those of color, figure, and hair, there are other physical distinctions proving a difference of race. They have less hair on the face and body. They secrete less by the kidneys, and more by the glands of the skin, which gives them a very strong and disagreeable odor. This greater degree of transpiration, renders them more tolerant of heat, and less so of cold than the whites. Perhaps, too, a difference of structure in the pulminary apparatus, which a late ingenious experimentalist has discovered to be the principal regulator of animal heat, may have disabled them from extricating, in the act of inspiration, so much of that fluid from the outer air, or obliged them in expiration, to part with more of it. They seem to require less sleep. A black after hard labor through the day, will be induced by the slightest amusements to sit up till midnight, or later, though knowing he must be out with the first dawn of the morning. They are at least as brave, and more adventuresome. But this may perhaps proceed from a want of forethought, which prevents their seeing a danger till it be present. When present, they do not go through it with more coolness or steadiness than the whites. They are more ardent after their female; but love seems with them to be more an eager desire, than a tender delicate mixture of sentiment and sensation.

Their griefs are transient. Those numberless afflictions, which render it doubtful whether heaven has given life to us in mercy or in wrath, are less felt, and sooner forgotten with them. In general, their existence appears to participate more of sensation than reflection. To this must be ascribed their disposition to sleep when abstracted from their diversions, and unemployed in labor. An animal whose body is at rest, and who does not reflect, must be disposed to sleep of course. Comparing them by their faculties of memory, reason, and imagination, it appears to me that in memory they are equal to the whites; in reason much inferior, as I think one could scarcely be found capable of tracing and comprehending the investigations of Euclid; and that in imagination they are dull, tasteless, and anomalous. It would be unfair to follow them to Africa for this investigation. We will consider them here, on the same stage with the whites, and where the facts are not apochryphal on which a judgment is to be formed. It will be right to make great allowances for the difference of condition, of education, of conversation, of the sphere in which they move. Many millions of them have been brought to, and born in America. Most of them, indeed, have been confined to tillage, to their own homes, and their own society; yet many have been so situated, that they might have availed themselves of the conversation of their masters; many have been brought up to the handicraft arts, and from that circumstance have always been associated with the whites. Some have been liberally educated, and all have lived in countries where the arts and sciences are cultivated to a considerable degree, and all have had before their eyes samples of the best works from abroad. . . . But never yet could I find that a black had uttered a thought above the level of plain narration; never saw even an elementary trait of painting or sculpture. In music they are more generally gifted than the whites with accurate ears for tune and time, and they have been found capable of imagining a small catch. Whether they will be equal to the composition of a more extensive run of melody, or of complicated harmony, is yet to be proved. Misery is often the parent of the most affecting touches in poetry. Among the blacks is misery enough, God knows, but no poetry. Love is the peculiar œstrum of the poet. Their love is ardent, but it kindles the senses only, not the imagination. . . . The improvement of the blacks in body and mind, in the first instance of their mixture with the whites, has been observed by every one, and proves that their inferiority is not the effect merely of their condition of life. We know that among the Romans, about the Augustan age especially, the condition of their slaves was much more deplorable than that of the blacks on the continent of America. The two sexes were confined in separate apartments, because to raise a child cost the master more than to buy one. Cato, for a very restricted indulgence to his slaves in this particular, took from them a certain price. But in this country the slaves multiply as fast as the free inhabitants. Their situation and manners place the commerce between the two sexes almost without restraint. The same Cato, on a principle of economy, always sold his sick and superannuated slaves. He gives it as a standing precept to a master visiting his farm, to sell his old oxen, old wagons, old tools, old and diseased servants, and everything else become useless. . . . Yet notwithstanding these and other discouraging circumstances among the Romans, their slaves were often their rarest artists. They excelled too in science, insomuch as to be usually employed as tutors to their master's children. Epictetus, Terence, and Phædrus, were slaves. But they were of the race of whites. It is not their condition then, but nature, which has produced the distinction. Whether further observation will or will not verify the conjecture, that nature has been less bountiful to them in the endowments of the head, I believe that in those of the heart she will be found to have done them justice. That disposition to theft with which they have been branded, must be ascribed to their situation, and not to any depravity of the moral sense. The man in whose favor no laws of property exist, probably feels himself less bound to respect those made in favor of others. When arguing for ourselves, we lay it down as a fundamental, that laws, to be just, must give a reciprocation of right; that, without this, they are mere arbitrary rules of conduct, founded in force, and not in conscience; and it is a problem which I give to the master to solve, whether the religious precepts against the violation of property were not framed for him as well as his slave? And whether the slave may not as justifiably take a little from one who has taken all from him, as he may slay one who would slay him? That a change in the relations in which a man is placed should change his ideas of moral right or wrong, is neither new, nor peculiar to the color of the blacks. Homer tells us it was so two thousand six hundred years ago. . . .

But the slaves of which Homer speaks were whites. Notwith-standing these considerations which must weaken their respect for the laws of property, we find among them numerous instances of the most rigid integrity, and as many as among their better in-structed masters, of benevolence, gratitude, and unshaken fidelity. The opinion that they are inferior in the faculties of reason and imagination, must be hazarded with great diffidence. To justify a general conclusion, requires many observations, even where the subject may be submitted to the anatomical knife, to optical glasses, to analysis by fire or by solvents. How much more then where it is a faculty, not a substance, we are examining; where it eludes the research of all the senses; where the conditions of its existence are various and variously combined; where the effects of those which are present or absent bid defiance to calculation; let me add too, as a circumstance of great tenderness, where our conclusion would de-grade a whole race of men from the rank in the scale of beings which their Creater may perhaps have given them. To our reproach it must be said, that though for a century and a half we have had under our eyes the races of black and of red men, they have never yet been viewed by us as subjects of natural history. I advance it, therefore, as a suspicion only, that the blacks, whether originally a distinct race, or made distinct by time and circumstances, are inferior to the whites in the endowments both of body and mind. It is not against experience to suppose that different species of the same genus, or varieties of the same species, may possess different qualifications. Will not a lover of natural history then, one who views the gradations in all the races of animals with the eye of philosophy, excuse an effort to keep those in the department of man as distinct as nature has formed them? This unfortunate differ-ence of color, and perhaps of faculty, is a powerful obstacle to the emancipation of these people. Many of their advocates, while they wish to vindicate the liberty of human nature, are anxious also to pre-serve its dignity and beauty. Some of these, embarrassed by the question, "What further is to be done with them?" join them-selves in opposition with those who are actuated by sordid avarice only. Among the Romans emancipation required but one effort. The slave, when made free, might mix with, without staining the blood of his master. But with us a second is necessary, unknown to history. When freed, he is to be removed beyond the reach of mixture.

D. Debate on the Importation of Negroes, South Carolina House of Representatives (1785)

In the lower South, slaves were regarded as subhuman animals, fit only for labor in the swampland rice and indigo plantations—where mortality rates and profit rates were both high. Accordingly, when slavery was discussed at all it was discussed as an economic, not a moral, question. One such discussion arose in the South Carolina legislature in 1785. For a variety of reasons, South Carolina planters were in temporary economic difficulties, and it was proposed that the importation of slaves be prohibited for three years, until planters could clear themselves from debt. The debates on the proposal (September 27, October 5, 1785) illustrate the attitudes of South Carolinians toward slavery:

. . . Mr. J. Rutledge was against the proposed measure of restricting the importation of Negroes for any given time into this state; he had been of opinion for many years, that Negroes were an increase of our wealth; what number of slaves had been imported since the peace? not above 7000, take these on an average at £50 a piece, would amount in the whole to about £400,000 and surely that was not a sum sufficient to have occasioned the present national calamities; was the above sum in any proportion to the immense quantities of dry goods which had been imported, certainly not, it was there the evil originated, and it was there a speedy remedy was necessary; However, as the business to which the House was now confined was what must originate in this committee, and as at present there was nothing before the house, he should vote for the motion, although when the report was made he should be at full liberty to oppose it in the house if he were so inclined, the report was then read and agreed on. . . .

Mr. Bee . . . thought the manner in which negroes had been lately imported threw the ballance of trade greatly against us, and therefore was the one great cause of our present calamities. He understood that last year we imported negroes to the value of £300,000 our exports for that period amounted to £400,000 now we had also imported in this time a very extensive quantity of goods which we had left only £100,000 to pay for with. Was this wise, was it politic? undoubtedly not. There were articles of foreign production that were indispensibly necessary for us to procure, especially whilst there appeared so great a backwardness amongst the people for establish-

SOURCE: *Charleston Evening Gazette*, September 28, October 18, 1785.

ing manufactories, such as those of the coarser kind, which we must have, but if we went on and imported luxuries, it was unreasonable to suppose we should ever be out of debt. The great quantity of negroes now pouring in upon us, occasions every planter to wish an increase of his stock, the sight of a negroe yard was to[o] great a temptation for a planter to withstand, he could not leave it without purchasing; in short, there seemed to be a rage for negroes, without any consideration how they were to be paid for. He did not object to this increase of slaves when we were out of debt; let that happy period arrive, wait with patience until we can clear ourselves, and then it would be time enough to permit importation. . . .

Judge Pendleton: . . . We wanted a large supply of negroes, and superfluities, when we could not devise means to pay for those we were already in possession of. . . . In a debate last year upon this subject, it had been said, and he did not doubt but the argument would be used this day, that negroes should be considered as the riches of a country, but this was an opinion he could by no means assent to. They might indeed constitute the strength of it, but its riches should be estimated by the number of its white inhabitants, for it was upon them that our commerce, our agriculture, and manufacture depended. . . .

General Pinckney went extensively into the question. He made a clear enumeration of the negroes imported, and their value on an average. He thought the strength of this country constituted its riches; that this sort of strength once saved this city, in the war, was the case when Prevost over-ran the country: 'twas true he only looked at us and went away, but what was this owing to—why to the number of bastions hastily thrown up, a service performed entirely by the negroe pioneers. This country was not capable of being cultivated by white men; as appeared on the attempt made in Georgia, during General Oglethorp's administration, but entirely failed, and ended in the white people emigrating from that state into this, where they could have negroes to cultivate their lands. Such part of this country was unhealthy as had not yet been cleared, so that the useful labours of negroes contributed to promote salubrity in the air. Much had been said about our exports being inferior to our imports, but this measure tended to diminish the exports still more, and of course prevents a great deal of specie from being brought into the state. Negroes were to this country what raw materials were to another country, they increased the staple commodity, a point well worth gentlemen's attention, as was also the large duty paid to the state for negroes imported; being about £3 per head. Who was it that wanted negroes? why those brave men that had suffered by the war; they had the general misfortune to find, on being released from captivity, there plantations plundered, and every negroe swept away. Was it not well understood, that no planter could cultivate his land without slaves? and yet is he not oblidged to pay his land tax? Is it not a moral impossibility for any planter to pay that or any other tax when by passing of this proposition they deprive of the means! Another observation of material consequence was, that to shut our ports against the importation of negroes, the whole of our trade would center in Georgia and North Carolina; they would keep their ports open while ours were shut; and so drain us of all our produce—was this the intention of gentlemen? surely not! and yet this would be the consequence if the committee agreed with the proposition. He concluded his speech with a declaration that he would vote against the proposition.

. . . Dr. Ramsey . . . It was frequently the case that a planter on his way to the treasury with his taxes, unluckily stumbled on a negro yard the temptation was too great for his philosophy to withstand, and he purchased negroes with the money that ought to have been devoted to payment of his debts. . . .

19. On the Limits and Distribution of Power

In the new republic, the lion's share of public discussion was devoted not to humanitarian or social or economic issues, but to the question of the nature, limit, and distribution of governmental power. Most particularly, in the 1780's debate centered on two subjects: the proper distribution of power in the federal system, and the proper limits (if any) to be placed on the actions of democratic or popular branches of government.

A. Commonwealth v. Caton, et al. (1782)

In time, American practice came to hold that the will of popular majorities, expressed through legislatures, was limited by written constitutions, and that it was the function of the courts to determine when leg-

SOURCE: Virginia Reports (1782), IV Call 5.

islation exceeded the bounds of constitutionality. Six or eight precedents for this doctrine of "judicial review" were established before 1789. One of the first was in Virginia, where a man named Caton was convicted of treason and pardoned by one but not the other branch of the legislature. The state court passed on the validity of the pardon, and in process announced that it would also pass on the constitutionality of properly enacted statutes:

Wythe, J.: Among all the advantages which have arisen to mankind, from the study of letters, and the universal diffusion of knowledge, there is none of more importance, than the tendency they have had to produce discussion upon the respective rights of the sovereign and the subject; and upon the powers which the different branches of the government may exercise. For, by this means, tyranny has been sapped, the departments kept within their own spheres, the citizens protected, and general liberty promoted. But this beneficial result attains to higher perfection, when those who hold the purse and the sword, differing as to the powers which each may exercise, the tribunals, who hold neither, are called upon to declare the law impartially between them. For thus the pretensions of each party are fairly examined, their respective powers ascertained, and the boundaries of authority peaceably established. Under these impressions I approach the question which has been submitted to us: and although it was said the other day by one of the judges that, imitating that great and good man Lord Hale, he would sooner quit the bench than determine it, I feel no alarm; but will meet the crisis as I ought; and in the language of my oath of office, will decide it according to the best of my skill and judgement.

I have heard of an English chancellor who said, and it was nobly said, that it was his duty to protect the rights of the subject against the encroachments of the crown; and that he would do it at every hazard. But if it was his duty to protect a solitary individual against the rapacity of the sovereign, surely it is equally mine to protect one branch of the legislature and, consequently, the whole community, against the usurpations of the other; and whenever the proper occasion occurs, I shall feel the duty; and fearlessly perform it. Whenever traitors shall be fairly convicted, by the verdict of their peers, before the competent tribunal, if one branch of the legislature, without the concurrence of the other, shall attempt to rescue the offenders from the sentence of the law, I shall not hesitate, sitting in this place, to say to the general court, *Fiat justitia, ruat coelum;* and, to the usurping branch of the legislature, you attempt worse than a vain thing; for although you cannot succeed, you set an example which may convulse society to its centre. Nay more, if the whole legislature, an event to be deprecated, should attempt to overleap the bounds prescribed to them by the people, I, in administering the public justice of the country, will meet the united powers at my seat in this tribunal; and, pointing to the constitution, will say to them, here is the limit of your authority; and, hither shall you go, but no further. . . .

I am therefore of the opinion that the pardon pleaded by the prisoners, is not valid; and that it ought to be so certified to the general court.

B. Ruling of the Pennsylvania Council of Censors (1784)

Most legislatures took the position that their power could not be checked by the courts, and when judges attempted to overrule states they were ignored or even impeached. In Pennsylvania, whose government was by far the most democratic in the United States, the proponents of legislative supremacy went even further. In 1784 the state Council of Censors dealt with the question of the sanctity of public contracts: whether a people could, through its legislature, commit itself by granting a charter and then revoke the commitment. The council, denying that an act altering the charter of the University of Pennsylvania was unconstitutional, gave among its reasons the following:

Because that although we highly reprobate all intermeddling of the General Assembly with the estates, interests or misdeeds of individuals, who are by the bill of rights secured the privilege of trial by jury, unless the matter be strictly within the cognizance of the House, or be proceeded on by orderly impeachment, yet we have no idea that corporations, which are the creatures of society, can, under the bill of rights, plead any exemption from legislative regulation.

Cases may be supposed with the highest probability, wherein, without breaking any law that may be divised, a body corporate might become not only a nuisance but dangerous; and therefore we

SOURCE: Journal of the Council of Censors, vol. II, August 27, 1784, in Public Records Division, Harrisburg, Pa.

cannot concede, that a charter obtained perhaps by fraud or impo- sition, or granted through the facility of our representatives, cannot be altered or repealed by any succeeding General Assembly. Of this the University of Oxford, left improvidently in the reign of William the third of England, in the hands of the disaffected, is a striking proof. If this doctrine were true, and verdicts ascertaining the abuse of charters were previously necessary, the extravagant inequality of representation in the English parliament could never be reduced to original principles, nor the rotten boroughs, as they are called, be deprived of their mischievous privileges. For it is plain, that this evil can only be cured by a law, which shall pass through all their charters. Nay, at this rate, should the Bank of North America, or any other corporation, become a monster of Weight and influence, and be able to counteract and overrule our legislative proceedings, nothing less than a general rising of the people would be equal to the exigence.

We consider that these *imperii in imperio*, these governments within the government of the state, holding common estates of large value, and exercising the power of making bye laws, as against the spirit and the policy of democracy, are only to be endured in order to obtain advantages which may greatly counterbalance the inconveniences and dangers which accompany them.

In Pennsylvania we have not a sole executive officer of perma- nency and weight, sufficient to restrain, and whose interest it is to keep those communities in awe; they may, therefore gradually pro- duce an indirect, yet firm aristocracy over the state, before we be aware of the mischief.

In England a Charter misused may be dissolved in a court of law upon the verdict of a Jury; and if the King be deceived by false suggestions of the grantees, the Court of Chancery has authority to repeal the charter, so obtained by fraud. But will it be said, that an act of incorporation passed here can be forfeited, or repealed for imposition on the House, unless by the Legislature? In fine, this doctrine, that the General Assembly ought not to interfere with a Corporate body, till a verdict of misuser has been found against it, involves this absurdity, that one House of General Assembly can enact a law that no succeeding General Assembly can alter, amend or repeal without the consent of the corporators, who may be highly interested in opposing the interposition of the Legislature.

20. Shays' Rebellion (1786–1787)

The ultimate challenge to governmental power arose in New England, and especially Massachusetts, in the fall of 1786. Most of the region was plagued by economic difficulties and saddled with crushing burdens of government debts, and in September 1786 armed bands attempted to stop the proceedings of government by preventing the sitting of county courts. During this phase of the uprising, the rebels held conventions to express their grievances and state their demands. Two such statements follow:

A. An Address to the People of the several towns in the county of Hampshire, now at arms (1786)

GENTLEMEN,

We have thought proper to inform you of some of the principal causes of the late risings of the people, and also of their present movement, viz.

1st. The present expensive mode of collecting debts, which by reason of the great scarcity of cash, will of necessity fill our gaols with unhappy debtors; and thereby a reputable body of people rendered incapable of being serviceable either to themselves or the community.

2d. The monies raised by impost and excise being appropriated to discharge the interest of governmental securities, and not the foreign debt, when these securities are not subject to taxation.

3d. A suspension of the writ of Habeas Corpus, by which those persons who have stepped forth to assert and maintain the rights of the people, are liable to be taken and conveyed even to the most distant parts of the Commonwealth, and thereby subjected to an unjust punishment.

4th. The unlimited power granted to Justices of the Peace and Sheriffs, Deputy Sheriffs, and Constables, by the Riot Act, indemnifying them to the prosecution thereof; when perhaps, wholly actuated from a principle of revenge, hatred, and envy.

SOURCE: G. R. Minot, History of the Insurrection in Massachusetts (Worcester, Mass., 1788), pp. 82 ff.

Furthermore, Be assured, that this body, now at arms, despise the idea of being instigated by British emissaries, which is so strenuously propagated by the enemies of our liberties: And also wish the most proper and speedy measures may be taken, to discharge both our foreign and domestick debt.

     Per Order,

DANIEL GRAY, Chairman of the Committee

B. *To the Printer of the* Hampshire Herald *(1786)*

Sir,

It has some how or other fallen to my lot to be employed in a more conspicuous manner than some others of my fellow citizens, in stepping forth on defence of the rights and privileges of the people, more especially of the county of Hampshire.

Therefore, upon the desire of the people now at arms, I take this method to publish to the world of mankind in general, particularly the people of this Commonwealth, some of the principal grievances we complain of. . . .

In the first place, I must refer you to a draught of grievances drawn up by a committee of the people, now at arms, under the signature of Daniel Gray, chairman, which is heartily approved of; some others also are here added, viz.

1st. The General Court, for certain obvious reasons, must be removed out of the town of Boston.

2d. A revision of the constitution is absolutely necessary.

3d. All kinds of governmental securities, now on interest, that have been bought of the original owners for two shillings, and the highest for six shillings and eight pence on the pound, and have received more interest than the principal cost the speculator who purchased them—that if justice was done, we verily belive, nay positively know, it would save this Commonwealth thousands of pounds.

4th. Let the lands belonging to this Commonwealth, at the eastward, be sold at the best advantage to pay the remainder of our domestick debt.

5th. Let the monies arising from impost and excise be appropriated to discharge the foreign debt.

6th. Let that act, passed by the General Court last June by a

SOURCE: *Ibid.*

small majority of only seven, called the Supplementary Act, for twenty-five years to come, be repealed.

7th. The total abolition of the Inferiour Court of Common Pleas and General Sessions of the Peace.

8th. Deputy Sheriffs totally set aside, as a useless set of officers in the community; and Constables who are really necessary, be empowered to do the duty, by which means a large swarm of lawyers will be banished from their wonted haunts, who have been more damage to the people at large, especially the common farmers, than the savage beasts of prey.

To this I boldly sign my proper name, as a hearty wellwisher to the real rights of the people.

Worcester, December 7, 1786   THOMAS GROVER

C. Report on the Rebellion: General William Shepard to Governor James Bowdoin, January 26, 1787

During the winter of 1786–87 the protest movement was transformed into armed insurrection. Possibly 3,000 men, commanded by Captain Daniel Shays of Pelham, drilled and prepared to march, though no one was certain just what the objectives of the rebellion were. A volunteer army, loyal to the state government, was formed and marched toward Springfield to battle the rebels. On January 25, 1787, the armies met and the rebels were quickly routed, as General Shepard's account indicates:

Sir,

The unhappy time is come in which we have been obliged to shed blood. Shays, who was at the head of about twelve hundred men, marched yesterday afternoon about four o'clock, towards the public buildings, in battle array.—He marched his men in an open column by plattoons. I sent several times by one of my Aids, and two other gentlemen, Captains Buffington and Woodbridge, to him to know what he was after, or what he wanted. His reply was, He wanted barracks, and barracks he would have, and stores. The answer returned was, He must purchase them dear, if he had them. He still proceeded on his march, untill he approached within two hundred and fifty yards of the arsenal. He then made a halt. I immediately sent Major Lyman, one of my Aids, and Capt Buffington, to inform him not to march his troops any nearer the arsenal on his peril, as I was stationed here by order of your Excellency

SOURCE: *Connecticut Courant*, February 5, 1787.

and the Secretary at War, for the defence of the public property; in case he did, I should surely fire on him and his men. A Mr. Wheeler, who appeared to be one of Shay's [sic] Aids, met Mr. Lyman, after he had delivered my orders in the most peremptory manner, and made answer, that that was all he wanted. Mr. Lyman returned with his answer.

Shays immediately put his troops in motion, and marched on rapidly near one hundred yards. I then ordered Major Stephens, who commanded the artillery, to fire upon them, he accordingly did. The two first shot he endeavoured to over-shoot them, in hopes they would have taken warning without firing among them, but it had no effect on them. Major Stephens then directed his shot thro' the centre of his column. The fourth or fifth shot put the whole column into the utmost confusion. Shays made an attempt to display the column, but in vain. We had one howit which was loaded with grape shot, which, when fired, gave them great uneasiness. Had I been disposed to destroy them, I might have charged upon their rear and flanks, with my infantry and the two field-pieces, and could have killed the greater part of his whole army within twenty-five minutes. There was not a single musket fired on either side.

I found three men dead on the spot, and one wounded, who is since dead. One of our artillerymen, by inattention, was badly wounded.

Three muskets were taken up with the dead, which were all deeply loaded. I have received no reinforcement yet, and expect to be attacked this day by their whole force combined. [The attack never materialized; the rebels disbanded and returned to their homes, and their leaders fled the state.]

Even as the tumults in Massachusetts were reaching a climax, so was another sequence of events that would, in time, lead to a radical alteration of the federal system, with the adoption of the Constitution. After a 1785 meeting between delegates from Virginia and Maryland had worked out a satisfactory agreement over navigation of the Potomac, Virginia in 1786 issued a call for a general convention to discuss all America's commercial problems—much as the Massachusetts legislature had proposed a year earlier. But now, because of worsening economic conditions in New England and the tobacco-growing states, because of the fear of domestic insurrection, and because of the total ineptitude of Congress, there was a somewhat more general response. Delegates to Virginia's proposed commercial convention were elected by several state legislatures, and delegates from five states showed up for the convention in Annapolis, Maryland, in September 1786. The Annapolis Convention declared that efforts to patch together a commercial agreement were futile, and resolved to request Congress and the several states to call a general convention of delegates "to take into consideration the situation of the United States, to devise such further provisions as shall appear to them necessary to render the constitution of the Foederal Government adequate to the exigencies of the Union."

The first reaction to the resolutions of the Annapolis Convention was far from enthusiastic. But then, stimulated by exaggerated accounts of the uprising in Massachusetts, as well as by the news that New York's legislature had sealed the doom of the Confederation Congress by rejecting the impost amendment of 1783, twelve of the thirteen states voted to send delegates to the proposed convention.

PART FOUR:

The Constitutional Convention, May-September 1787

The general convention was scheduled to meet in Philadelphia on the second Monday in May 1787. It actually began its formal deliberations on Monday, May 28. Fifty-five men participated in the convention at one time and another, average attendance being about thirty-five to forty. The delegates were, as a body, perhaps the most able group of statesmen ever assembled for a single occasion.

21. William Pierce's Sketches of the Delegates (1787)

One of the delegates, William Pierce, a merchant from Savannah, Georgia, recorded his impressions of his fellow delegates:

CHARACTERS IN THE CONVENTION OF THE STATES HELD AT
PHILADELPHIA, MAY 1787

From New Hampshire
John Langdon Esq. and Nicholas Gilman Esquire.

Mr. Langdon is a Man of considerable fortune, possesses a liberal mind, and a good plain understanding.—about 40 years old.[1]

Mr. Gilman is modest, genteel, and sensible. There is nothing brilliant or striking in his character, but there is something respectable and worthy in the man.—about 30 years of age.

SOURCE: Max Farrand, ed., *Records of the Federal Convention of 1787* (3 vols., New Haven, Conn., 1911), III, 91ff.

[1] Pierce's statements of age, throughout the paper, are only approximately correct—Farrand's note.

From Massachusetts

Rufus King, Nathaniel Gorham, [Elbridge] Gerry and [Caleb] Strong Esquires.

Mr. King is a Man much distinguished for his eloquence and great parliamentary talents. He was educated in Massachusetts, and is said to have good classical as well as legal knowledge. He has served for three years in the Congress of the United States with great and deserved applause, and is at this time high in the confidence and approbation of his Country-men. This Gentleman is about thirty three years of age, about five feet ten Inches high, well formed, an handsome face, with a strong expressive Eye, and a sweet high toned voice. In his public speaking there is something peculiarly strong and rich in his expression, clear, and convincing in his arguments, rapid and irresistible at times in his eloquence but he is not always equal. His action is natural, swimming, and graceful, but there is a rudeness of manner sometimes accompanying it. But take him *tout en semble*, he may with propriety be ranked among the Luminaries of the present Age.

Mr. Gorham is a Merchant in Boston, high in reputation, and much in the esteem of his Country-men. He is a Man of very good sense, but not much improved in his education. He is eloquent and easy in public debate, but has nothing fashionable or elegant in his style;—all he aims at is to convince, and where he fails it never is from his auditory not understanding him, for no Man is more perspicuous and full. He has been President of Congress, and three years a Member of that Body. Mr. Gorham is about 46 years of age, rather lusty, and has an agreable and pleasing manner.

Mr. Gerry's character is marked for integrity and perseverance. He is a hesitating and laborious speaker;—possesses a great degree of confidence and goes extensively into all subjects that he speaks on, with respect to elegance or flower of diction. He is connected and sometimes clear in his arguments, conceives well, and cherishes as his first virtue, a love for his Country. Mr. Gerry is very much of a Gentleman in his principles and manners;—he has been engaged in the mercantile line and is a Man of property. He is about 37 years of age.

Mr. Strong is a Lawyer of some eminence,—he has received a liberal education, and has good connections to recommend him. As a Speaker he is feeble, and without confidence. This Gentleman is about thirty five years of age, and greatly in the esteem of his Colleagues.

From Connecticut

[William Samuel] Johnson, Roger Sherman, and [Oliver] Elsworth Esquires.

Dr. Johnson is a character much celebrated for his legal knowledge; he is said to be one of the first classics in America, and certainly possesses a very strong and enlightened understanding.

As an Orator in my opinion, there is nothing in him that warrants the high reputation which he has for public speaking. There is something in the tone of his voice not pleasing to the Ear,—but he is eloquent and clear,—always abounding with information and instruction. He was once employed as an Agent for the State of Connecticut to state her claims to certain landed territory before the British House of Commons; this Office he discharged with so much dignity, and made such an ingenious display of his powers, that he laid the foundation of a reputation which will probably last much longer than his own life. Dr. Johnson is about sixty years of age, possesses the manners of a Gentleman, and engages the Hearts of Men by the sweetness of his temper, and that affectionate style of address with which he accosts his acquaintance.

Mr. Sherman exhibits the oddest shaped character I ever remember to have met with. He is awkward, un-meaning, and unaccountably strange in his manner. But in his train of thinking there is something regular, deep, and comprehensive; yet the oddity of his address, the vulgarisms that accompany his public speaking, and that strange new England cant which runs through his public as well as his private speaking make everything that is connected with him grotesque and laughable;—and yet he deserves infinite praise,—no Man has a better Heart or a clearer Head. If he cannot embellish he can furnish thoughts that are wise and useful. He is an able politician, and extremely artful in accomplishing any particular object;—it is remarked that he seldom fails. I am told he sits on the Bench in Connecticut, and is very correct in the discharge of his Judicial functions. In the early part of his life he was a Shoe-maker; —but despising the lowness of his condition, he turned Almanack maker, and so progressed upwards to a Judge. He has been several years a Member of Congress, and discharged the duties of his Office with honor and credit to himself, and advantage to the State he represented. He is about 60.

Mr. Elsworth is a Judge of the Supreme Court in Connecticut;—he is a Gentleman of a clear, deep, and copious understanding; eloquent, and connected in public debate; and always attentive to his duty. He is very happy in a reply, and choice in selecting such parts of his adversary's arguments as he finds make the strongest impressions,—in order to take off the force of them, so as to admit the power of his own. Mr. Elsworth is about 37 years of age, a Man much respected for his integrity, and venerated for his abilities.

From New York

Alexander Hamilton, [Robert] Yates, and [John] Lansing Esquires.

Colonel Hamilton is deservedly celebrated for his talents. He is a practitioner of the Law, and reputed to be a finished Scholar. To a clear and strong judgment he unites the ornaments of fancy, and whilst he is able, convincing, and engaging in his eloquence the Heart and Head sympathize in approving him. Yet there is something too feeble in his voice to be equal to the strains of oratory;—it is my opinion that he is rather a convincing Speaker, that [than] a blazing Orator. Colonel Hamilton requires time to think,—he enquires into every part of his subject with the searchings of phylosophy, and when he comes forward he comes highly charged with interesting matter, there is no skimming over the surface of a subject with him, he must sink to the bottom to see what foundation it rests on.—His language is not always equal, sometimes didactic like Bolinbroke's, at others light and tripping like Stern's. His eloquence is not so defusive as to trifle with the senses, but he rambles just enough to strike and keep up the attention. He is about 33 years old, of small stature, and lean. His manners are tinctured with stiffness, and sometimes with a degree of vanity that is highly disagreable.

Mr. Yates is said to be an able Judge. He is a Man of great legal abilities, but not distinguished as an Orator. Some of his Enemies say he is an anti-federal Man, but I discovered no such disposition in him. He is about 45 years old, and enjoys a great share of health.

Mr. Lansing is a practicing Attorney at Albany, and Mayor of that Corporation. He has a hisitation in his speech, that will prevent his being an Orator of any eminence;—his legal knowledge I am told is not extensive, nor his education a good one. He is however a Man of good sense, plain in his manners, and sincere in his friendships. He is about 32 years of age.

From New Jersey
    William Livingston, David Brearly, William Patterson, and
    Jonathan Dayton, Esquires.[2]

Governor Livingston is confessedly a Man of the first rate talents, but he appears to me rather to indulge a sportiveness of wit, than a strength of thinking. He is however equal to anything, from the extensiveness of his education and genius. His writings teem with satyr and a neatness of style. But he is no Orator, and seems little acquainted with the guiles of policy. He is about 60 years old, and remarkably healthy.

Mr. Brearly is a man of good, rather than of brilliant parts. He is a Judge of the Supreme Court of New Jersey, and is very much in the esteem of the people. As an Orator he has little to boast of, but as a Man he has every virtue to recommend him. Mr. Brearly is about 40 years of age.

Mr. Patterson is one of those kind of Men whose powers break in upon you, and create wonder and astonishment. He is a Man of great modesty, with looks that bespeak talents of no great extent,— but he is a Classic, a Lawyer, and an Orator;—and of a disposition so favorable to his advancement that every one seemed ready to exalt him with their praises. He is very happy in the choice of time and manner of engaging in a debate, and never speaks but when he understands his subject well. This Gentleman is about 34 years of age, of a very low stature.

Captain Dayton is a young Gentleman of talents, with ambition to exert them. He possesses a good education and some reading; he speaks well, and seems desirous of improving himself in Oratory. There is an impetuosity in his temper that is injurious to him; but there is an honest rectitude about him that makes him a valuable Member of Society, and secures to him the esteem of all good Men. He is about 30 years old, served with me as a Brother Aid to General Sullivan in the Western expedition of '79.

From Pennsylvania
    Benjamin Franklin, Thomas Mifflin, Robert Morris, George
    Clymer, Thomas Fitzsimons, Jared Ingersol, James Wilson,
    Governeur Morris.

Dr. Franklin is well known to be the greatest phylosopher of the present age;—all the operations of nature he seems to understand, —the very heavens obey him, and the Clouds yield up their Light-

[2] W. C. Houstoun omitted—Farrand's note.

ning to be imprisoned in his rod. But what claim he has to the politician, posterity must determine. It is certain that he does not shine much in public Council,—he is no Speaker, nor does he seem to let politics engage his attention. He is, however, a most extraordinary Man, and tells a story in a style more engaging than anything I ever heard. Let his Biographer finish his character. He is 82 years old, and possesses an activity of mind equal to a youth of 25 years of age.

General Mifflin is well known for the activity of his mind, and the brilliancy of his parts. He is well informed and a graceful Speaker. The General is about 40 years of age, and a very handsome man.

Robert Morris is a merchant of great eminence and wealth; an able Financier, and a worthy Patriot. He has an understanding equal to any public object, and possesses an energy of mind that few Men can boast of. Although he is not learned, yet he is as great as those who are. I am told that when he speaks in the Assembly of Pennsylvania, that he bears down all before him. What could have been his reason for not Speaking in the Convention I know not,— but he never once spoke on any point. This Gentleman is about 50 years old.

Mr. Clymer is a lawyer of some abilities;—he is a respectable Man, and much esteemed. Mr. Clymer is about 40 years old.

Mr. Fitzsimons is a Merchant of considerable talents, and speaks very well I am told, in the Legislature of Pennsylvania. He is about 40 years old.

Mr. Ingersol is a very able Attorney, and possesses a clear legal understanding. He is well aducated in the Classic's, and is a Man of very extensive reading. Mr. Ingersol speaks well, and comprehends his subject fully. There is a modesty in his character that keeps him back. He is about 36 years old.

Mr. Wilson ranks among the foremost in legal and political knowledge. He has joined to a fine genius all that can set him off and show him to advantage. He is well acquainted with Man, and understands all the passions that influence him. Government seems to have been his peculiar Study, all the political institutions of the World he knows in detail, and can trace the causes and effects of every revolution from the earliest stages of the Grecian commonwealth down to the present time. No man is more clear, copious, and comprehensive than Mr. Wilson, yet he is no great Orator. He draws the attention not by the charm of his eloquence, but by the force of his reasoning. He is about 45 years old.

Mr. Governeur Morris is one of those Genius's in whom every species of talents combine to render him conspicuous and flourishing in public debate:—He winds through all the mazes of rhetoric, and throws around him such a glare that he charms, captivates, and leads away the senses of all who hear him. With an infinite streach of fancy he brings to view things when he is engaged in deep argumentation, that render all the labor of reasoning easy and pleasing. But with all these powers he is fickle and inconstant,—never pursuing one train of thinking,—nor ever regular. He has gone through a very extensive course of reading, and is acquainted with all the sciences. No Man has more wit,—nor can any one engage the attention more than Mr. Morris. He was bred to the Law, but I am told he disliked the profession, and turned Merchant. He is engaged in some great mercantile matters with his namesake Mr. Robert Morris. This Gentleman is about 38 years old, he has been unfortunate in losing one of his Legs, and getting all the flesh taken off his right arm by a scald, when a youth.

From Delaware

> John Dickinson, Gunning Bedford, George Read, Richard Bassett, and Jacob Broom Esquires.

Mr. Dickinson has been famed through all America, for his Farmers Letters; he is a Scholar, and said to be a Man of very extensive information. When I saw him in the Convention I was induced to pay the greatest attention to him whenever he spoke. I had often heard that he was a great Orator, but I found him an indifferent Speaker. With an affected air of wisdom he labors to produce a trifle,—his language is irregular and incorrect,—his flourishes, (for he sometimes attempts them), are like expiring flames, they just shew themselves and go out;—no traces of them are left on the mind to chear or animate it. He is, however, a good writer and will be ever considered one of the most important characters in the United States. He is about 55 years old, and was bred a Quaker.

Mr. Bedford was educated for the Bar, and in his profession I am told, has merit. He is a bold and nervous Speaker, and has a very commanding and striking manner;—but he is warm and impetuous in his temper, and precipitate in his judgment. Mr. Bedford is about 32 years old, and very corpulant.

Mr. Read is a Lawyer and a Judge;—his legal abilities are said to be very great, but his powers of Oratory are fatiguing and tiresome to the last degree;—his voice is feeble, and his articulation so bad that few can have patience to attend to him. He is a very good Man, and bears an amiable character with those who know him. Mr. Read is about 50, of a low stature, and a weak constitution.

Mr. Bassett is a religious enthusiast, lately turned Methodist, and serves his Country because it is the will of the people that he should do so. He is a Man of plain sense, and has modesty enough to hold his Tongue. He is a Gentlemanly Man, and is in high estimation among the Methodists. Mr. Bassett is about 36 years old.

Mr. Broom is a plain good Man, with some abilities, but nothing to render him conspicuous. He is silent in public, but chearful and conversable in private. He is about 35 years old.

From Maryland
 Luther Martin, James McHenry, Daniel of St. Thomas Jenifer,
 and Daniel Carrol Esquires.[3]

Mr. Martin was educated for the Bar, and is Attorney general for the State of Maryland. This Gentleman possesses a good deal of information, but he has a very bad delivery, and so extremely prolix, that he never speaks without tiring the patience of all who hear him. He is about 34 years of age.

Mr. McHenry was bred a physician, but he afterwards turned Soldier and acted as Aid to General Washington and the Marquis de la Fayette. He is a Man of specious talents, with nothing of genious to improve them. As a politician there is nothing remarkable in him, nor has he any of the graces of the Orator. He is however, a very respectable young Gentleman, and deserves the honor which his Country has bestowed on him. Mr. McHenry is about 32 years of age.

Mr. Jenifer is a Gentleman of fortune in Maryland;—he is always in good humour, and never fails to make his company pleased with him. He sits silent in the Senate, and seems to be conscious that he is no politician. From his long continuance in single life, no doubt but he has made the vow of celibacy. He speaks warmly of the Ladies notwithstanding. Mr. Jenifer is about 55 years of Age, and once served as an Aid de Camp to Major General Lee.

Mr. Carrol is a Man of large fortune, and influence in his State. He possesses plain good sense, and is in the full confidence of his Countrymen. This Gentleman is about years of age.

[3] John Francis Mercer omitted—Farrand's note.

From Virginia

General George Washington, George Wythe, George Mason, James Maddison junior, John Blair, Edmund Randolph, and James McClurg.

General Washington is well known as the Commander in chief of the late American Army. Having conducted these States to independence and peace, he now appears to assist in framing a Government to make the People happy. Like Gustavus Vasa, he may be said to be the deliverer of his Country;—like Peter the great he appears as the politician and the States-man; and like Cincinnatus he returned to his farm perfectly contented with being only a plain Citizen, after enjoying the highest honor of the Confederacy,—and now only seeks for the approbation of his Countrymen by being virtuous and useful. The General was conducted to the Chair as President of the Convention by the unanimous voice of its Members. He is in the 52nd year of his age.

Mr. Wythe is the famous Professor of Law at the University of William and Mary. He is confessedly one of the most learned legal Characters of the present age. From his close attention to the study of general learning he has acquired a compleat knowledge of the dead languages and all the sciences. He is remarked for his examplary life, and universally esteemed for his good principles. No Man it is said understands the history of Government better than Mr. Wythe,—nor any one who understands the fluctuating condition to which all societies are liable better than he does, yet from his too favorable opinion of Men, he is no great politician. He is a neat and pleasing Speaker, and a most correct and able Writer. Mr. Wythe is about 55 years of age.

Mr. Mason is a Gentleman of remarkable strong powers, and possesses a clear and copious understanding. He is able and convincing in debate, steady and firm in his principles, and undoubtedly one of the best politicians in America. Mr. Mason is about 60 years old, with a fine strong constitution.

Mr. Maddison is a character who has long been in public life; and what is very remarkable every Person seems to acknowledge his greatness. He blends together the profound politician, with the Scholar. In the management of every great question he evidently took the lead in the Convention, and tho' he cannot be called an Orator, he is a most agreable, eloquent, and convincing Speaker. From a spirit of industry and application which he possesses in a most eminent degree, he always comes forward the best informed Man of any point in debate. The affairs of the United States, he perhaps, has the most correct knowledge of, of any Man in the Union. He has been twice a Member of Congress, and was always thought one of the ablest Members that ever sat in that Council. Mr. Maddison is about 37 years of age, a Gentleman of great modesty,—with a remarkable sweet temper. He is easy and unreserved among his acquaintance, and has a most agreable style of conversation.

Mr. Blair is one of the most respectable Men in Virginia, both on account of his Family as well as fortune. He is one of the Judges of the Supreme Court in Virginia, and acknowledged to have a very extensive knowledge of the Laws. Mr. Blair is however, no Orator, but his good sense, and most excellent principles, compensate for other deficiencies. He is about 50 years of age.

Mr. Randolph is Governor of Virginia,—a young Gentleman in whom unite all the accomplishments of the Scholar, and the Statesman. He came forward with the postulata, or first principles, on which the Convention acted, and he supported them with a force of eloquence and reasoning that did him great honor. He has a most harmonious voice, a fine person and striking manners.

Mr. Randolph is about 32 years of age.

Mr. [McClurg] is a learned physician, but having never appeared before in public life his character as a politician is not sufficiently known. He attempted once or twice to speak, but with no great success. It is certain that he has a foundation of learning, on which, if he pleases, he may erect a character of high renown. The Doctor is about 38 years of age, a Gentleman of great respectability, and of a fair and unblemished character.

North Carolina

> William Blount, Richard Dobbs Spaight, Hugh Williamson, William R. [Davie], and [Alexander] Martin Esquires.

Mr. Blount is a character strongly marked for integrity and honor. He has been twice a Member of Congress, and in that office discharged his duty with ability and faithfulness. He is no Speaker, nor does he possess any of those talents that make Men shine;—he is plain, honest, and sincere. Mr. Blount is about 36 years of age.

Mr. Spaight is a worthy Man, of some abilities, and fortune. Without possessing a Genius to render him briliant, he is able to discharge any public trust that his Country may repose in him. He is about 31 years of age.

Mr. Williamson is a Gentleman of education and talents. He enters freely into public debate from his close attention to most subjects, but he is no Orator. There is a great degree of good humour and pleasantry in his character; and in his manners there is a strong trait of the Gentleman. He is about 48 years of age.

[Mr. Davie] is a Lawyer of some eminence in his State. He is said to have a good classical education, and is a Gentleman of considerable literary talents. He was silent in the Convention, but his opinion was always respected. [Mr. Davie] is about 30 years of age.

Mr. Martin was lately Governor of North Carolina, which office he filled with credit. He is a Man of sense, and undoubtedly is a good politician, but he is not formed to shine in public debate, being no Speaker. Mr. Martin was once a Colonel in the American Army, but proved unfit for the field. He is about 40 years of age.

South Carolina

John Rutledge, Charles Cotesworth Pinckney, Charles Pinckney, and Pierce Butler Esquires.

Mr. Rutledge is one of those characters who was highly mounted at the commencement of the late revolution;—his reputation in the first Congress gave him a distinguished rank among the American Worthies. He was bred to the Law, and now acts as one of the Chancellors of South Carolina. This Gentleman is much famed in his own State as an Orator, but in my opinion he is too rapid in his public speaking to be denominated an agreeable Orator. He is undoubtedly a man of abilities, and a Gentleman of distinction and fortune. Mr. Rutledge was once Governor of South Carolina. He is about 48 years of age.

Mr. Charles Cotesworth Pinckney is a Gentleman of Family and fortune in his own State. He has received the advantage of a liberal education, and possesses a very extensive degree of legal knowledge. When warm in a debate he sometimes speaks well,—but he is generally considered an indifferent Orator. Mr. Pinckney was an Officer of high rank in the American Army, and served with great reputation through the War. He is now about 40 years of age.

Mr. Charles Pinckney is a young Gentleman of the most promising talents. He is, altho' only 24 years of age, in possession of a very great variety of knowledge. Government, Law, History and Phylosophy are his favorite studies, but he is intimately acquainted with every species of polite learning, and has a spirit of application and industry beyond most men. He speaks with great neatness and perspicuity, and treats every subject as fully, without running into prolixity, as it requires. He has been a member of Congress, and served in that Body with ability and eclat.

Mr. Butler is a character much respected for the many excellent virtues which he possesses. But as a politician or an Orator, he has no pretentions to either. He is a Gentleman of fortune, and takes rank among the first in South Carolina. He has been appointed to Congress, and is now a Member of the Legislature of South Carolina. Mr. Butler is about 40 years of age; an Irishman by birth.

For Georgia

William Few, Abraham Baldwin, William Pierce, and William Houstoun Esquires.

Mr. Few possesses a strong natural Genius, and from application has acquired some knowledge of legal matters;—he practises at the bar of Georgia, and speaks tolerably well in the Legislature. He has been twice a Member of Congress, and served in that capacity with fidelity to his State, and honor to himself. Mr. Few is about 35 years of age.

Mr. Baldwin is a Gentleman of superior abilities, and joins in a public debate with great art and eloquence. Having laid the foundation of a compleat classical education at Harvard College, he pursues every other study with ease. He is well acquainted with Books and Characters, and has an accomodating turn of mind, which enables him to gain the confidence of Men, and to understand them. He is a practising Attorney in Georgia, and has been twice a Member of Congress. Mr. Baldwin is about 38 years of age.

Mr. Houstoun is an Attorney at Law, and has been Member of Congress for the State of Georgia. He is a Gentleman of Family, and was educated in England. As to his legal or political knowledge he has very little to boast of. Nature seems to have done more for his corporeal than mental powers. His Person is striking, but his mind very little improved with useful or elegant knowledge. He has none of the talents requisite for the Orator, but in public debate is confused and irregular. Mr. Houstoun is about 30 years of age of an amiable and sweet temper, and of good and honorable principles.

My own character I shall not attempt to draw, but leave those who may choose to speculate on it, to consider it in any light that their fancy or imagination may depict. I am conscious of having discharged my duty as a Soldier through the course of the late revolution with honor and propriety; and my services in Congress and the Convention were bestowed with the best intention towards the interest of Georgia, and towards the general welfare of the Confederacy. I possess ambition, and it was that, and the flattering opinion which some of my Friends had of me, that gave me a seat in the wisest Council in the World, and furnished me with an opportunity of giving these short Sketches of the Characters who composed it.

22. The Randolph or Virginia Plan, May 29, 1787

Governor Edmund Randolph of Virginia "opened the main business" of the convention with a speech analyzing the defects of the Confederation and proposing a plan for altering the system. The plan was a joint effort, the principal author being Randolph's fellow delegate from Virginia, James Madison.

(The proceedings were secret, but several delegates took notes and Madison kept a rather full journal of the debates, which was published a half century later. This selection and the ones that follow—Documents 23 through 35—are taken from Madison's Journal):

MR. RANDOLPH then opened the main business.

. . .

He expressed his regret, that it should fall to him, rather than those, who were of longer standing in life and political experience, to open the great subject of their mission. But, as the convention had originated from Virginia, and his colleagues supposed that some proposition was expected from them, they had imposed this task on him.

He then commented on the difficulty of the crisis, and the necessity of preventing the fulfilment of the prophecies of the American downfal.

He observed that in revising the fœderal system we ought to inquire 1. into the properties, which such a government ought to possess, 2. the defects of the confederation, 3. the danger of our situation & 4. the remedy.

SOURCE: Madison's *Journal*, in Farrand, ed., *Records of the Federal Convention*, as dated.

1. The Character of such a government ought to secure 1. against foreign invasion: 2. against dissentions between members of the Union, or seditions in particular states: 3. to procure to the several States various blessings, of which an isolated situation was incapable: 4. to be able to defend itself against incroachment: & 5. to be paramount to the state constitutions.

2. In speaking of the defects of the confederation he professed a high respect for its authors, and considered them, as having done all that patriots could do, in the then infancy of the science, of constitutions, & of confederacies,—when the inefficiency of requisitions was unknown—no commercial discord had arisen among any states —no rebellion had appeared as in Massachusetts—foreign debts had not become urgent—the havoc of paper money had not been foreseen—treaties had not been violated—and perhaps nothing better could be obtained from the jealousy of the states with regard to their sovereignty.

He then proceeded to enumerate the defects: 1. that the confederation produced no security against foreign invasion; congress not being permitted to prevent a war nor to support it by their own authority—Of this he cited many examples; most of which tended to shew, that they could not cause infractions of treaties or of the law of nations, to be punished: that particular states might by their conduct provoke war without controul; and that neither militia nor draughts being fit for defence on such occasions, inlistments only could be successful, and these could not be executed without money.

2. that the fœderal government could not check the quarrels between states, nor a rebellion in any, not having constitutional power nor means to interpose according to the exigency:

3. that there were many advantages, which the U. S. might acquire, which were not attainable under the confederation—such as a productive impost—counteraction of the commercial regulations of other nations—pushing of commerce ad libitum—etc. etc.

4. that the fœderal government could not defend itself against the incroachments from the states.

5. that it was not even paramount to the state constitutions, ratified, as it was in ma[n]y of the states.

3. He next reviewed the danger of our situation, appealed to the sense of the best friends of the U. S.—the prospect of anarchy from the laxity of government every where; and to other considerations.

4. He then proceeded to the remedy; the basis of which he said must be the republican principle

He proposed as conformable to his ideas the following resolutions, which he explained one by one. . . .

1. Resolved that the Articles of Confederation ought to be so corrected & enlarged as to accomplish the objects proposed by their institution; namely, "common defence, security of liberty, and general welfare."

2. Resolved therefore that the rights of suffrage in the National Legislature ought to be proportioned to the Quotas of contribution, or to the number of free inhabitants, as the one or the other rule may seem best in different cases.

3. Resolved that the National Legislature ought to consist of two branches.

4. Resolved that the members of the first branch of the National Legislature ought to be elected by the people of the several States every   for the term of   ; to be of the age of   years at least, to receive liberal stipends by which they may be compensated for the devotion of their time to public service; to be ineligible to any office established by a particular State, or under the authority of the United States, except those peculiarly belonging to the functions of the first branch, during the term of service, and for the space of   after its expiration; to be incapable of reelection for the space of   after the expiration of their term of service, and to be subject to recall.

5. Resolved that the members of the second branch of the National Legislature ought to be elected by those of the first, out of a proper number of persons nominated by the individual Legislatures, to be of the age of   years at least; to hold their offices for a term sufficient to ensure their independency; to receive liberal stipends, by which they may be compensated for the devotion of their time to public service; and to be ineligible to any office established by a particular State, or under the authority of the United States, except those peculiarly belonging to the functions of the second branch, during the term of service, and for the space of   after the expiration thereof.

6. Resolved that each branch ought to possess the right of originating Acts; that the National Legislature ought to be impowered to enjoy the Legislative Rights vested in Congress by the Confed-

eration & moreover to legislate in all cases to which the separate States are incompetent, or in which the harmony of the United States may be interrupted by the exercise of individual Legislation; to negative all laws passed by the several States, contravening in the opinion of the National Legislature the articles of Union; and to call forth the force of the Union against any member of the Union failing to fulfill its duty under the articles thereof.

7. Resolved that a National Executive be instituted; to be chosen by the National Legislature for the term of   years, to receive punctually at stated times, a fixed compensation for the services rendered, in which no increase or diminution shall be made so as to affect the Magistracy, existing at the time of increase or diminution, and to be ineligible a second time; and that besides a general authority to execute the National laws, it ought to enjoy the Executive rights vested in Congress by the Confederation.

8. Resolved that the Executive and a convenient number of the National Judiciary, ought to compose a Council of revision with authority to examine every act of the National Legislature before it shall operate, & every act of a particular Legislature before a Negative thereon shall be final; and that the dissent of the said Council shall amount to a rejection, unless the Act of the National Legislature be again passed, or that of a particular Legislature be again negatived by   of the members of each branch.

9. Resolved that a National Judiciary be established to consist of one or more supreme tribunals, and of inferior tribunals to be chosen by the National Legislature, to hold their offices during good behaviour; and to receive punctually at stated times fixed compensation for their services, in which no increase or diminution shall be made so as to affect the persons actually in office at the time of such increase or diminution; that the jurisdiction of the inferior tribunals shall be to hear & determine in the first instance, and of the supreme tribunal to hear and determine in the dernier resort, all piracies & felonies on the high seas, captures from an enemy, cases in which foreigners or citizens of other States applying to such jurisdictions may be interested, or which respect the collection of the National revenue; impeachments of any National officers, and questions which may involve the national peace and harmony.

10. Resolved that provision ought to be made for the admission of States lawfully arising within the limits of the United States, whether from a voluntary junction of Government & Territory or

otherwise, with the consent of a number of voices in the National legislature less than the whole.

11. Resolved that a Republican Government & the territory of each State, except in the instance of a voluntary junction of Government & territory, ought to be guarantied by the United States to each State

12. Resolved that provision ought to be made for the continuance of Congress and their authorities and privileges, until a given day after the reform of the articles of Union shall be adopted, and for the completion of all their engagements.

13. Resolved that provision ought to be made for the amendment of the Articles of Union whensoever it shall seem necessary, and that the assent of the National Legislature ought not to be required thereto.

14. Resolved that the Legislative Executive & Judiciary powers within the several States ought to be bound by oath to support the articles of Union.

15. Resolved that the amendments which shall be offered to the Confederation, by the Convention ought at a proper time, or times, after the approbation of Congress to be submitted to an assembly or assemblies of Representatives, recommended by the several Legislatures to be expressly chosen by the people, to consider & decide thereon.

He concluded with an exhortation, not to suffer the present opportunity of establishing general peace, harmony, happiness and liberty in the U. S. to pass away unimproved.

23. Debates in Constitutional Convention, June 6, 1787

The convention resolved itself into a committee of the whole house and debated Randolph's resolutions for two weeks. The most controverted issue was the proposal to split Congress into two branches, to be elected by the people rather than the legislatures. The following selection concerns that issue:

Wednesday, June 6. In Committee of the whole

Mr. PINKNEY . . . moved "that the first branch of the national

Legislature be elected by the State Legislatures, and not by the people." contending that the people were less fit Judges in such a case, and that the Legislatures would be less likely to promote the adoption of the new Government, if they were to be excluded from all share in it.

Mr. RUTLIDGE seconded the motion.

Mr. GERRY. Much depends on the mode of election. In England, the people will probably lose their liberty from the smallness of the proportion having a right of suffrage. Our danger arises from the opposite extreme: hence in Massachusetts the worst men get into the Legislature. Several members of that Body had lately been convicted of infamous crimes. Men of indigence, ignorance & baseness, spare no pains, however dirty to carry their point against men who are superior to the artifices practised. He was not disposed to run into extremes. He was as much principled as ever against aristocracy and monarchy. It was necessary on the one hand that the people should appoint one branch of the Government in order to inspire them with the necessary confidence. But he wished the election on the other to be so modified as to secure more effectually a just preference of merit. His idea was that the people should nominate certain persons in certain districts, out of whom the State Legislatures should make the appointment.

Mr. WILSON. He wished for vigor in the Government, but he wished that vigorous authority to flow immediately from the legitimate source of all authority. The Government ought to possess not only first the *force*, but secondly the *mind* or *sense* of the people at large. The Legislature ought to be the most exact transcript of the whole Society. Representation is made necessary only because it is impossible for the people to act collectively. The opposition was to be expected he said from the *Governments*, not from the Citizens of the States. The latter had parted as was observed (by Mr. King) with all the necessary powers; and it was immaterial to them, by whom they were exercised, if well exercised. The State officers were to be the losers of power. The people he supposed would be rather more attached to the national Government than to the State Governments as being more important in itself, and more flattering to their pride. There is no danger of improper elections if made by *large* districts. Bad elections proceed from the smallness of the districts which give an opportunity to bad men to intrigue themselves into office.

Mr. Sherman. If it were in view to abolish the State Governments the elections ought to be by the people. If the State Governments are to be continued, it is necessary in order to preserve harmony between the National & State Governments that the elections to the former should be made by the latter. The right of participating in the National Government would be sufficiently secured to the people by their election of the State Legislatures. The objects of the Union, he thought were few. 1. defence against foreign danger. 2. against internal disputes & a resort to force. 3. Treaties with foreign nations. 4. regulating foreign commerce, & drawing revenue from it. These & perhaps a few lesser objects alone rendered a Confederation of the States necessary. All other matters civil & criminal would be much better in the hands of the States. The people are more happy in small than large States. States may indeed be too small as Rhode Island, & thereby be too subject to faction. Some others were perhaps too large, the powers of Government not being able to pervade them. He was for giving the General Government power to legislate and execute within a defined province.

Colonel Mason. Under the existing Confederacy, Congress represent the *States* not the *people* of the States: their acts operate on the *States*, not on the individuals. The case will be changed in the new plan of Government. The people will be represented; they ought therefore to choose the Representatives. The requisites in actual representation are that the Representatives should sympathize with their constituents; should think as they think, & feel as they feel; and that for these purposes should even be residents among them. Much he said had been alleged against democratic elections. He admitted that much might be said; but it was to be considered that no Government was free from imperfections & evils; and that improper elections in many instances, were inseparable from Republican Governments. But compare these with the advantage of this Form in favor of the rights of the people, in favor of human nature. He was persuaded there was a better chance for proper elections by the people, if divided into large districts, than by the State Legislatures. . . .

Mr. Madison considered an election of one branch at least of the Legislature by the people immediately, as a clear principle of free Government and that this mode under proper regulations had the additional advantage of securing better representatives, as well as of avoiding too great an agency of the State Governments in the

General one.—He differed from the member from Connecticut [Mr. Sherman] in thinking the objects mentioned to be all the principal ones that required a National Government. Those were certainly important and necessary objects; but he combined with them the necessity of providing more effectually for the security of private rights, and the steady dispensation of Justice. Interferences with these were evils which had more perhaps than any thing else, produced this convention. Was it to be supposed that republican liberty could long exist under the abuses of it practised in some of the States. The gentleman [Mr. Sherman] had admitted that in a very small State, faction & oppression would prevail. It was to be inferred then that wherever these prevailed the State was too small. Had they not prevailed in the largest as well as the smallest tho' less than in the smallest; and were we not thence admonished to enlarge the sphere as far as the nature of the Government would admit. This was the only defence against the inconveniencies of democracy consistent with the democratic form of Government. All civilized Societies would be divided into different Sects, Factions, & interests, as they happened to consist of rich & poor, debtors & creditors, the landed, the manufacturing, the commercial interests, the inhabitants of this district or that district, the followers of this political leader or that political leader, the disciples of this religious Sect or that religious Sect. In all cases where a majority are united by a common interest or passion, the rights of the minority are in danger. What motives are to restrain them? A prudent regard to the maxim that honesty is the best policy is found by experience to be as little regarded by bodies of men as by individuals. Respect for character is always diminished in proportion to the number among whom the blame or praise is to be divided. Conscience, the only remaining tie, is known to be inadequate in individuals: In large numbers, little is to be expected from it. Besides, Religion itself may become a motive to persecution & oppression.—These observations are verified by the Histories of every Country antient & modern. In Greece & Rome the rich & poor, the creditors & debtors, as well as the patricians & plebians alternately oppressed each other with equal unmercifulness. What a source of oppression was the relation between the parent cities of Rome, Athens & Carthage, & their respective provinces: the former possessing the power, & the latter being sufficiently distinguished to be separate objects of it? Why was America so justly apprehensive of Parliamentary injustice?

Because Great Britain had a separate interest real or supposed, & if her authority had been admitted, could have pursued that interest at our expence. We have seen the mere distinction of colour made in the most enlightened period of time, a ground of the most oppressive dominion ever exercised by man over man. What has been the source of those unjust laws complained of among ourselves? Has it not been the real or supposed interest of the major number? Debtors have defrauded their creditors. The landed interest has borne hard on the mercantile interest. The Holders of one species of property have thrown a disproportion of taxes on the holders of another species. The lesson we are to draw from the whole is that where a majority are united by a common sentiment, and have an opportunity, the rights of the minor party become insecure. In a Republican Government the Majority if united have always an opportunity. The only remedy is to enlarge the sphere, & thereby divide the community into so great a number of interests & parties, that in the first place a majority will not be likely at the same moment to have a common interest separate from that of the whole or of the minority; and in the second place, that in case they should have such an interest, they may not be apt to unite in the pursuit of it. It was incumbent on us then to try this remedy, and with that view to frame a republican system on such a scale and in such form as will controul all the evils which have been experienced.

Mr. DICKENSON considered it as essential that one branch of the Legislature should be drawn immediately from the people; and as expedient that the other should be chosen by the Legislatures of the States. This combination of the State Governments with the national Government was as politic as it was unavoidable. In the formation of the Senate we ought to carry it through such a refining process as will assimilate it as near as may be to the House of Lords in England. He repeated his warm eulogiums on the British Constitution. He was for a strong National Government but for leaving the States a considerable agency in the System. . . .

Mr. READ. Too much attachment is betrayed to the State Governments. We must look beyond their continuance. A national Government must soon of necessity swallow all of them up. . . . He was against patching up the old federal System; he hoped the idea would be dismissed. It would be like putting new cloth on an old garment. The confederation was founded on temporary principles. It cannot last: it cannot be amended. If we do not establish a good Government on new principles, we must either go to ruin, or have the work to do over again. The people at large are wrongly suspected of being averse to a General Government. The aversion lies among interested men who possess their confidence.

24. The Paterson or Small States Plan, June 15, 1787

The delegates from five states opposed the proposal to discard the system of equal representation in Congress and substitute representation based on population. After the committee of the whole had revised and reported on the Randolph Plan, William Paterson of New Jersey presented an alternate plan based on equal representation, but vastly increasing the power of the national government:

Friday, June 15

Mr. PATTERSON, laid before the Convention the plan which he said several of the deputations wished to be substituted in place of that proposed by Mr. Randolph. After some little discussion of the most proper mode of giving it a fair deliberation it was agreed that it should be referred to a Committee of the whole, and that in order to place the two plans in due comparison, the other should be recommitted. At the earnest desire of Mr. Lansing & some other gentlemen, it was also agreed that the Convention should not go into Committee of the whole on the subject till tomorrow, by which delay the friends of the plan proposed by Mr. Patterson would be better prepared to explain & support it, and all would have an opportunity of taking copies.[1]

[1] This plan had been concerted among the deputations or members thereof, from Connecticut, New York, New Jersey, Delaware, and perhaps Mr. Martin from Maryland who made with them a common cause on different principles. Connecticut and New York were against a departure from the principle of the Confederation, wishing rather to add a few new powers to Congress than to substitute a National Government. The States of New Jersey and Delaware were opposed to a National Government because its patrons considered a proportional representation of the States as the basis of it. The eagourness displayed by the members opposed to a National Government from these different motives began now to produce serious anxiety for the result of the Convention. Mr. Dickenson said to Mr. Madison—You see the consequence of pushing things too far. Some of the members from the small States wish for two branches in the General Legislature, and are

The propositions from N. Jersey moved by Mr. Patterson were in the words following.

1. Resolved that the articles of Confederation ought to be so revised, corrected & enlarged, as to render the federal Constitution adequate to the exigencies of Government, & the preservation of the Union.

2. Resolved that in addition to the powers vested in the United States in Congress, by the present existing articles of Confederation, they be authorized to pass acts for raising a revenue, by levying a duty or duties on all goods or merchandizes of foreign growth or manufacture, imported into any part of the United States, by Stamps on paper, vellum or parchment, and by a postage on all letters or packages passing through the general post-office, to be applied to such federal purposes as they shall deem proper & expedient; to make rules & regulations for the collection thereof; and the same from time to time, to alter & amend in such manner as they shall think proper: to pass Acts for the regulation of trade & commerce as well with foreign nations as with each other: provided that all punishments, fines, forfeitures & penalties to be incurred for contravening such acts rules and regulations shall be adjudged by the Common law Judiciaries of the State in which any offence contrary to the true intent & meaning of such Acts rules & regulations shall have been committed or perpetrated, with liberty of commencing in the first instance all suits & prosecutions for that purpose in the superior common law Judiciary in such State, subject nevertheless, for the correction of all errors, both in law & fact in rendering Judgment, to an appeal to the Judiciary of the United States.

3. Resolved that whenever requisitions shall be necessary, instead of the rule for making requisitions mentioned in the articles of Confederation, the United States in Congress be authorized to make such requisitions in proportion to the whole number of white & other free citizens & inhabitants of every age sex and condition including those bound to servitude for a term of years & three fifths of all other persons not comprehended in the foregoing description, except Indians not paying taxes; that if such requisitions be not complied with, in the time specified therein, to direct the collection

friends to a good National Government; but we would sooner submit to a foreign power than submit to be deprived of an equality of suffrage, in both branches of the legislature, and thereby be thrown under the domination of the large States—Madison's note.

thereof in the non complying States & for that purpose to devise and pass acts directing & authorizing the same; provided that none of the powers hereby vested in the United States in Congress shall be exercised without the consent of at least   States, and in that proportion if the number of Confederated States should hereafter be increased or diminished.

4. Resolved that the United States in Congress be authorized to elect a federal Executive to consist of   persons, to continue in office for the term of   years, to receive punctually at stated times a fixed compensation for their services, in which no increase or diminution shall be made so as to affect the persons composing the Executive at the time of such increase or diminution, to be paid out of the federal treasury; to be incapable of holding any other office or appointment during their time of service and for   years thereafter; to be ineligible a second time, & removeable by Congress on application by a majority of the Executives of the several States; that the Executives besides their general authority to execute the federal acts ought to appoint all federal officers not otherwise provided for, & to direct all military operations; provided that none of the persons composing the federal Executive shall on any occasion take command of any troops, so as personally to conduct any enterprise as General or in other capacity.

5. Resolved that a federal Judiciary be established to consist of a supreme Tribunal the Judges of which to be appointed by the Executive, & to hold their offices during good behaviour, to receive punctually at stated times a fixed compensation for their services in which no increase or diminution shall be made, so as to affect the persons actually in office at the time of such increase or diminution; that the Judiciary so established shall have authority to hear & determine in the first instance on all impeachments of federal officers, & by way of appeal in the dernier resort in all cases touching the rights of Ambassadors, in all cases of captures from an enemy, in all cases of piracies & felonies on the high Seas, in all cases in which foreigners may be interested, in the construction of any treaty or treaties, or which may arise on any of the Acts for regulation of trade, or the collection of the federal Revenue: that none of the Judiciary shall during the time they remain in office be capable of receiving or holding any other office or appointment during their time of service, or for   thereafter.

6. Resolved that all Acts of the United States in Congress made

by virtue & in pursuance of the powers hereby & by the articles of Confederation vested in them, and all Treaties made & ratified under the authority of the United States shall be the supreme law of the respective States so far forth as those Acts or Treaties shall relate to the said States or their Citizens, and that the Judiciary of the several States shall be bound thereby in their decisions, any thing in the respective laws of the Individual States to the contrary notwithstanding; and that if any State, or any body of men in any State shall oppose or prevent the carrying into execution such acts or treaties, the federal Executive shall be authorized to call forth the power of the Confederated States, or so much thereof as may be necessary to enforce and compel an obedience to such Acts, or an observance of such Treaties.

7. Resolved that provision be made for the admission of new States into the Union.

8. Resolved the rule for naturalization ought to be the same in every State.

9. Resolved that a Citizen of one State committing an offense in another State of the Union, shall be deemed guilty of the same offense as if it had been committed by a Citizen of the State in which the offense was committed.

25. Debate on the Randolph and Paterson Plans, June 16, 1787

The next day, the merits of the two plans were debated. Delegates from Connecticut, New York, New Jersey, Delaware, and Maryland supported the Paterson Plan, and delegates from the other six—the so-called "large states"—supported the Randolph Plan:[1]

[1] In fact, excluding the extremes (Virginia, the most populous state, and Delaware, the least populous), the average population of the states in the "large-state" bloc was 307,000, and that of the "small" roughly 278,000—a difference of only 10 per cent. The alignment was more precisely one of "landed" versus "landless" states: the states in the "large-state" bloc had access, through colonial charters or some other means, to enormous surpluses of unoccupied lands, and the other states had no such lands. The "small states" expected, through preservation of equal representation, to obtain a share of these vacant lands. As George Read of Delaware said on

Saturday, June 16. In Committee of the whole

Mr. LANSING called for the reading of the first resolution of each plan, which he considered as involving principles directly in contrast; that of Mr. Patterson says he sustains the sovereignty of the respective States, that of Mr. Randolph distroys it: the latter requires a negative on all the laws of the particular States; the former, only certain general powers for the general good. The plan of Mr. Randolph in short absorbs all power except what may be exercised in the little local matters of the States which are not objects worthy of the supreme cognizance. He grounded his preference of Mr. Patterson's plan, chiefly on two objections against that of Mr. Randolph. 1. want of power in the Convention to discuss & propose it. 2. the improbability of its being adopted. . . .

Mr. PATTERSON, said as he had on a former occasion given his sentiments on the plan proposed by Mr. Randolph he would now avoiding repetition as much as possible give his reasons in favor of that proposed by himself. He preferred it because it accorded 1. with the powers of the Convention, 2. with the sentiments of the people. If the confederacy was radically wrong, let us return to our States, and obtain larger powers, not assume them of ourselves. . . . Our object is not such a Government as may be best in itself, but such a one as our Constituents have authorized us to prepare, and as they will approve. If we argue the matter on the supposition that no Confederacy at present exists, it can not be denied that all the States stand on the footing of equal sovereignty. All therefore must concur before any can be bound. If a proportional representation be right, why do we not vote so here? If we argue on the fact that a federal compact actually exists, and consult the articles of it we still find an equal Sovereignty to be the basis of it. He reads the fifth article of Confederation giving each State a vote—& the thirteenth declaring that no alteration shall be made without unanimous consent. This is the nature of all treaties. What is unanimously done, must be unanimously undone. It was observed (by Mr. Wilson) that the larger States gave up the point, not because it was right, but because the circumstances of the moment urged

---

June 25, give the small states an equal share of "the common lands . . . the great States have appropriated to themselves, and then if you please, proportion the representation, and we shall not be jealous of one another."

the concession. Be it so. Are they for that reason at liberty to take it back. Can·the donor resume his gift without the consent of the donee. This doctrine may be convenient, but it is a doctrine that will sacrifice the lesser States. The large States acceded readily to the confederacy. It was the small ones that came in reluctantly and slowly. New Jersey & Maryland were the two last, the former objecting to the want of power in Congress over trade: both of them to the want of power to appropriate the vacant territory to the benefit of the whole.—If the sovereignty of the States is to be maintained, the Representatives must be drawn immediately from the States, not from the people: and we have no power to vary the idea of equal sovereignty. The only expedient that will cure the difficulty, is that of throwing the States into Hotchpot. To say that this is impracticable, will not make it so. Let it be tried, and we shall see whether the Citizens of Massachusetts, Pennsylvania, & Virginia accede to it. It will be objected that Coercion will be impracticable. But will it be more so in one plan than the other? Its efficacy will depend on the quantum of power collected, not on its being drawn from the States, or from the individuals; and according to his plan it may be exerted on individuals as well as according that of Mr. Randolph. A distinct executive & Judiciary also were equally provided by his plan. It is urged that two branches in the Legislature are necessary. Why? for the purpose of a check. But the reason of the precaution is not applicable to this case. Within a particular State, where party heats prevail, such a check may be necessary. In such a body as Congress it is less necessary, and besides, the delegations of the different States are checks on each other. Do the people at large complain of Congress? No, what they wish is that Congress may have more power. If the power now proposed be not enough, the people hereafter will make additions to it. With proper powers Congress will act with more energy & wisdom than the proposed National Legislature; being fewer in number, and more secreted & refined by the mode of election. The plan of Mr. Randolph will also be enormously expensive. Allowing Georgia & Delaware two representatives each in the popular branch the aggregate number of that branch will be 180. Add to it half as many for the other branch and you have 270. members coming once at least a year from the most distant as well as the most central parts of the republic. In the present deranged state of our finances can so expensive a system be seriously thought of? By enlarging the powers of Congress the greatest part of this expence will be saved, and all purposes will be answered. At least a trial ought to be made.

Mr. WILSON entered into a contrast of the principal points of the two plans so far he said as there had been time to examine the one last proposed. These points were 1. in the Virginia plan there are two & in some degree three branches in the Legislature: in the plan from N. J. there is to be a *single* legislature only—2. Representation of the people at large is the basis of the one:—the State Legislatures, the pillars of the other—3. proportional representation prevails in one:—equality of suffrage in the other—4. A single Executive Magistrate is at the head of the one:—a plurality is held out in the other.—5. in the one the majority of the people of the U. S. must prevail:—in the other a minority may prevail. 6. the National Legislature is to make laws in all cases to which the separate States are incompetent &—:—in place of this Congress are to have additional power in a few cases only—7. A negative on the laws of the States:—in place of this coertion to be substituted—8. The Executive to be removeable on impeachment & conviction;—in one plan: in the other to be removeable at the instance of majority of the Executives of the States—9. Revision of the laws provided for in one:—no such check in the other—10. inferior national tribunals in one:—none such in the other. 11. In the one jurisdiction of National tribunals to extend &c—; an appellate jurisdiction only allowed in the other. 12. Here the jurisdiction is to extend to all cases affecting the National peace & harmony: there, a few cases only are marked out. 13. finally the ratification is in this to be by the people themselves:—in that by the legislative authorities according to the thirteenth article of Confederation.

With regard to the *power of the Convention*, he conceived himself authorized to *conclude nothing*, but to be at liberty to *propose any thing*. In this particular he felt himself perfectly indifferent to the two plans.

With regard to the sentiments of the people, he conceived it difficult to know precisely what they are. Those of the particular circle in which one moved, were commonly mistaken for the general voice. He could not persuade himself that the State Governments & Sovereignties were so much the idols of the people, nor a National Government so obnoxious to them, as some supposed. Why should a National Government be unpopular? Has it less dignity? will each Citizen enjoy under it less liberty or protection? Will a Citizen of

Delaware be degraded by becoming a Citizen of the *United States?* Where do the people look at present for relief from the evils of which they complain? Is it from an internal reform of their Governments? no, Sir. It is from the National Councils that relief is expected. For these reasons he did not fear, that the people would not follow us into a national Government and it will be a further recommendation of Mr. Randolph's plan that it is to be submitted to *them*, and not to the *Legislatures*, for ratification.

Proceeding now to the first point on which he had contrasted the two plans, he observed that anxious as he was for some augmentation of the federal powers, it would be with extreme reluctance indeed that he could ever consent to give powers to Congress he had two reasons either of which was sufficient. 1. Congress as a Legislative body does not stand on the people. 2. it is a *single* body. 1. He would not repeat the remarks he had formerly made on the principles of Representation. he would only say that an inequality in it, has ever been a poison contaminating every branch of Government . . . 2. *Congress is a single Legislature.* Despotism comes on Mankind in different Shapes, sometimes in an Executive, sometimes in a Military, one. Is there no danger of a Legislative despotism? Theory & practice both proclaim it. If the Legislative authority be not restrained, there can be neither liberty nor stability; and it can only be restrained by dividing it within itself, into distinct and independent branches. In a single House there is no check, but the inadequate one, of the virtue & good sense of those who compose it.

On another great point, the contrast was equally favorable to the plan reported by the Committee of the whole. It vested the Executive powers in a single Magistrate. The plan of New Jersey, vested them in a plurality. In order to controul the Legislative authority, you must divide it. In order to controul the Executive you must unite it. One man will be more responsible than three. . . .

Mr. PINKNEY, the whole comes to this, as he conceived. Give New Jersey an equal vote, and she will dismiss her scruples, and concur in the National system. He thought the Convention authorized to go any length in recommending, which they found necessary to remedy the evils which produced this Convention.

. . .

Mr. RANDOLPH, was not scrupulous on the point of power. When the salvation of the Republic was at stake, it would be treason to our trust, not to propose what we found necessary. He painted in strong colours, the imbecility of the existing Confederacy, & the danger of delaying a substantial reform. . . . There are certainly seasons of a peculiar nature where the ordinary cautions must be dispensed with; and this is certainly one of them. He would not as far as depended on him leave any thing that seemed necessary, undone. The present moment is favorable, and is probably the last that will offer.

The true question is whether we shall adhere to the federal plan, or introduce the national plan. The insufficiency of the former has been fully displayed by the trial already made. There are but two modes, by which the end of a General Government can be attained: the first is by coercion as proposed by Mr. Patterson's plan, 2. by real legislation as proposed by the other plan. Coercion he pronounced to be *impracticable, expensive, cruel to individuals.* It tended also to habituate the instruments of it to shed the blood & riot in the spoils of their fellow Citizens, and consequently trained them up for the service of ambition. We must resort therefor to a National *Legislation over individuals,* for which Congress are unfit. To vest such power in them, would be blending the Legislative with the Executive, contrary to the recognized maxim on this subject: If the Union of these powers heretofore in Congress has been safe, it has been owing to the general impotency of that body. Congress are moreover not elected by the people, but by the Legislatures who retain even a power of recall. They have therefore no will of their own, they are a mere diplomatic body, and are always obsequious to the views of the States, who are always encroaching on the authority of the United States. A provision for harmony among the States, as in trade, naturalization, etc.—for crushing rebellion whenever it may rear its crest—and for certain other general benefits, must be made. The powers for these purposes, can never be given to a body, inadequate as Congress are in point of representation, elected in the mode in which they are, and possessing no more confidence than they do; for notwithstanding what has been said to the contrary, his own experience satisfied him that a rooted distrust of Congress pretty generally prevailed. A National Government alone, properly constituted, will answer the purpose; and he begged it to be considered that the present is the last moment for establishing one. After this select experiment, the people will yield to despair.

26. The Hamilton Plan, June 18, 1787

Disgusted with the "low tone" of the proceedings so far, Alexander Hamilton delivered a brilliant speech denouncing both plans, outlining his theories of government, and proposing his own plan, which included an executive chosen for life. As William Samuel Johnson of Connecticut noted, Hamilton was "praised by everybody . . . supported by none."

Monday, June 18. In Committee of the whole

. . . Mr. HAMILTON. . . . The great question is what provision shall we make for the happiness of our Country? He would first make a comparative examination of the two plans—prove that there were essential defects in both—and point out such changes as might render a *national* one, efficacious.—The great & essential principles necessary for the support of Government are 1. an active & constant interest in supporting it. This principle does not exist in the States in favor of the federal Government . . . They constantly pursue internal interests adverse to those of the whole. . . . 2. The love of power. Men love power. The same remarks are applicable to this principle. The States have constantly shewn a disposition rather to regain the powers delegated by them than to part with more, or to give effect to what they had parted with. The ambition of their demagogues is known to hate the controul of the General Government. It may be remarked too that the Citizens have not that anxiety to prevent a dissolution of the General Government as of the particular Governments. A dissolution of the latter would be fatal; of the former would still leave the purposes of Government attainable to a considerable degree. . . . 3. An habitual attachment of the people. The whole force of this tie is on the side of the State Government. Its sovereignty is immediately before the eyes of the people: its protection is immediately enjoyed by them. From its hand distributive justice, and all those acts which familiarize & endear Government to a people, are dispensed to them. 4. *Force* by which may be understood a *coertion* of laws or *coertion* of arms. Congress have not the former except in few cases. In particular

States, this coercion is nearly sufficient; though he held it in most cases, not entirely so. A certain portion of military force is absolutely necessary in large communities. Massachusetts is now feeling this necessity & making provision for it. But how can this force be exerted on the States collectively. It is impossible. It amounts to a war between the parties. Foreign powers also will not be idle spectators. They will interpose, the confusion will increase, and a dissolution of the Union ensue. 5. *influence.* he did not mean corruption, but a dispensation of those regular honors & emoluments, which produce an attachment to the Government. Almost all the weight of these is on the side of the States; and must continue so as long as the States continue to exist. All the passions then we see, of avarice, ambition, interest, which govern most individuals, and all public bodies, fall into the current of the States, and do not flow in the stream of the General Government. The former therefore will generally be an overmatch for the General Government and render any confederacy, in its very nature precarious. Theory is in this case fully confirmed by experience. [Here Hamilton cites the Amphictyonic Council, the German Confederacy and the German Diet, and the Swiss cantons.] How then are all these evils to be avoided? only by such a compleat sovereignty in the general Government as will turn all the strong principles & passions above mentioned on its side. Does the scheme of New Jersey produce this effect? does it afford any substantial remedy whatever? On the contrary it labors under great defects, and the defect of some of its provisions will destroy the efficacy of others. It gives a direct revenue to Congress but this will not be sufficient. The balance can only be supplied by requisitions: which experience proves can not be relied on. If States are to deliberate on the mode, they will also deliberate on the object of the supplies, and will grant or not grant as they approve or disapprove of it. The delinquency of one will invite and countenance it in others. Quotas too must in the nature of things be so unequal as to produce the same evil. To what standard will you resort? [Hamilton considers and rejects land, number of inhabitants, and geographical situation, and mentions commerce.] Another destructive ingredient in the plan, is that equality of suffrage which is so much desired by the small States. It is not in human nature that Virginia & the large States should consent to it, or if they did that they should long abide by it. It shocks too much the ideas of Justice, and every human feeling. Bad principles in a Government tho slow are sure in their operation and will gradually destroy it. . . . If the powers proposed were adequate, the organization of Congress is such that they could never be properly & effectually exercised. The members of Congress being chosen by the States & subject to recall, represent all the local prejudices. Should the powers be found effectual, they will from time to time be heaped on them, till a tyrannic sway shall be established. The general power whatever be its form if it preserves itself, must swallow up the State powers. Otherwise it will be swallowed up by them. It is against all the principles of a good Government to vest the requisite powers in such a body as Congress. Two Sovereignties can not co-exist within the same limits. Giving powers to Congress must eventuate in a bad Government or in no Government. The plan of New Jersey therefore will not do. What then is to be done? Here he was embarrassed. The extent of the Country to be governed, discouraged him. The expence of a general Government was also formidable; unless there were such a diminution of expence on the side of the State Governments as the case would admit. If they were extinguished, he was persuaded that great œconomy might be obtained by substituting a general Government. He did not mean however to shock the public opinion by proposing such a measure. On the other hand he saw no other necessity for declining it. They are not necessary for any of the great purposes of commerce, revenue, or agriculture. Subordinate authorities he was aware would be necessary. There must be district tribunals: corporations for local purposes. But cui bono, the vast & expensive apparatus now appertaining to the States. The only difficulty of a serious nature which occurred to him, was that of drawing representatives from the extremes to the center of the Community. What inducements can be offered that will suffice? The moderate wages for the first branch would only be a bait to little demagogues. Three dollars or thereabouts he supposed would be the utmost. The Senate he feared from a similar cause, would be filled by certain undertakers who wish for particular offices under the Government. This view of the subject almost led him to despair that a Republican Government could be established over so great an extent. He was sensible at the same time that it would be unwise to propose one of any other form. In his private opinion he had no scruple in declaring, supported as he was by the opinions of so many of the wise & good, that the British Government was the best in the world: and that he doubted much whether any thing short of it would do in America. He hoped Gentlemen of different opinions would bear with him in this, and begged them to recollect the change of opinion on this subject which had taken place and was still going on. It was once thought that the power of Congress was amply sufficient to secure the end of their institution. The error was now seen by every one. The members most tenacious of republicanism, he observed, were as loud as any in declaiming against the vices of democracy. This progress of the public mind led him to anticipate the time, when others as well as himself would join in the praise bestowed by Mr. Neckar on the British Constitution, namely, that it is the only Government in the world "which unites public strength with individual security."—In every community where industry is encouraged, there will be a division of it into the few & the many. Hence separate interests will arise. There will be debtors & creditors etc. Give all power to the many, they will oppress the few. Give all power to the few, they will oppress the many. Both therefore ought to have power, that each may defend itself against the other. To the want of this check we owe our paper money, instalment laws, etc. To the proper adjustment of it the British owe the excellence of their Constitution. Their house of Lords is a most noble institution. Having nothing to hope for by a change, and a sufficient interest by means of their property, in being faithful to the national interest, they form a permanent barrier against every pernicious innovation, whether attempted on the part of the Crown or of the Commons. No temporary Senate will have firmness enough to answer the purpose. . . . Gentlemen differ in their opinions concerning the necessary checks, from the different estimates they form of the human passions. They suppose seven years a sufficient period to give the senate an adequate firmness, from not duly considering the amazing violence & turbulence of the democratic spirit. When a great object of Government is pursued, which seizes the popular passions, they spread like wild fire, and become irresistable. He appealed to the gentlemen from the New England States whether experience had not there verified the remark.—As to the Executive, it seemed to be admitted that no good one could be established on Republican principles. Was not this giving up the merits of the question: for can there be a good Government without a good Executive. The English model was the only good one on this subject. The Hereditary interest of the King was so interwoven with that of the Nation, and his personal emoluments so great, that he was placed above the danger of being corrupted from abroad—and at the same time was both sufficiently independent and sufficiently controuled, to answer the purpose of the institution at home. one of the weak sides of Republics was their being liable to foreign influence & corruption. Men of little character, acquiring great power become easily the tools of intermedling Neibours. . . . What is the inference from all these observations? That we ought to go as far in order to attain stability and permanency, as republican principles will admit. Let one branch of the Legislature hold their places for life or at least during good behaviour. Let the Executive also be for life. He appealed to the feelings of the members present whether a term of seven years, would induce the sacrifices of private affairs which an acceptance of public trust would require, so as to ensure the services of the best Citizens. On this plan we should have in the Senate a permanent will, a weighty interest, which would answer essential purposes. But is this a Republican Government, it will be asked? Yes if all the Magistrates are appointed, and vacancies are filled, by the people, or a process of election originating with the people. He was sensible that an Executive constituted as he proposed would have in fact but little of the power and independence that might be necessary. On the other plan of appointing him for seven years, he thought the Executive ought to have but little power. He would be ambitious, with the means of making creatures; and as the object of his ambition would be to *prolong* his power, it is probable that in case of a war, he would avail himself of the emergency, to evade or refuse a degradation from his place. An Executive for life has not this motive for forgetting his fidelity, and will therefore be a safer depository of power. It will be objected probably, that such an Executive will be an *elective Monarch*, and will give birth to the tumults which characterize that form of Government. He would reply that *Monarch* is an indefinite term. It marks not either the degree or duration of power. If this Executive Magistrate would be a monarch for life—the other proposed by the Report from the Committee of the whole, would be a monarch for seven years. The circumstance of being elective was also applicable to both. It had been observed by judicious writers that elective monarchies would be the best if they could be guarded against the *tumults* excited by the ambition and intrigues of competitors. He was not sure that tumults were an inseparable evil. He rather thought this character of Elective Monarchies had been taken rather from particular cases than from general principles. . . . Might not such a mode of election be devised among ourselves as will defend the community against these effects in any dangerous degree? Having made these observations he would read to the Committee a sketch of a plan which he should prefer to either of those under consideration. He was aware that it went beyond the ideas of most members. But will such a plan be adopted out of doors? In return he would ask will the people adopt the other plan? At present they will adopt neither. But he sees the Union dissolving or already dissolved—he sees evils operating in the States which must soon cure the people of their fondness for democracies—he sees that a great progress has been already made & is still going on in the public mind. He thinks therefore that the people will in time be unshackled from their prejudices; and whenever that happens, they will themselves not be satisfied at stopping where the plan of Mr. Randolph would place them, but be ready to go as far at least as he proposes. He did not mean to offer the paper he had sketched as a proposition to the Committee. It was meant only to give a more correct view of his ideas, and to suggest the amendments which he should probably propose to the plan of Mr. Randolph in the proper stages of its future discussion. He read his sketch in the words following: towit

I. "The Supreme Legislative power of the United States of America to be vested in two different bodies of men; the one to be called the Assembly, the other the Senate who together shall form the Legislature of the United States with power to pass all laws whatsoever subject to the Negative hereafter mentioned.

II. The Assembly to consist of persons elected by the people to serve for three years.

III. The Senate to consist of persons elected to serve during good behaviour; their election to be made by electors chosen for that purpose by the people: in order to this the States to be divided into election districts. On the death, removal or resignation of any Senator his place to be filled out of the district from which he came.

IV. The supreme Executive authority of the United States to be vested in a Governour to be elected to serve during good behaviour —the election to be made by Electors chosen by the people in the Election Districts aforesaid—The authorities & functions of the Executive to be as follows: to have a negative on all laws about to be passed, and the execution of all laws passed, to have the direction of war when authorized or begun; to have with the advice and approbation of the Senate the power of making all treaties; to have the sole appointment of the heads or chief officers of the departments of Finance, War, and Foreign Affairs; to have the nomination of all other officers (Ambassadors to foreign Nations included) subject to the approbation or rejection of the Senate; to have the power of pardoning all offences except Treason; which he shall not pardon without the approbation of the Senate.

V. On the death, resignation or removal of the Governour his authorities to be exercised by the President of the Senate till a Successor be appointed.

VI. The Senate to have the sole power of declaring war, the power of advising and approving all Treaties, the power of approving or rejecting all appointments of officers except the heads or chiefs of the departments of Finance, War, and foreign affairs.

VII. The supreme Judicial authority to be vested in Judges to hold their offices during good behaviour with adequate and permanent salaries. This Court to have original jurisdiction in all causes of capture, and an appellative jurisdiction in all causes in which the revenues of the general Government or the Citizens of foreign Nations are concerned.

VIII. The Legislature of the United States to have power to institute Courts in each State for the determination of all matters of general concern.

IX. The Governour, Senators, and all officers of the United States to be liable to impeachment for mal- and corrupt conduct; and upon conviction to be removed from office, & disqualified for holding any place of trust or profit—All impeachments to be tried by a Court to consist of the Chief   or Judge of the superior Court of Law of each State, provided such Judge shall hold his place during good behavior, and have a permanent salary.

X. All laws of the particular States contrary to the Constitution or laws of the United States to be utterly void; and the better to prevent such laws being passed, the Governour or president of each State shall be appointed by the General Government and shall have a negative upon the laws about to be passed in the State of which he is Governour or President.

XI. No State to have any forces land or Naval; and the Militia of all the States to be under the sole and exclusive direction of the

United States, the officers of which to be appointed and commissioned by them."

On these several articles he entered into explanatory observations corresponding with the principles of his introductory reasoning.

27. Charles Pinckney, Debate on Representation, June 25, 1787

Still another plan was presented by the erratic young South Carolina aristocrat Charles Pinckney. Pinckney's plan was not formally discussed by the convention and no copy of it survives—though apparently several of its features did find their way into the finished Constitution—but in the following speech, delivered during the continuing debate on representation, Pinckney gives his philosophy of government and his analysis of America's needs:

Monday, June 25. In Convention

Resolution 4 [concerning the basis of representation in the second branch of the legislature] being taken up.

Mr. PINKNEY spoke as follows—The efficacy of the System will depend on this article. In order to form a right judgment in the case, it will be proper to examine the situation of this Country more accurately than it has yet been done. The people of the United States are perhaps the most singular of any we are acquainted with. Among them there are fewer distinctions of fortune & less of rank, than among the inhabitants of any other nation. Every freeman has a right to the same protection & security; and a very moderate share of property entitles them to the possession of all the honors and privileges the public can bestow: hence arises a greater equality, than is to be found among the people of any other country, and an equality which is more likely to continue—I say this equality is likely to continue, because in a new Country, possessing immense tracts of uncultivated lands, where every temptation is offered to emigration & where industry must be rewarded with competency, there will be few poor, and few dependent—Every member of the Society almost, will enjoy an equal power of arriving at the supreme offices & consequently of directing the strength & sentiments of the whole Community. None will be excluded by birth, & few by fortune, from voting for proper persons to fill the offices of Government—the whole community will enjoy in the fullest sense that kind of political liberty which consists in the power the members of the State reserve to themselves, of arriving at the public offices, or at least, of having votes in the nomination of those who fill them.

If this State of things is true & the prospect of its continuing probable, it is perhaps not politic to endeavour too close an imitation of a Government calculated for a people whose situation is, & whose views ought to be extremely different.

Much has been said of the Constitution of Great Britain. I will confess that I believe it to be the best Constitution in existence; but at the same time I am confident it is one that will not or can not be introduced into this Country, for many centuries.—If it were proper to go here into a historical dissertation on the British Constitution, it might easily be shewn that the peculiar excellence, the distinguishing feature of that Government can not possibly be introduced into our System—that its balance between the Crown & the people can not be made a part of our Constitution.—that we neither have or can have the members to compose it, nor the rights, privileges & properties of so distinct a class of Citizens to guard.—that the materials for forming this balance or check do not exist, nor is there a necessity for having so permanent a part of our Legislative, until the Executive power is so constituted as to have something fixed & dangerous in its principle—By this I mean a sole, hereditary, though limited Executive.

That we cannot have a proper body for forming a Legislative balance between the inordinate power of the Executive and the people, is evident from a review of the accidents & circumstances which gave rise to the peerage of Great Britain. [Pinckney then briefly sketched the growth of the nobility and commons.]

I have said that such a body cannot exist in this Country for ages, and that untill the situation of our people is exceedingly changed no necessity will exist for so permanent a part of the Legislature. To illustrate this I have remarked that the people of the United States are more equal in their circumstances than the people of any other Country—that they have very few rich men among them,— by rich men I mean those whose riches may have a dangerous influence, or such as are esteemed rich in Europe—perhaps there are not one hundred such on the Continent; that it is not probable this number will be greatly increased: that the genius of the people, their mediocrity of situation & the prospects which are afforded their industry in a Country which must be a new one for centuries are unfavorable to the rapid distinction of ranks. The destruction of the right of primogeniture & the equal division of the property of Intestates will also have an effect to preserve this mediocrity; for laws invariably affect the manners of a people. On the other hand that vast extent of unpeopled territory which opens to the frugal & industrious a sure road to competency & independence will effectually prevent for a considerable time the increase of the poor or discontented, and be the means of preserving that equality of condition which so eminently distinguishes us.

If equality is as I contend the leading feature of the United States, where then are the riches & wealth whose representation & protection is the peculiar province of this permanent body. Are they in the hands of the few who may be called rich; in the possession of less than a hundred citizens? certainly not. They are in the great body of the people, among whom there are no men of wealth, and very few of real poverty.—Is it probable that a change will be created, and that a new order of men will arise? If under the British Government, for a century no such change was probable, I think it may be fairly concluded it will not take place while even the semblance of Republicanism remains.—How is this change to be effected? Where are the sources from whence it is to flow? From the landed interest? No. That is too unproductive & too much divided in most of the States. From the Monied interest? If such exists at present, little is to be apprehended from that source. Is it to spring from commerce? I believe it would be the first instance in which a nobility sprang from merchants. Besides, Sir, I apprehend that on this point the policy of the United States has been much mistaken. We have unwisely considered ourselves as the inhabitants of an old instead of a new country. We have adopted the maxims of a State full of people & manufactures & established in credit. We have deserted our true interest, and instead of applying closely to those improvements in domestic policy which would have ensured the future importance of our commerce, we have rashly & prematurely engaged in schemes as extensive as they are imprudent. This however is an error which daily corrects itself & I have no doubt that a few more severe trials will convince us, that very different commercial principles ought to govern the conduct of these States.

The people of this country are not only very different from the inhabitants of any State we are acquainted with in the modern world; but I assert that their situation is distinct from either the people of Greece or Rome, or of any State we are acquainted with among the antients. . . .

Our true situation appears to me to be this.—a new extensive Country containing within itself the materials for forming a Government capable of extending to its citizens all the blessings of civil & religious liberty—capable of making them happy at home. This is the great end of Republican Establishments. We mistake the object of our Government, if we hope or wish that it is to make us respectable abroad. Conquest or superiority among other powers is not or ought not ever to be the object of republican systems. If they are sufficiently active & energetic to rescue us from contempt & preserve our domestic happiness & security, it is all we can expect from them,—it is more than almost any other Government ensures to its citizens.

I believe this observation will be found generally true:—that no two people are so exactly alike in their situation or circumstances as to admit the exercise of the same Government with equal benefit: that a system must be suited to the habits & genius of the people it is to govern, and must grow out of them.

The people of the U. S. may be divided into three classes—*Professional men* who must from their particular pursuits always have a considerable weight in the Government while it remains popular —*Commercial men*, who may or may not have weight as a wise or injudicious commercial policy is pursued.—If that commercial policy is pursued which I conceive to be the true one, the merchants of this Country will not or ought not for a considerable time to have much weight in the political scale.—The third is the *landed interest*, the owners and cultivators of the soil, who are and ought ever to be the governing spring in the system.—These three classes, however distinct in their pursuits are individually equal in the political scale, and may be easily proved to have but one interest. The dependence of each on the other is mutual. The merchant depends on the planter. Both must in private as well as public affairs be connected with the professional men; who in their turn must in some measure depend upon them. Hence it is clear from this manifest connection, & the equality which I before stated exists, & must for the reasons then assigned, continue, that after all there is one, but one great & equal body of citizens composing the inhabitants of this Country among whom there are no distinctions of rank, and very few or none of fortune.

For a people thus circumstanced are we then to form a government & the question is what kind of Government is best suited to them.

Will it be the British Government? No. Why? Because Great Britain contains three orders of people distinct in their situation, their possessions & their principles.—These orders combined form the great body of the Nation. . . . Each therefore must of necessity be represented by itself, or the sign of itself; and this accidental mixture has certainly formed a Government admirably well balanced.

But the United States contain but one order that can be assimilated to the British Nation,—this is the order of Commons. They will not surely then attempt to form a Government consisting of three branches, two of which shall have nothing to represent. They will not have an Executive & Senate (hereditary) because the King & Lords of England are so. The same reasons do not exist and therefore the same provisions are not necessary.

We must as has been observed suit our Government to the people it is to direct. These are I believe as active, intelligent & susceptible of good Government as any people in the world. The Confusion which has produced the present relaxed State is not owing to them. It is owing to the weakness & (defects) of a Government incapable of combining the various interests it is intended to unite, and destitute of energy.—All that we have to do then is to distribute the powers of Government in such a manner, and for such limited periods, as while it gives a proper degree of permanency to the Magistrate, will reserve to the people, the right of election they will not or ought not frequently to part with.—I am of opinion that this may be easily done; and that with some amendments the propositions before the Committee will fully answer this end.

No position appears to me more true than this; that the General Government can not effectually exist without reserving to the States the possession of their local rights. They are the instruments upon which the Union must frequently depend for the support &

execution of their powers, however immediately operating upon the people, and not upon the States.

Much has been said about the propriety of abolishing the distinction of State Governments, & having but one general System. Suffer me for a moment to examine this question.[1]

28. Debates of June 26, 1787

The convention continued to be deadlocked on the question of representation. Madison argued that diversity, incorporated into the system of representation, was the safest guarantee of liberty; Roger Sherman of Connecticut that frequent elections were the surest safeguard; Hamilton that liberty would ensue from making the government as "high toned" as possible:

Mr. MADISON. In order to judge of the form to be given to this institution, it will be proper to take a view of the ends to be served by it. These were first to protect the people against their rulers: secondly to protect the people against the transient impressions into which they themselves might be led. A people deliberating in a temperate moment, and with the experience of other nations before them, on the plan of Government most likely to secure their happiness, would first be aware, that those charged with the public happiness, might betray their trust. An obvious precaution against this danger would be to divide the trust between different bodies of men, who might watch & check each other. In this they would be governed by the same prudence which has prevailed in organizing the subordinate departments of Government, where all business liable to abuses is made to pass through separate hands, the one being a check on the other. It would next occur to such a people, that they themselves were liable to temporary errors, through want of information as to their true interest, and that men chosen for a short term, & employed but a small portion of that in public affairs, might err from the same cause. This reflection would naturally suggest that the Government be so constituted, as that one of its

[1] Madison failed to record the remainder of Pinckney's speech—Ed.

branches might have an opportunity of acquiring a competent knowledge of the public interests. Another reflection equally becoming a people on such an occasion, would be that they themselves, as well as a numerous body of Representatives, were liable to err also, from fickleness and passion. A necessary fence against this danger would be to select a portion of enlightened citizens, whose limited number, and firmness might seasonably interpose against impetuous councils. It ought finally to occur to a people deliberating on a Government for themselves, that as different interests necessarily result from the liberty meant to be secured, the major interest might under sudden impulses be tempted to commit injustice on the minority. In all civilized Countries the people fall into different classes having a real or supposed difference of interests. There will be creditors & debtors, farmers, merchants, & manufacturers. There will be particularly the distinction of rich & poor. It was true as had been observed (by Mr. Pinkney) we had not among us those hereditary distinctions, of rank which were a great source of the contests in the ancient Governments as well as the modern States of Europe, nor those extremes of wealth or poverty which characterize the latter. We cannot however be regarded even at this time, as one homogeneous mass, in which every thing that affects a part will affect in the same manner the whole. In framing a system which we wish to last for ages, we should not lose sight of the changes which ages will produce. An increase of population will of necessity increase the proportion of those who will labour under all the hardships of life, & secretly sigh for a more equal distribution of its blessings. These may in time outnumber those who are placed above the feelings of indigence. According to the equal laws of suffrage, the power will slide into the hands of the former. No agrarian attempts have yet been made in this Country, but symtoms, of a leveling spirit, as we have understood, have sufficiently appeared in a certain quarter to give notice of the future danger. How is this danger to be guarded against on republican principles? How is the danger in all cases of interested coalitions to oppress the minority to be guarded against? Among other means by the establishment of a body in the Government sufficiently respectable for its wisdom & virtue, to aid on such emergences, the preponderance of justice by throwing its weight into that scale. Such being the objects of the second branch in the proposed Government he thought a considerable duration ought to be given to it.

He did not conceive that the term of nine years could threaten any real danger; but in pursuing his particular ideas on the subject, he should require that the long term allowed to the second branch should not commence till such a period of life, as would render a perpetual disqualification to be reelected little inconvenient either in a public or private view. He observed that as it was more than probable we were now digesting a plan which in its operation would decide for ever the fate of Republican Government we ought not only to provide every guard to liberty that its preservation could require, but be equally careful to supply the defects which our own experience had particularly pointed out.

Mr. SHERMAN. Government is instituted for those who live under it. It ought therefore to be so constituted as not to be dangerous to their liberties. The more permanency it has the worse if it be a bad Government. Frequent elections are necessary to preserve the good behavior of rulers. They also tend to give permanency to the Government, by preserving that good behavior, because it ensures their re-election. . . . He wished to have provision made for steadiness & wisdom in the system to be adopted; but he thought six or four years would be sufficient. He should be content with either.

. . .

Mr. HAMILTON. He did not mean to enter particularly into the subject. He concurred with Mr. Madison in thinking we were now to decide for ever the fate of Republican Government; and that if we did not give to that form due stability and wisdom, it would be disgraced & lost among ourselves, disgraced & lost to mankind for ever. He acknowledged himself not to think favorably of Republican Government; but addressed his remarks to those who did think favorably of it, in order to prevail on them to tone their Government as high as possible. He professed himself to be as zealous an advocate for liberty as any man whatever, and trusted he should be as willing a martyr to it though he differed as to the form in which it was most eligible.

29. Madison's Remarks on Liberty and Power,
June 28, 1787

Continuing to try to persuade the small states to abandon equal representation, Madison made the profound observation that the weakest members of society are best protected by a strong government, not a weak one:

Mr. MADISON, said he was much disposed to concur in any expedient not inconsistent with fundamental principles, that could remove the difficulty concerning the rule of representation. But he could neither be convinced that the rule contended for was just, nor necessary for the safety of the small States against the large States. . . . The fallacy of the reasoning drawn from the equality of Sovereign States in the formation of compacts, lay in confounding mere Treaties, in which were specified certain duties to which the parties were to be bound, and certain rules by which their subjects were to be reciprocally governed in their intercourse, with a compact by which an authority was created paramount to the parties, and making laws for the government of them. . . . That it is not necessary to secure the small States against the large ones he conceived to be equally obvious: Was a combination of the large ones dreaded? this must arise either from some interest common to Virginia, Massachusetts, and Pennsylvania and distinguishing them from the other States or from the mere circumstance of similarity of size. Did any such common interest exist? In point of situation they could not have been more effectually separated from each other by the most jealous citizen of the most jealous State. In point of manners, Religion, and the other circumstances which sometimes beget affection between different communities, they were not more assimilated than the other States.—In point of the staple productions they were as dissimilar as any three other States in the Union. The Staple of Massachusetts was *fish*, of Pennsylvania *flour*, of Virginia *tobacco*. Was a combination to be apprehended from the mere circumstance of equality of size? Experience suggested no such danger. . . . Experience rather taught a contrary lesson. Among individuals of superior eminence & weight in Society, rivalships were much more frequent than coalitions. Among independent nations, pre-eminent over their neighbours, the same remark was verified. . . . Were the large States formidable *singly* to their smaller neighbours? On this supposition the latter ought to wish for such a general Government as will operate with equal energy on the former as on themselves. The more lax the band, the more liberty the larger will have to avail themselves of their superior force. Here again Experience was an instructive monitor. What is the situation of the weak compared with the strong in those stages of civilization in which the violence of individuals is least controuled by an efficient Government? . . . Is not the danger to the former exactly in proportion to their weakness. . . . In a word; the two extremes before us are a perfect separation & a perfect incorporation, of the thirteen States. In the first case they would be independent nations subject to no law, but the law of nations. In the last, they would be mere counties of one entire republic, subject to one common law. In the first case the smaller States would have every thing to fear from the larger. In the last they would have nothing to fear. The true policy of the small States therefore lies in promoting those principles & that form of Government which will most approximate the States to the condition of counties. Another consideration may be added. If the General Government be feeble, the large States distrusting its continuance, and foreseeing that their importance & security may depend on their own size & strength, will never submit to a partition. Give to the General Government sufficient energy & permanency, & you remove the objection. Gradual partitions of the large, & junctions of the small States will be facilitated, and time may effect that equalization, which is wished for by the small States now, but can never be accomplished at once. . . .

30. Gouverneur Morris on the Senate as an
Aristocracy, July 2, 1787

Hopelessly deadlocked, on July 2 the convention resolved to submit the question of representation to a committee, to seek a compromise solution. Gouverneur Morris agreed to the commitment, and urged that the committee make one branch democratic, the other aristocratic:

Mr. GOVERNEUR MORRIS thought a Committee adviseable as the Convention had been equally divided. He had a stronger reason also. The mode of appointing the second branch tended he was sure to defeat the object of it. What is this object? to check the precipitation, changeableness, and excesses of the first branch. Every man of observation had seen in the democratic branches of the State Legislatures, precipitation—in Congress changeableness, in every department excesses against personal liberty, private property, & personal safety. What qualities are necessary to constitute a check in this case? *Abilities* and *virtue*, are equally necessary in both branches. Something more then is now wanted. In the first place, the checking branch must have a personal interest in checking the other branch, one interest must be opposed to another interest. Vices as they exist, must be turned against each other. In the second place, it must have great personal property, it must have the aristocratic spirit; it must love to lord it through pride, pride is indeed the great principle that actuates both the poor & the rich. It is this principle which in the former resists, in the latter abuses authority. In the third place, it should be independent. In Religion the Creature is apt to forget its Creator. That it is otherwise in political affairs, the late debates here are an unhappy proof. The aristocratic body, should be as independent & as firm as the democratic. If the members of it are to revert to a dependence on the democratic choice, the democratic scale will preponderate. All the guards contrived by America have not restrained the Senatorial branches of the Legislatures from a servile complaisance to the democratic. If the second branch is to be dependent we are better without it. To make it independent, it should be for life. It will then do wrong, it will be said. He believed so: He hoped so. The Rich will strive to establish their dominion & enslave the rest. They always did. They always will. The proper security against them is to form them into a separate interest. The two forces will then controul each other. Let the rich mix with the poor and in a Commercial Country, they will establish an oligarchy. Take away commerce, and the democracy will triumph. Thus it has been all the world over. So it will be among us. Reason tells us we are but men: and we are not to expect any particular interference of Heaven in our favor. By thus combining & setting apart, the aristocratic interest, the popular interest will be combined against it. There will be a mutual check and mutual security. In the fourth place, an independence for life, involves the necessary permanency. If we change our measures no body will trust us: and how avoid a change of measures, but by avoiding a change of men. Ask any man if he confides in Congress, if he confides in the State of Pennsylvania, if he will lend his money or enter into contract? He will tell you no. He sees no stability. He can repose no confidence. If Great Britain were to explain her refusal to treat with us, the same reasoning would be employed.—He disliked the exclusion of the second branch from holding offices. It is dangerous. It is like the imprudent exclusion of the military officers during the war, from civil appointments. It deprives the Executive of the principal source of influence. If danger be apprehended from the Executive what a left-handed way is this of obviating it? If the son, the brother or the friend can be appointed, the danger may be even increased, as the disqualified father etc. can then boast of a disinterestedness which he does not possess. Besides shall the best, the most able, the most virtuous citizens not be permitted to hold offices? Who then are to hold them? He was also against paying the Senators. They will pay themselves if they can. If they can not they will be rich and can do without it. Of such the second branch ought to consist; and none but such can compose it if they are not to be paid —He contended that the Executive should appoint the Senate & fill up vacancies. This gets rid of the difficulty in the present question. You may begin with any ratio you please; it will come to the same thing. The members being independent & for life, may be taken as well from one place as from another.—It should be considered too how the scheme could be carried through the States. He hoped there was strength of mind enough in this House to look truth in the face. He did not hesitate therefore to say that loaves &

fishes must bribe the Demagogues. They must be made to expect higher offices under the general than the State Governments. A Senate for life will be a noble bait. Without such captivating prospects, the popular leaders will oppose & defeat the plan. He perceived that the first branch was to be chosen by the people of the States: the second by those chosen by the people. Is not here a Government by the States. A Government by Compact between Virginia in the first & second branch; Massachusetts in the first & second branch etc. This is going back to mere treaty. It is no Government at all. It is altogether dependent on the States, and will act over again the part which Congress has acted. A firm Government alone can protect our liberties. He fears the influence of the rich. They will have the same effect here as elsewhere if we do not by such a Government keep them within their proper sphere. We should remember that the people never act from reason alone. The Rich will take advantage of their passions & make these the instruments for oppressing them. The Result of the Contest will be a violent aristocracy, or a more violent despotism. The schemes of the Rich will be favored by the extent of the Country. The people in such distant parts can not communicate & act in concert. They will be the dupes of those who have more knowledge & intercourse. The only security against encroachments will be a select & sagacious body of men, instituted to watch against them on all sides. He meant only to hint these observations, without grounding any motion on them.

31. Debate on the Proposed Compromise on Representation, July 5, 1787

The committee brought in a compromise proposal, suggested by Franklin, that would provide proportional representation (one congressman for every 40,000 inhabitants) in the lower house, equal representation in the upper, and give the lower house exclusive power over taxes and expenditures. Madison and Morris led a fierce opposition to the proposal, and it was rejected:

Mr. MADISON could not regard the exclusive privilege of originating money bills as any concession on the side of the small States.

Experience proved that it had no effect. If seven States in the upper branch wished a bill to be originated, they might surely find some member from some of the same States in the lower branch who would originate it. The restriction as to amendments was of as little consequence. Amendments could be handed privately by the Senate to members in the other house. . . .

Mr. GOVERNEUR MORRIS thought the form as well as the matter of the Report objectionable. . . . He conceived the whole aspect of it to be wrong. He came here as a Representative of America; he flattered himself he came here in some degree as a Representative of the whole human race; for the whole human race will be affected by the proceedings of this Convention. He wished gentlemen to extend their views beyond the present moment of time; beyond the narrow limits of place from which they derive their political origin. If he were to believe some things which he had heard, he should suppose that we were assembled to truck and bargain for our particular States. . . . Much has been said of the sentiments of the people. They were unknown. They could not be known. All that we can infer is that if the plan we recommend be reasonable & right; all who have reasonable minds and sound intentions will embrace it, notwithstanding what had been said by some gentlemen. Let us suppose that the larger States shall agree; and that the smaller refuse: and let us trace the consequences. The opponents of the system in the smaller States will no doubt make a party, and a noise for a time, but the ties of interest, of kindred & of common habits which connect them with the other States will be too strong to be easily broken. In New Jersey particularly he was sure a great many would follow the sentiments of Pennsylvania & New York. This Country must be united. If persuasion does not unite it, the sword will. He begged that this consideration might have its due weight. The scenes of horror attending civil commotion can not be described, and the conclusion of them will be worse than the term of their continuance. The stronger party will then make traytors of the weaker; and the Gallows & Halter will finish the work of the sword. How far foreign powers would be ready to take part in the confusions he would not say. Threats that they will be invited have it seems been thrown out. . . . But returning to the Report he could not think it in any respect calculated for the public good. . . . State attachments, and State importance have been the bane of this Country. We can not annihilate; but we may perhaps take out the teeth of the serpents. He wished our ideas to be enlarged to the true interest of man, instead of being circumscribed within the narrow compass of a particular Spot. And after all how little can be the motive yielded by selfishness for such a policy. Who can say whether he himself, much less whether his children, will the next year be an inhabitant of this or that State. . . .

The first proposition in the report for fixing the representation in the first branch, one member for every 40,000 inhabitants, being taken up.

Mr. GOVERNEUR MORRIS objected to that scale of apportionment. He thought property ought to be taken into the estimate as well as the number of inhabitants. Life & liberty were generally said to be of more value, than property. An accurate view of the matter would nevertheless prove that property was the main object of Society. The savage State was more favorable to liberty than the Civilized; and sufficiently so to life. It was preferred by all men who had not acquired a taste for property; it was only renounced for the sake of property which could only be secured by the restraints of regular Government.

32. Debate on the Executive Branch, July 19, 1787

On July 16 the convention compromised on representation at last, providing equal representation in the lower house and giving each state two seats in the upper. Forthwith, the delegates became entangled in another dispute, the manner of choosing and length of service of the executive. The aristocratic Gouverneur Morris favored popular election; Randolph and King disagreed:

Thursday, July 19. In Convention

On reconsideration of the vote rendering the Executive re-eligible a second time, Mr. MARTIN moved to reinstate the words, "to be ineligible a second time."

Mr. GOVERNEUR MORRIS. It is necessary to take into one view all that relates to the establishment of the Executive; on the due formation of which must depend the efficacy & utility of the Union among the present and future States. It has been a maxim in Political Science that Republican Government is not adapted to a large extent of Country, because the energy of the Executive Magistracy can not reach the extreme parts of it. Our Country is an extensive one. We must either then renounce the blessings of the Union, or provide an Executive with sufficient vigor to pervade every part of it. This subject was of so much importance that he hoped to be indulged in an extensive view of it. One great object of the Executive is to controul the Legislature. The Legislature will continually seek to aggrandize & perpetuate themselves. . . . It is necessary then that the Executive Magistrate should be the guardian of the people, even of the lower classes, against Legislative tyranny, against the Great & the wealthy who in the course of things will necessarily compose the Legislative body. . . . The check provided in the second branch was not meant as a check on Legislative usurpations of power, but . . . on the propensity in the first branch to legislate too much to run into projects of paper money & similar expedients. It is no check on Legislative tyranny. On the contrary it may favor it, and if the first branch can be seduced may find the means of success. The Executive therefore ought to be so constituted as to be the great protector of the Mass of the people.—It is the duty of the Executive to appoint the officers & to command the forces of the Republic. . . . Who will be the best Judges whether these appointments be well made? The people at large, who will know, will see, will feel the effects of them. . . . He finds too that the Executive is not to be re-eligible. What effect will this have? 1. It will destroy the great incitement to merit public esteem by taking away the hope of being rewarded with a reappointment. It may give a dangerous turn to one of the strongest passions in the human breast. The love of fame is the great spring to noble & illustrious actions. Shut the Civil road to Glory & he may be compelled to seek it by the sword. 2. It will tempt him to make the most of the short space of time allotted him, to accumulate wealth and provide for his friends. 3. It will produce violations of the very constitution it is meant to secure. In moments of pressing danger the tried abilities and established character of a favorite Magistrate will prevail over respect for the forms of the Constitution. The Executive is also to be impeachable. . . . It will hold him in such dependence that he will be no check on the Legislature, will not be a firm guardian of the people and of the public interest. He will be the tool of a faction, of some leading demagogue in the Legislature. These then are the faults of the Executive establishment as now proposed. Can no better establishment be devised? If he is to be the Guardian of the people let him be appointed by the people. If he is to be a check on the Legislature let him not be impeachable. Let him be of short duration, that he may with propriety be re-eligible. It has been said that the candidates for this office will not be known to the people. If they be known to the Legislature, they must have such a notoriety and eminence of Character, that they can not possibly be unknown to the people at large. It cannot be possible that a man shall have sufficiently distinguished himself to merit this high trust without having his character proclaimed by fame throughout the Empire. As to the danger from an unimpeachable magistrate he could not regard it as formidable. . . . He suggested a biennial election of the Executive . . . by the people at large. . . . He saw no alternative for making the Executive independent of the Legislature but either to give him his office for life, or make him eligible by the people—Again, it might be objected that two years would be too short a duration. But he believes that as long as he should behave himself well, he would be continued in his place. The extent of the Country would secure his re-election against the factions & discontents of particular States. It deserved consideration also that such an ingredient in the plan would render it extremely palatable to the people. These were the general ideas which occurred to him on the subject, and which led him to wish & move that the whole constitution of the Executive might undergo reconsideration.

Mr. RANDOLPH urged the motion of Mr. Luther Martin for restoring the words making the Executive ineligible a second time. If he ought to be independent, he should not be left under a temptation to court a re-appointment. . . . He thought an election by the Legislature with an incapacity to be elected a second time would be more acceptable to the people than the plan suggested by Mr. Governeur Morris.

Mr. KING did not like the ineligibility. He thought . . . that he who has proved himself to be most fit for an Office, ought not to be excluded by the constitution from holding it. He would therefore prefer any other reasonable plan that could be substituted. He was much disposed to think that in such cases the people at large would chuse wisely. There was indeed some difficulty arising from the improbability of a general concurrence of the people in favor of any one man. On the whole he was of opinion that an appointment by electors chosen by the people for the purpose, would be liable to fewest objections.

33. Debate on the Powers of the Judiciary, July 21, 1787

On July 21, there followed a vigorous debate on the question of the role of the courts in vetoing or invalidating acts of Congress:

Mr. WILSON moved as an amendment to Resolution 10 that the supreme National Judiciary should be associated with the Executive in the Revisionary [veto] power. This proposition had been before made and failed: but he was so confirmed by reflection in the opinion of its utility, that he thought it incumbent on him to make another effort: The Judiciary ought to have an opportunity of remonstrating against projected encroachments on the people as well as on themselves. It had been said that the Judges, as expositors of the Laws would have an opportunity of defending their constitutional rights. There was weight in this observation; but this power of the Judges did not go far enough. Laws may be unjust, may be unwise, may be dangerous, may be destructive; and yet may not be so unconstitutional as to justify the Judges in refusing to give them effect. Let them have a share in the Revisionary power, and they will have an opportunity of taking notice of these characters of a law, and of counteracting, by the weight of their opinions the improper views of the Legislature.—

Mr. MADISON seconded the motion.

Mr. GORHAM did not see the advantage of employing the Judges in this way. As Judges they are not to be presumed to possess any peculiar knowledge of the mere policy of public measures. Nor can it be necessary as a security for their constitutional rights. The Judges in England have no such additional provision for their defence, yet their jurisdiction is not invaded. He thought it would be best to let the Executive alone be responsible, and at most to authorize him to call on Judges for their opinions.

Mr. ELLSWORTH approved heartily of the motion. The aid of the Judges will give more wisdom & firmness to the Executive. They will possess a systematic and accurate knowledge of the Laws, which the

Executive can not be expected always to possess. The law of Nations also will frequently come into question. Of this the Judges alone will have competent information.

Mr. MADISON considered the object of the motion as of great importance to the meditated Constitution. It would be useful to the Judiciary department by giving it an additional opportunity of defending itself against Legislative encroachments; It would be useful to the Executive, by inspiring additional confidence & firmness in exerting the revisionary power: It would be useful to the Legislature by the valuable assistance it would give in preserving a consistency, conciseness, perspicuity & technical propriety in the laws, qualities peculiarly necessary; & yet shamefully wanting in our republican Codes. It would moreover be useful to the Community at large as an additional check against a pursuit of those unwise & unjust measures which constituted so great a portion of our calamities. If any solid objection could be urged against the motion, it must be on the supposition that it tended to give too much strength either to the Executive or Judiciary. He did not think there was the least ground for this apprehension. It was much more to be apprehended that notwithstanding this co-operation of the two departments, the Legislature would still be an over-match for them. Experience in all the States had evinced a powerful tendency in the Legislature to absorb all power into its vortex. This was the real source of danger to the American Constitutions; & suggested the necessity of giving every defensive authority to the other departments that was consistent with republican principles.

. . . Mr. GERRY did not expect to see this point which had undergone full discussion, again revived. . . . The motion was liable to strong objections. It was combining & mixing together the Legislative & the other departments. It was establishing an improper coalition between the Executive & Judiciary departments. It was making Statesmen of the Judges; and setting them up as the guardians of the Rights of the people. He relied for his part on the Representatives of the people as the guardians of their Rights & interests. It was making the Expositors of the Laws the Legislators, which ought never to be done. . . .

Mr. GOVERNEUR MORRIS. Some check being necessary on the Legislature, the question is in what hands it should be lodged. On one side it was contended that the Executive alone ought to exercise it. He did not think that an Executive appointed for six years, and impeachable whilst in office would be a very effectual check. On the other side it was urged that he ought to be reinforced by the Judiciary department. Against this it was objected that Expositors of laws ought to have no hand in making them, and arguments in favor of this had been drawn from England. What weight was due to them might be easily determined by an attention to facts. The truth was that the Judges in England had a great share in the Legislation. They are consulted in difficult & doubtful cases. They may be & some of them are members of the Legislature. They are or may be members of the privy Council, and can there advise the Executive as they will do with us if the motion succeeds. The influence the English Judges may have in the latter capacity in strengthening the Executive check can not be ascertained, as the King by his influence in a manner dictates the laws. There is one difference in the two Cases however which disconcerts all reasoning from the British to our proposed Constitution. The British Executive has so great an interest in his prerogatives and such powerful means of defending them that he will never yield any part of them. The interest of our Executive is so inconsiderable & so transitory, and his means of defending it so feeble, that there is the justest ground to fear his want of firmness in resisting incroachments. He was extremely apprehensive that the auxiliary firmness & weight of the Judiciary would not supply the deficiency. He concurred in thinking the public liberty in greater danger from Legislative usurpations than from any other source. It had been said that the Legislature ought to be relied on as the proper Guardians of liberty. The answer was short and conclusive. Either bad laws will be pushed or not. On the latter supposition no check will be wanted. On the former a strong check will be necessary: And this is the proper supposition. Emissions of paper money, largesses to the people—a remission of debts and similar measures, will at some times be popular, and will be pushed for that reason. At other times such measures will coincide with the interests of the Legislature themselves, & that will be a reason not less cogent for pushing them. It may be thought that the people will not be deluded and misled in the latter case. But experience teaches another lesson. The press is indeed a great means of diminishing the evil, yet it is found to be unable to prevent it altogether.

Mr. LUTHER MARTIN. Considered the association of the Judges

with the Executive as a dangerous innovation; as well as one which could not produce the particular advantage expected from it. A knowledge of Mankind, and of Legislative affairs cannot be presumed to belong in a higher degree to the Judges than to the Legislature. And as to the Constitutionality of laws, that point will come before the Judges in their proper official character. In this character they have a negative on the laws. Join them with the Executive in the Revision and they will have a double negative. It is necessary that the Supreme Judiciary should have the confidence of the people. This will soon be lost, if they are employed in the task of remonstrating against popular measures of the Legislature. . . .

Mr. MADISON could not discover in the proposed association of the Judges with the Executive in the Revisionary check on the Legislative any violation of the maxim which requires the great departments of power to be kept separate & distinct. On the contrary he thought it an auxiliary precaution in favor of the maxim. If a Constitutional discrimination of the departments on paper were a sufficient security to each against encroachments of the others, all further provisions would indeed be superfluous. But experience had taught us a distrust of that security; and that it is necessary to introduce such a balance of powers and interests, as will guarantee the provisions on paper. Instead therefore of contenting ourselves with laying down the Theory in the Constitution that each department ought to be separate & distinct, it was proposed to add a defensive power to each which should maintain the Theory in practice. In so doing we did not blend the departments together. We erected effectual barriers for keeping them separate. The most regular example of this theory was in the British Constitution. Yet it was not only the practice there to admit the Judges to a seat in the legislature, and in the Executive Councils, and to submit to their previous examination all laws of a certain description, but it was a part of their Constitution that the Executive might negative any law whatever; a part of *their* Constitution which had been universally regarded as calculated for the preservation of the whole. The objection against a union of the Judiciary & Executive branches in the revision of the laws, had either no foundation or was not carried far enough. If such a Union was an improper mixture of powers, or such a Judiciary check on the laws, was inconsistent with the Theory of a free Constitution, it was equally so to admit the Executive to any participation in the making of laws; and the revisionary plan ought to be discarded altogether.

34. Continued Debate on the Executive Branch, July 25–26, 1787

The debate on the proper constitution of the proposed executive branch raged on, objections being raised to every method suggested:

Mr. MADISON. There are objections against every mode that has been, or perhaps can be proposed. The election must be made either by some existing authority under the National or State Constitutions—or by some special authority derived from the people—or by the people themselves.—The two Existing authorities under the National Constitution would be the Legislative & Judiciary. The latter he presumed was out of the question. The former was in his Judgment liable to insuperable objections. . . . The existing authorities in the States are the Legislative, Executive & Judiciary. The appointment of the National Executive by the first, was objectionable in many points of view, some of which had been already mentioned. He would mention one which of itself would decide his opinion. The Legislatures of the States had betrayed a strong propensity to a variety of pernicious measures. One object of the National Legislature was to controul this propensity. One object of the National Executive, so far as it would have a negative on the laws, was to controul the National Legislature, so far as it might be infected with a similar propensity. Refer the appointment of the National Executive to the State Legislatures, and this controuling purpose may be defeated. The Legislatures can & will act with some kind of regular plan, and will promote the appointment of a man who will not oppose himself to a favorite object. Should a majority of the Legislatures at the time of election have the same object, or different objects of the same kind, The National Executive would be rendered subservient to them.—An appointment by the State Executives, was liable among other objections to this insuperable one, that being standing bodies, they could & would be courted, and intrigued with by the Candidates, by their partizans, and by the Ministers of foreign powers. The State Judiciaries had not & he presumed would not be proposed as a proper source of appointment. The option before us then lay between an appointment by Electors chosen by the people—and an immediate appointment by the people. He thought the former mode free from many of the objections which had been urged against it, and greatly preferable to an appointment by the National Legislature. As the electors would be chosen for the occasion, would meet at once, & proceed immediately to an appointment, there would be very little opportunity for cabal, or corruption. As a farther precaution, it might be required that they should meet at some place distinct from the seat of Government and even that no person within a certain distance of the place at the time should be eligible. This Mode however had been rejected so recently and by so great a majority that it probably would not be proposed anew. The remaining mode was an election by the people or rather by the qualified part of them at large: With all its imperfections he liked this best. . . .

Mr. GOVERNEUR MORRIS was against a rotation in every case. . . . A change of men is ever followed by a change of measures. . . . He considered an election by the people as the best, by the Legislature as the worst, mode. . . .

Thursday, July 26. In Convention

Colonel MASON. In every Stage of the Question relative to the Executive, the difficulty of the subject and the diversity of the opinions concerning it have appeared. Nor have any of the modes of constituting that department been satisfactory. 1. It has been proposed that the election should be made by the people at large; that is that an act which ought to be performed by those who know most of Eminent characters, and qualifications, should be performed by those who know least. 2. That the election should be made by the Legislatures of the States. 3. By the Executives of the States. Against these modes also strong objections have been urged. 4. It has been proposed that the elections should be made by Electors chosen by the people for that purpose. This was at first agreed to: But on further consideration has been rejected. 5. Since which, the mode of Mr. Williamson, requiring each freeholder to vote for several candidates has been proposed. This seemed like many other propositions, to carry a plausible face, but on closer inspection is liable to fatal objections. A popular election in any form, as Mr. Gerry has observed, would throw the appointment into the hands of the Cincinnati, a Society for the members of which he had a great respect; but which he never wished to have a preponderating influence in the Government. 6. Another expedient was proposed by Mr. Dickenson, which is liable to so palpable & material an inconvenience that he had little doubt of its being by this time rejected by himself. It would exclude every man who happened not to be popular within his own State; though the causes of his local unpopularity might be of such a nature as to recommend him to the States at large. 7. Among other expedients, a lottery has been introduced. But as the tickets do not appear to be in much demand, it will probably, not be carried on, and nothing therefore need be said on that subject. After reviewing all these various modes, he was led to conclude, that an election by the National Legislature as originally proposed, was the best. If it was liable to objections, it was liable to fewer than any other. He conceived at the same time that a second election ought to be absolutely prohibited. Having for his primary object, for the polestar of his political conduct, the preservation of the rights of the people, he held it as an essential point, as the very palladium of Civil liberty, that the great officers of State, and particularly the Executive should at fixed periods return to that mass from which they were at first taken, in order that they may feel & respect those rights & interests, which are again to be personally valuable to them. He concluded with moving that the constitution of the Executive as reported by the Committee of the whole be re-instated, viz. "that the Executive be appointed for seven years, & be ineligible a second time"

Mr. DAVIE seconded the motion

Doctor FRANKLIN. It seems to have been imagined by some that the returning to the mass of the people was degrading the magistrate. This he thought was contrary to republican principles. In free Governments the rulers are the servants, and the people their superiors & sovereigns. For the former therefore to return among the latter was not to *degrade* but to *promote* them. And it would be imposing an unreasonable burden on them, to keep them always in a State of servitude, and not allow them to become again one of the Masters.

Question on Colonel Masons motion as above; which passed in the affirmative

35. Debate on the Navigation Acts, August 29, 1787

By July 26 the convention had gone as far as it could in dealing with general principles; it was now time to pull its resolutions together in the form of a concrete system. The proceedings were turned over to a five-man Committee of Detail, which put together twenty-three resolutions as the framework of a constitution. The delegates resumed their deliberations on August 6, and debates continued for the next five weeks. Much of the time was spent on continued argument about the executive branch. The remainder was mainly devoted to efforts to reconcile conflicting economic and sectional interests. The debates of August 29 illustrate the conflict:

Art. vii, sect. 6,[1] by the Committee of eleven reported to be struck out (see the 24 instant) being now taken up,

Mr. PINCKNEY moved to postpone the Report in favor of the foling proposition—"That no act of the Legislature for the purpose of regulating the commerce of the United States with foreign powers, or among the several States, shall be passed without the assent of two thirds of the members of each House." He remarked that there were five distinct commercial interests. 1. The fisheries and West India trade, which belonged to the New England States. 2. The interest of New York lay in a free trade. 3. Wheat and flour the staples of the two middle States (N. J. and Penn.). 4. Tobacco the staple of Maryland and Virginia, and partly of North Carolina. 5. Rice and indigo, the staples of South Carolina and Georgia. These different interests would be a source of oppressive regulations if no check to a bare majority should be provided. States pursue their interests with less scruple than individuals. The power of regulating commerce was a pure concession on the part of the southern States.

[1] The requirement of a two-thirds majority for a navigation Act—Madison's note.

They did not need the protection of the northern States at present.

Mr. MARTIN seconded the motion.

General PINCKNEY said it was the true interest of the southern States to have no regulation of commerce; but considering the loss brought on the commerce of the eastern States by the Revolution, their liberal conduct towards the views[2] of South Carolina, and the interest the weak southern States had in being united with the strong eastern States, he thought it proper that no fetters should be imposed on the power of making commercial regulations; and that his constituents, though prejudiced against the eastern States, would be reconciled to this liberality. He had himself, he said, prejudices against the eastern States before he came here, but would acknowledge that he had found them as liberal and candid as any men whatever.

Mr. CLYMER. The diversity of commercial interests of necessity creates difficulties, which ought not to be increased by unnecessary restrictions. The northern and middle States will be ruined, if not enabled to defend themselves against foreign regulations.

Mr. SHERMAN, alluding to Mr. Pinckney's enumeration of particular interests as requiring a security against abuse of the power, observed that the diversity was of itself a security, adding that to require more than a majority to decide a question was always embarrassing, as had been experienced in cases requiring the votes of nine States in Congress.

Mr. PINCKNEY replied that his enumeration meant the five minute interests. It still left the two great divisions of northern and southern interests.

Mr. GOVERNEUR MORRIS opposed the object of the motion as highly injurious. Preferences to American ships will multiply them, till they can carry the southern produce cheaper than it is now carried. A navy was essential to security, particularly of the southern States, and can only be had by a Navigation Act encouraging American bottoms and seamen. In those points of view then alone, it is the interest of the southern States that navigation acts should be

[2] He meant the permission to import slaves. And understanding on the two subjects of *navigation* and *slavery* had taken place between those parts of the Union, which explains the vote on the motion depending, as well as the language of General Pinckney and others. [This is Madison's note, and not an entirely accurate appraisal. See Forrest McDonald, *E Pluribus Unum* (New York, 1965), pp. 183–184.]

facilitated. Shipping, he said, was the worst and most precarious kind of property, and stood in need of public patronage.

Mr. WILLIAMSON was in favor of making two-thirds instead of a majority requisite, as more satisfactory to the southern people. No useful measure he believed had been lost in Congress for want of nine votes. As to the weakness of the southern States, he was not alarmed on that account. The sickliness of their climate for invaders would prevent their being made an object. He acknowledged that he did not think the motion requiring two-thirds necessary in itself, because if a majority of the northern States should push their regulations too far, the southern States would build ships for themselves: but he knew the southern people were apprehensive on this subject and would be pleased with the precaution. . . .

Mr. BUTLER differed from those who considered the rejection of the motion as no concession on the part of the southern States. He considered the interests of these and of the eastern States to be as different as the interests of Russia and Turkey. Being notwithstanding desirous of conciliating the affections of the eastern States, he should vote against requiring two-thirds instead of a majority.

Colonel MASON. If the government is to be lasting, it must be founded in the confidence and affections of the people, and must be so constructed as to obtain these. The majority will be governed by their interests. The southern States are the minority in both Houses. Is it to be expected that they will deliver themselves bound hand and foot to the eastern States, and enable them to exclaim, in the words of Cromwell on a certain occasion—"the Lord hath delivered them into our hands"?

Mr. WILSON took notice of the several objections and remarked that if every peculiar interest was to be secured, unanimity ought to be required. The majority, he said, would be no more governed by interest than the minority. It was surely better to let the latter be bound hand and foot than the former. Great inconveniences had, he contended, been experienced in Congress from the Articles of Confederation requiring nine votes in certain cases.

Mr. MADISON went into a pretty full view of the subject. He observed that the disadvantage to the southern States from a Navigation Act lay chiefly in a temporary rise of freight, attended, however, with an increase of southern as well as northern shipping, with the emigration of northern seamen and merchants to the southern States, and with a removal of the existing and injurious retaliations among the States on each other. The power of foreign nations to obstruct our retaliating measures on them by a corrupt influence would also be less, if a majority should be made competent than if two-thirds of each House should be required to legislative acts in this case. An abuse of the power would be qualified with all these good effects. But he thought an abuse was rendered improbable by the provision of two branches, by the independence of the Senate, by the negative of the Executive, by the interest of Connecticut and New Jersey, which were agricultural, not commercial States; by the interior interest which was also agricultural in the most commercial States, and by the accession of western States which would be altogether agricultural. He added that the southern States would derive an essential advantage in the general security afforded by the increase of our maritime strength. He stated the vulnerable situation of them all, and of Virginia in particular. The increase of the coasting trade, and of seamen, would also be favorable to the southern States, by increasing the consumption of their produce. If the wealth of the eastern should in a still greater proportion be augmented, that wealth would contribute the more to the public wants, and be otherwise a national benefit.

Mr. RUTLEDGE was against the motion of his colleague. It did not follow from a grant of the power to regulate trade, that it would be abused. At the worst a Navigation Act could bear hard a little while only on the southern States. As we are laying the foundation for a great empire, we ought to take a permanent view of the subject and not look at the present moment only. He reminded the House of the necessity of securing the West India trade to this country. That was the great object, and a Navigation Act was necessary for obtaining it.

Mr. RANDOLPH said that there were features so odious in the Constitution as it now stands, that he doubted whether he should be able to agree to it. A rejection of the motion would compleat the deformity of the system. He took notice of the argument in favor of giving the power over trade to a majority, drawn from the opportunity foreign powers would have of obstructing retaliatory measures, if two-thirds were made requisite. He did not think there was weight in that consideration. The difference between a majority and two-thirds did not afford room for such an opportunity. Foreign influence would also be more likely to be exerted on the President, who could require three-fourths by his negative. He did not mean, however, to enter into the merits. What he had in view was merely to pave the way for a declaration which he might be hereafter obliged to make if an accumulation of obnoxious ingredients should take place, that he could not give his assent to the plan.

Mr. GORHAM. If the Government is to be so fettered as to be unable to relieve the eastern States, what motive can they have to join in it, and thereby tie their own hands from measures which they could otherwise take for themselves? The eastern States were not led to strengthen the Union by fear for their own safety. He deprecated the consequences of disunion, but if it should take place it was the southern part of the Continent that had most reason to dread them. He urged the improbability of a combination against the interest of the southern States, the different situations of the northern and middle States being a security against it. It was moreover certain that foreign ships would never be altogether excluded, especially those of nations in treaty with us.

On the question to postpone in order to take up Mr. Pinckney's motion,

N. H. no. Mass. no. Conn. no. N. J. no. Pa. no. Del. no. Md. ay. Va. ay. N. C. ay. S. C. no. Geo. ay.

The Report of the Committee for striking out sect. 6, requiring two-thirds of each House to pass a Navigation Act, was then agreed to, *nem. con.*

36. Comments from Outside the Convention, September 1787

As the convention moved toward a climax the general public, totally lacking news of the proceedings, waited anxiously. Many rumors circulated: one held that the convention proposed to divide the nation into regional confederations, another that the members were sounding out various European princes with a view toward inviting one to become king of the United States.

A. *"Rusticus," in the* New York Journal, *September 13, 1787*

Most of the newspaper comment assured readers that good things would emerge because the delegates were such a wise and virtuous group. An anonymous *New Yorker* agreed that some of the delgates were wise and virtuous, but that:

. . . There are too many having a very different character; perfect Bashaws! (saving a want of power) who would trample on the most sacred rights of the people, without the least reluctance or remorse. . . . (Only) a certain Aristocratical junto (spoke so highly of the delegates, and) the greatest part of the publications alluded to, are artfully calculated to prepare the minds of the people, implicitly to receive any *form* of government that may be offered them. . . .

B. Jonas Phillips to the President and Members of the Convention, September 7, 1787

Perhaps, however, this letter written by a Philadelphian epitomized the hopes and fears of Americans:

Sires

With leave and submission I address myself To those in whome there is wisdom understanding and knowledge. they are the honourable personages appointed and Made overseers of a part of the terrestrial globe of the Earth, Namely the 13 united states of america in Convention Assembled, the Lord preserve them amen—

I the subscriber being one of the people called Jews of the City of Philadelphia, a people scattered and despersed among all nations do behold with Concern that among the laws in the Constitution of Pennsylvania their is a Clause Sect. 10 to viz—I do believe in one God the Creature and governour of the universe the Rewarder of the good and the punisher of the wicked—and I do acknowledge the scriptures of the old and New testament to be given by a devine inspiration—to swear and believe that the new testament was given by devine inspiration is absolutly against the Religious principle of a Jew. and is against his Conscience to take any such oath—By the above law a Jew is deprived of holding any publick office or place of Goverment which is a Contridectory to the bill of Right Sect 2. viz

That all men have a natural and unalienable Right To worship

SOURCE: *Documentary History of the Constitution,* I, 281–283.

almighty God according to the dectates of their own Conscience and understanding, and that no man aught or of Right can be Compelled to attend any Relegious Worship or Erect or support any place of worship or Maintain any minister contrary to or against his own free will and Consent nor Can any man who acknowledges the being of a God be Justly deprived or abridged of any Civil Right as a Citizen on account of his Religious sentiments or peculiar mode of Religious Worship, and that no authority Can or aught to be vested in or assumed by any power what ever that shall in any Case interfere or in any manner Controul the Right of Conscience in the free Exercise of Religious Worship—

It is well known among all the Citizens of the 13 united States that the Jews have been true and faithful whigs, and during the late Contest with England they have been foremost in aiding and assisting the States with their lifes and fortunes, they have supported the Cause, have bravely faught and bleed for liberty which they Can not Enjoy—

Therefore if the honourable Convention shall in ther Wisdom think fit and alter the said oath and leave out the words to viz—and I do acknoweledge the scripture of the new testament to be given by devine inspiration then the Israeletes will think them self happy to live under a goverment where all Relegious societys are on an Eaquel footing—I solecet this favour for my self my Childreen and posterity and for the benefit of all the Isrealetes through the 13 united States of america

My prayers is unto the Lord. May the people of this States Rise up as a great and young lion, May they prevail against their Enemies, May the degrees of honour of his Excellencey the president of the Convention George Washington, be Extollet and Raise up. May Every one speak of his glorious Exploits. May God prolong his days among us in this land of Liberty— May he lead the armies against his Enemys as he has done hereuntofore— May God Extend peace unto the united States— May they get up to the highest Prosperetys— May God Extend peace to them and their seed after them so long as the Sun and moon Endureth—and may the almighty God of our father Abraham Isaac and Jacob endue this Noble Assembly with wisdom Judgement and unamity in their Councells, and may they have the Satisfaction to see that their present toil and labour for the wellfair of the united States may be approved of, Through all the world and perticular by the united States of america is the ardent prayer of Sires

Your Most devoted obed Servant

JONAS PHILLIPS

Philadelphia 24th Ellul 5547 or Sepr 7th 1787

37. The Constitution of the United States, September 17, 1787

The convention had agreed on a Constitution by September 10. The rough draft was turned over to a Committee on Style, headed by Gouverneur Morris, which drafted the finished version. On September 17 the final document was signed by thirty-nine of the forty-two delegates present:

We the People of the United States, in order to form a more perfect Union, establish justice, insure domestic tranquillity, provide for the common defence, promote the general welfare, and secure the blessings of liberty to ourselves and our posterity, do ordain and establish this Constitution for the United States of America.

ARTICLE I

Section 1. All legislative powers herein granted, shall be vested in a Congress of the United States, which shall consist of a Senate and House of Representatives.

Section 2. The House of Representatives shall be composed of members chosen every second year by the people of the several States; and the electors in each State shall have the qualifications requisite for electors of the most numerous branch of the State Legislature.

No person shall be a representative who shall not have attained the age of twenty-five years, and been seven years a citizen of the United States, and who shall not, when elected, be an inhabitant of that State in which he shall be chosen.

Representatives and direct taxes shall be apportioned among the

SOURCE: Original in the National Archives.

several States which may be included within this Union, according to their respective numbers, which shall be determined by adding to the whole number of free persons, including those bound to service for a term of years, and excluding Indians not taxed, three fifths of all other persons. The actual enumeration shall be made within three years after the first meeting of the Congress of the United States, and within every subsequent term of ten years, in such manner as they shall by law direct. The number of representatives shall not exceed one for every thirty thousand, but each State shall have at least one representative, and until such enumeration shall be made, the state of New Hampshire shall be entitled to choose three, Massachusetts eight, Rhode Island and Providence Plantations one, Connecticut five, New York six, New Jersey four, Pennsylvania eight, Delaware one, Maryland six, Virginia ten, North Carolina five, South Carolina five, and Georgia three.

When vacancies happen in the representation from any State, the Executive authority thereof shall issue writs of election to fill such vacancies.

The House of Representatives shall choose their speaker and other officers; and shall have the sole power of impeachment.

Section 3. The Senate of the United States shall be composed of two Senators from each State, chosen by the Legislature thereof, for six years; and each Senator shall have one vote.

Immediately after they shall be assembled, in consequence of the first election, they shall be divided as equally as may be into three classes. The seats of the Senators of the first class shall be vacated at the expiration of the second year, of the second class at the expiration of the fourth year, and of the third class at the expiration of the sixth year, so that one third may be chosen every second year; and if vacancies happen by resignation, or otherwise, during the recess of the Legislature of any State, the Executive thereof may make temporary appointments until the next meeting of the Legislature, which shall then fill such vacancies.

No person shall be a Senator who shall not have attained to the age of thirty years, and been nine years a citizen of the United States, and who shall not, when elected, be an inhabitant of that State for which he shall be chosen.

The Vice President of the United States shall be president of the Senate, but shall have no vote, unless they be equally divided.

The Senate shall choose their other officers, and also a president *pro tempore*, in the absence of the Vice President, or when he shall exercise the office of President of the United States.

The Senate shall have the sole power to try all impeachments. When sitting for that purpose, they shall be on oath or affirmation. When the President of the United States is tried, the Chief Justice shall preside; and no person shall be convicted without the concurrence of two thirds of the members present.

Judgment in cases of impeachment shall not extend further than to removal from office, and disqualification to hold and enjoy any office of honour, trust or profit, under the United States; but the party convicted shall nevertheless be liable and subject to indictment, trial, judgment, and punishment according to law.

Section 4. The times, places and manner of holding elections for Senators and Representatives, shall be prescribed in each State by the Legislature thereof; but the Congress may at any time by law make or alter such regulations, except as to the places of choosing Senators.

The Congress shall assemble at least once in every year, and such meeting shall be on the first Monday in December, unless they shall by law appoint a different day.

Section 5. Each House shall be the judge of the elections, returns, and qualifications of its own members, and a majority of each shall constitute a quorum to do business; but a smaller number may adjourn from day to day, and may be authorized to compel the attendance of absent members, in such manner, and under such penalties, as each House may provide.

Each House may determine the rules of its proceedings, punish its members for disorderly behaviour, and, with the concurrence of two thirds, expel a member.

Each House shall keep a journal of its proceedings, and from time to time publish the same, excepting such parts as may, in their judgment, require secrecy; and the yeas and nays of the members of either House on any question, shall, at the desire of one fifth of those present, be entered on the journal.

Neither House, during the session of Congress, shall, without the consent of the other, adjourn for more than three days, nor to any other place than that in which the two Houses shall be sitting.

Section 6. The Senators and Representatives shall receive a compensation for their services, to be ascertained by law, and paid out of the Treasury of the United States. They shall, in all cases, except treason, felony, and breach of the peace, be privileged from arrest during their attendance at the session of their respective Houses, and in going to, and returning from, the same; and for any speech or debate in either House, they shall not be questioned in any other place.

No Senator or Representative shall, during the time for which he was elected, be appointed to any civil office under the authority of the United States, which shall have been created, or the emoluments whereof shall have been increased during such time; and no person holding any office under the United States, shall be a member of either House during his continuance in office.

Section 7. All bills for raising revenue shall originate in the House of Representatives; but the Senate may propose or concur with amendments as on other bills.

Every bill which shall have passed the House of Representatives and the Senate, shall, before it become a law, be presented to the President of the United States; if he approve he shall sign it, but if not he shall return it, with his objections, to that House in which it shall have originated, who shall enter the objections at large on their journal, and proceed to reconsider it. If after such reconsideration two thirds of that House shall agree to pass the bill, it shall be sent, together with the objections, to the other House, by which it shall likewise be reconsidered, and if approved by two thirds of that House, it shall become a law. But in all such cases the votes of both Houses shall be determined by yeas and nays, and the names of the persons voting for and against the bill shall be entered on the journal of each House respectively. If any bill shall not be returned by the President within ten days, (Sundays excepted,) after it shall have been presented to him, the same shall be a law, in like manner as if he had signed it, unless the Congress by their adjournment prevent its return, in which case it shall not be a law.

Every order, resolution, or vote, to which the concurrence of the Senate and House of Representatives may be necessary, (except on a question of adjournment,) shall be presented to the President of the United States; and before the same shall take effect, shall be approved by him, or being disapproved by him, shall be re-passed by two thirds of the Senate and House of Representatives, according to the rules and limitations prescribed in the case of a bill.

Section 8. The Congress shall have power To lay and collect taxes, duties, imposts and excises, to pay the debts, and provide for the common defence and general welfare of the United States; but all duties, imposts, and excises shall be uniform throughout the United States:

To borrow money on the credit of the United States:

To regulate commerce with foreign nations, and among the several States, and with the Indian tribes:

To establish an uniform rule of naturalization, and uniform laws on the subject of bankruptcies throughout the United States:

To coin money, regulate the value thereof, and of foreign coin, and fix the standard of weights and measures:

To provide for the punishment of counterfeiting the securities and current coin of the Unted States:

To establish post-offices and post-roads:

To promote the progress of science and useful arts, by securing, for limited times, to authors and inventors, the exclusive right to their respective writings and discoveries:

To constitute tribunals inferior to the Supreme Court:

To define and punish piracies and felonies committed on the high seas, and offences against the law of nations:

To declare war, grant letters of marque and reprisal, and make rules concerning captures on land and water:

To raise and support armies: but no appropriation of money to that use shall be for a longer term than two years:

To provide and maintain a navy:

To make rules for the government and regulation of the land and naval forces:

To provide for calling forth the militia to execute the laws of the Union, suppress insurrections and repel invasions:

To provide for organizing, arming, and disciplining the militia, and for governing such part of them as may be employed in the service of the United States, reserving to the States respectively, the appointment of the officers, and the authority of training the militia according to the discipline prescribed by Congress.

To exercise exclusive legislation, in all cases whatsoever, over such district (not exceeding ten miles square) as may by cession of particular States, and the acceptance of Congress, become the seat of the government of the United States, and to exercise like authority over all places purchased by the consent of the legislature of the State in which the same shall be, for the erection of forts, magazines, arsenals, dock-yards, and other needful buildings. And,

To make all laws which shall be necessary and proper for carrying into execution the foregoing powers, and all other powers vested by this Constitution in the government of the United States, or in any department or officer thereof.

Section 9. The migration or importation of such persons as any of the States now existing shall think proper to admit, shall not be prohibited by the Congress prior to the year one thousand eight hundred and eight; but a tax or duty may be imposed on such importation, not exceeding ten dollars for each person.

The privilege of the writ of *habeas corpus* shall not be suspended, unless when in cases of rebellion or invasion the public safety may require it.

No bill of attainder or *ex post facto* law shall be passed.

No capitation, or other direct tax, shall be laid, unless in proportion to the *census* or enumeration herein before directed to be taken.

No tax or duty shall be laid on articles exported from any State. No preference shall be given by any regulation of commerce or revenue to the ports of one State over those of another; nor shall vessels bound to, or from, one State be obliged to enter, clear, or pay duties in another.

No money shall be drawn from the treasury, but in consequence of appropriations made by law; and a regular statement and account of the receipts and expenditures of all public money shall be published from time to time.

No title of nobility shall be granted by the United States; and no person holding any office of profit or trust under them, shall, without the consent of the Congress, accept of any present, emolument, office, or title of any kind whatever, from any king, prince, or foreign state.

Section 10. No State shall enter into any treaty, alliance, or confederation; grant letters of marque and reprisal; coin money; emit bills of credit; make any thing but gold and silver coin a tender in payment of debts; pass any bill of attainder, *ex post facto* law, or law impairing the obligation of contracts, or grant any title of nobility.

No State shall, without the consent of the Congress, lay any imposts or duties on imports or exports, except what may be absolutely necessary for executing its inspection laws; and the net produce of all duties and imposts, laid by any State on imports or exports, shall be for the use of the treasury of the United States; and all such laws shall be subject to the revision and control of the Congress. No State shall, without the consent of Congress, lay any duty of tonnage, keep troops, or ships of war, in time of peace, enter into any agreement or compact with another State, or with a foreign power, on engage in war, unless actually invaded, or in such imminent danger as will not admit of delay.

ARTICLE II

Section 1. The executive power shall be vested in a President of the United States of America. He shall hold his office during the term of four years, and together with the Vice President, chosen for the same term, be elected as follows:

Each State shall appoint, in such manner as the legislature thereof may direct, a number of electors equal to the whole number of Senators and Representatives to which the State may be entitled in the Congress; but no Senator or Representative, or person holding an office of trust or profit under the United States, shall be appointed an elector.

The electors shall meet in their respective States, and vote by ballot for two persons, of whom one at least shall not be an inhabitant of the same State with themselves. And they shall make a list of all the persons voted for, and of the number of votes for each; which list they shall sign and certify, and transmit sealed to the seat of the government of the United States, directed to the President of the Senate. The President of the Senate shall, in the presence of the Senate and House of Representatives, open all the certificates, and the votes shall then be counted. The person having the greatest number of votes shall be the President, if such number be a majority of the whole number of electors appointed; and if there be more than one who have such majority, and have an equal number of votes, then the House of Representatives shall immediately choose by ballot one of them for President; and if no person have a majority, then from the five highest on the list the said House shall in like manner choose the President. But in choosing the President, the votes shall be taken by States, the representation from each State having one vote; a quorum for this purpose shall consist of a member or members from two thirds of the States, and a majority of all the States shall be necessary to a choice. In every case, after the choice of the President, the person having the greatest number of votes of the electors shall be the Vice President. But if there should remain two or more who have equal votes, the Senate shall choose from them by ballot the Vice President.

The Congress may determine the time of choosing the electors, and the day on which they shall give their votes; which day shall be the same throughout the United States.

No person except a natural born citizen, or a citizen of the United States, at the time of the adoption of this Constitution, shall be eligible to the office of President; neither shall any person be eligible to that office who shall not have attained to the age of thirty-five years, and been fourteen years a resident within the United States.

In case of the removal of the President from office, or of his death, resignation, or inability to discharge the powers and duties of the said office, the same shall devolve on the Vice President, and the Congress may by law provide for the case of removal, death, resignation, or inability, both of the President and Vice President, declaring what officer shall then act as President, and such officer shall act accordingly until the disability be removed, or a President shall be elected.

The President shall at stated times, receive for his services, a compensation, which shall neither be increased nor diminished during the period for which he shall have been elected, and he shall not receive within that period any other emolument from the United States or any of them.

Before he enter on the execution of his office, he shall take the following oath or affirmation:

"I do solemnly swear, (or affirm,) that I will faithfully execute the office of President of the United States, and will, to the best of my ability, preserve, protect, and defend the Constitution of the United States."

Section 2. The President shall be commander-in-chief of the army and navy of the United States, and of the militia of the several States, when called into the actual service of the United States; he may require the opinion, in writing, of the principal officer in each of the executive departments, upon any subject relating to the duties of their respective offices, and he shall have power to grant reprieves and pardons for offences against the United States, except in cases of impeachment.

He shall have power, by and with the advice and consent of the

Senate, to make treaties, provided two thirds of the Senators present concur; and he shall nominate, and by and with the advice and consent of the Senate, shall appoint ambassadors, other public ministers and consuls, judges of the Supreme Court, and all other officers of the United States, whose appointments are not herein otherwise provided for, and which shall be established by law. But the Congress may by law vest the appointment of such inferior officers, as they think proper, in the President alone, in the courts of law, or in the heads of departments.

The President shall have power to fill up all vacancies that may happen during the recess of the Senate, by granting commissions which shall expire at the end of their session.

Section 3. He shall, from time to time, give to the Congress information of the state of the Union, and recommend to their consideration such measures as he shall judge necessary and expedient. He may on extraordinary occasions, convene both Houses, or either of them; and in case of disagreement between them, with respect to the time of adjournment, he may adjourn them to such time as he shall think proper. He shall receive ambassadors and other public ministers. He shall take care that the laws be faithfully executed; and shall commission all the offcers of the United States.

Section 4. The President, Vice President, and all civil officers of the United States, shall be removed from office on impeachment for, and conviction of, treason, bribery, or other high crimes and misdemeanors.

ARTICLE III

Section 1. The judicial power of the United States shall be vested in one Supreme Court, and in such inferior courts as the Congress may, from time to time, ordain and establish. The judges, both of the Supreme and inferior courts, shall hold their offices during good behaviour; and shall, at stated times, receive for their services, a compensation, which shall not be diminished during their continuance in office.

Section 2. The judicial power shall extend to all cases, in law and equity, arising under this Constitution, the laws of the United States, and treaties made, or which shall be made, under their authority; to all cases affecting ambassadors, other public ministers, and consuls; to all cases of admiralty and maritime jurisdiction; to controversies to which the United States shall be a party; to controversies between two or more States, between a State and citizens of another State, between citizens of different States, between citizens of the same State claiming lands under grants of different States, and between a State, or the citizens thereof, and foreign States, citizens or subjects.

In all cases affecting ambassadors, other public ministers and consuls, and those in which a State shall be party, the Supreme Court shall have original jurisdiction. In all the other cases before mentioned, the Supreme Court shall have appellate jurisdiction, both as to law and fact, with such exceptions, and under such regulations, as the Congress shall make.

The trial of all crimes, except in cases of impeachment, shall be by jury; and such trial shall be held in the State where the said crimes shall have been committed; but when not committed within any State, the trial shall be at such place or places as the Congress may by law have directed.

Section 3. Treason against the United States, shall consist only in levying war against them, or in adhering to their enemies, giving them aid and comfort. No person shall be convicted of treason unless on the testimony of two witnesses to the same overt act, or on confession in open court.

The Congress shall have power to declare the punishment of treason, but no attainder of treason shall work corruption of blood, or forfeiture, except during the life of the person attainted.

ARTICLE IV

Section 1. Full faith and credit shall be given in each State to the public acts, records, and judicial proceedings of every other State. And the Congress may by general laws prescribe the manner in which such acts, records, and proceedings shall be proved, and the effect thereof.

Section 2. The citizens of each State shall be entitled to all privileges and immunities of citizens in the several States.

A person charged in any State with treason, felony, or other crime, who shall flee from justice, and be found in another State, shall, on demand of the executive authority of the State from which he fled, be delivered up, to be removed to the State having jurisdiction of the crime.

No person held to service or labour in one State, under the laws thereof, escaping into another, shall, in consequence of any law or regulation therein, be discharged from such service or labour, but shall be delivered up on claim of the party to whom such service or labour may be due.

Section 3. New States may be admitted by the Congress into this Union; but no new State shall be formed or erected within the jurisdiction of any other State; nor any State be formed by the junction of two or more States, or parts of States, without the consent of the legislatures of the States concerned, as well as of the Congress.

The Congress shall have power to dispose of and make all needful rules and regulations respecting the territory or other property belonging to the United States; and nothing in this Constitution shall be so construed as to prejudice any claims of the United States, or of any particular State.

Section 4. The United States shall guarantee to every State in this Union a republican form of government, and shall protect each of them against invasion; and on application of the legislature, or of the executive, (when the legislature cannot be convened) against domestic violence.

Article V

The Congress, whenever two thirds of both Houses shall deem it necessary, shall propose amendments to this Constitution, or, on the application of the legislatures of two thirds of the several States, shall call a convention for proposing amendments, which, in either case, shall be valid to all intents and purposes, as part of this Constitution, when ratified by the legislatures of three fourths of the several States, or by conventions in three fourths thereof, as the one or the other mode of ratification may be proposed by the Congress; provided, that no amendment, which may be made prior to the year one thousand eight hundred and eight, shall in any manner affect the first and fourth clauses in the ninth section of the first article; and that no State, without its consent, shall be deprived of its equal suffrage in the Senate.

Article VI

All debts contracted, and engagements entered into, before the adoption of this Constitution, shall be as valid against the United States, under this Constitution, as under the confederation.

This Constitution, and the laws of the United States which shall be made in pursuance thereof, and all treaties made, or which shall be made, under the authority of the United States, shall be the supreme law of the land: and the judges, in every State, shall be bound thereby, any thing in the Constitution or laws of any State to the contrary notwithstanding.

The Senators and Representatives before mentioned, and the members of the several State legislatures, and all executive and judicial officers, both of the United States and of the several States, shall be bound, by oath or affirmation, to support this Constitution; but no religious test shall ever be required as a qualification to any office or public trust under the United States.

Article VII

The ratification of the conventions of nine States, shall be sufficient for the establishment of this Constitution between the States so ratifying the same.

PART FIVE:

The Contest over Ratification, 1787-1790

The Constitution provided that it should go into force when specially elected conventions in nine states had ratified it. Before the end of 1787 Delaware, New Jersey, and Pennsylvania had ratified, the first two unanimously, the third by a 46 to 23 vote in convention. Georgia followed on January 2, 1787, again unanimously, and Connecticut ratified by a 128 to 40 vote on January 9. From then on the going was slower: Massachusetts ratified on February 8 by a 187 to 168 convention vote, Maryland on April 26 by 63 to 11, South Carolina on May 23 by 149 to 73, New Hampshire on June 21 by 57 to 47, Virginia on June 25 by 89 to 79, and New York on July 26 by 30 to 27. North Carolina and Rhode Island did not ratify until after the government under the Constitution had come into operation, the former in September 1789, the latter in May 1790.

The contest was marked by a long debate in the newspapers, in pamphlets, and in the several conventions. This debate was sometimes petty and ill-informed, but in the main it constituted an astonishingly profound public discussion on the theory and principles of popular government. The following four selections (Documents 38 through 41) illustrate the quality and nature of the discussion.

38. Address by James Wilson at the State House in Philadelphia, October 10, 1787 (favoring ratification)

It will be proper . . . before I enter into the refutation of the charges that are alleged, to mark the leading discrimination between the State constitutions and the constitution of the United States.

SOURCE: James Bach McMaster and Frederick Stone, *Pennsylvania and the Federal Constitution, 1787–1788* (Philadelphia, 1888), pp. 143–178.

When the people established the powers of legislation under their separate governments, they invested their representatives with every right and authority which they did not in explicit terms reserve; and therefore upon every question respecting the jurisdiction of the House of Assembly, if the frame of government is silent, the jurisdiction is efficient and complete. But in delegating federal powers, another criterion was necessarily introduced, and the congressional power is to be collected, not from tacit implication, but from the positive grant expressed in the instrument of the union. Hence, it is evident, that in the former case everything which is not reserved is given; but in the latter the reverse of the proposition prevails, and everything which is not given is reserved.

This distinction being recognized, will furnish an answer to those who think the omission of a bill of rights a defect in the proposed constitution; for it would have been superfluous and absurd to have stipulated with a federal body of our own creation, that we should enjoy those privileges of which we are not divested, either by the intention or the act that has brought the body into existence. For instance, the liberty of the press, which has been a copious source of declamation and opposition—what control can proceed from the Federal government to shackle or destroy that sacred palladium of national freedom? If, indeed, a power similar to that which has been granted for the regulation of commerce had been granted to regulate literary publications, it would have been as necessary to stipulate that the liberty of the press should be preserved inviolate, as that the impost should be general in its operation. . . . In truth, then, the proposed system possesses no influence whatever upon the press, and it would have been merely nugatory to have introduced a formal declaration upon the subject—nay, that very declaration might have been construed to imply that some degree of power was given, since we undertook to define its extent.

Another objection that has been fabricated against the new constitution, is expressed in this disingenious form—"The trial by jury is abolished in civil cases." . . . Let it be remembered . . . that the business of the Federal Convention was not local, but general—not limited to the views and establishments of a single State, but co-extensive with the continent, and comprehending the views and establishments of thirteen independent sovereignties. When, therefore, this subject was in discussion, we were involved in difficulties which pressed on all sides, and no precedent could be discovered to direct our course. The cases open to a trial by jury differed in the different States. It was therefore impracticable, on that ground, to have made a general rule. The want of uniformity would have rendered any reference to the practice of the States idle and useless; and it could not with any propriety be said that; "The trial by jury shall be as heretofore," since there has never existed any federal system of jurisprudence, to which the declaration could relate. Besides, it is not in all cases that the trial by jury is adopted in civil questions; for depending in courts of admiralty, such as relate to maritime captures, and such as are agitated in courts of equity, do not require the intervention of that tribunal. How, then was the line of discrimination to be drawn? The Convention found the task too difficult for them, and they left the business as it stands, in the fullest confidence that no danger could possibly ensue, since the proceedings of the Supreme Court are to be regulated by the Congress, which is a faithful representation of the people; and the oppression of government is effectually barred, by declaring that in all criminal cases the trial by jury shall be preserved.

This constitution, it has been further urged, is of a pernicious tendency, because it tolerates a standing army in the time of peace. This has always been a topic of popular declamation; and yet I do not know a nation in the world which has not found it necessary and useful to maintain the appearance of strength in a season of the most profound tranquility. Nor is it a novelty with us; for under the present articles of confederation, Congress certainly possesses this reprobated power, and the exercise of that power is proved at this moment by her cantonments along the banks of the Ohio. But what would be our national situation were it otherwise? Every principle of policy must be subverted, and the government must declare war, before they are prepared to carry on. Whatever may be the provocation, however important the object in view, and however necessary dispatch and secrecy may be, still the declaration must precede the preparation, and the enemy will be informed of your intention, not only before you are equipped for an attack, but even before you are fortified for a defence. The consequence is too obvious to require any further delineation, and no man who regards the dignity and safety of his country can deny the necessity of a military force, under the control and with the restrictions which the new constitution provides. . . .

The next accusation I shall consider is that which represents the federal constitution, as not only calculated, but designedly framed, to reduce the State governments to mere corporations, and eventually to annihilate them. Those who have employed the term corporation upon this occasion are not perhaps aware of its extent. In common parlance, indeed, it is generally applied to petty associations for the ease and convenience of a few individuals; but in its enlarged sense, it will comprehend the government of Pennsylvania, the existing union of the States, and even this projected system is nothing more than a formal act of incorporation. But upon what pretence can it be alleged that it was designed to annihilate the State governments? For I will undertake to prove that upon their existence depends the existence of the Federal plan. For this purpose, permit me to call your attention to the manner in which the President, Senate and House of Representatives are proposed to be appointed. The President is to be chosen by electors, nominated in such manner as the legislature of each State may direct; so that if there is no legislature there can be no electors, and consequently the office of President cannot be supplied.

The Senate is to be composed of two Senators from each State, chosen by the Legislature; and, therefore, if there is no Legislature, there can be no Senate. The House of Representatives is to be composed of members chosen every second year by the people of the several States, and the electors in each State shall have the qualifications requisite for electors of the most numerous branch of the State Legislature; unless, therefore, there is a State Legislature, that qualification cannot be ascertained, and the popular branch of the federal constitution must be extinct. From this view, then, it is evidently absurd to suppose that the annihilation of the separate governments will result from their union; or, that having that intention, the authors of the new system would have bound their connection with such indissoluble ties. Let me here advert to an arrangement highly advantageous, for you will perceive, without prejudice to the powers of the Legislature in the election of Senators, the people at large will acquire an additional privilege in returning members to the House of Representatives; whereas, by the present confederation, it is the Legislature alone that appoints the delegates to Congress.

The power of direct taxation has likewise been treated as an improper delegation to the federal government; but when we consider it as the duty of that body to provide for the national safety, to support the dignity of the union, and to discharge the debts contracted upon the collected faith of the States for their common benefit, it must be acknowledged that those upon whom such important obligations are imposed, ought in justice and in policy to possess every means requisite for a faithful performance of their trust. But why should we be alarmed with visionary evils? I will venture to predict that the great revenue of the United States must, and always will, be raised by impost, for, being at once less obnoxious and more productive, the interest of the government will be best promoted by the accommodation of the people. Still, however, the objects of direct taxation should be within reach in all cases of emergency; and there is no more reason to apprehend oppression in the mode of collecting a revenue from this resource, than in the form of an impost, which, by universal assent, is left to the authority of the federal government. In either case, the force of civil institutions will be adequate to the purpose; and the dread of military violence, which has been assiduously disseminated, must eventually prove the mere effusion of a wild imagination or a factious spirit. But the salutary consequences that must flow from thus enabling the government to receive and support the credit of the union, will afford another answer to the objections upon this ground. . . .

I will confess . . . that I am not a blind admirer of this plan of government, and that there are some parts of it which, if my wish had prevailed, would certainly have been altered. . . . If there are errors, it should be remembered that the seeds of reformation are sown in the work itself, and the concurrence of two-thirds of the Congress may at any time introduce alterations and amendments. Regarding it, then, in every point of view, with a candid and disinterested mind, I am bold to assert that it is the best form of government which has ever been offered to the world.

39. Richard Henry Lee: Letters from the Federal Farmer to the Republican. Letter III, October 10, 1787 (opposing ratification)

The great object of a free people must be so to form their government and laws and so to administer them, as to create a confidence in, and respect for the laws; and thereby induce the sensible and virtuous part of the community to declare in favor of the laws, and to support them without an expensive military force. I wish, though I confess I have not much hope, that this may be the case with the laws of congress under the new constitution. I am fully convinced that we must organize the national government on different principals, and make the parts of it more efficient, and secure in it more effectually the different interests in the community; or else leave in the state governments some powers propose to be lodged in it—at least till such an organization shall be found to be practicable. Not sanguine in my expectations of a good federal administration, and satisfied, as I am, of the impracticability of consolidating the states, and at the same time of preserving the rights of the people at large, I believe we ought still to leave some of these powers in the state governments, in which the people, in fact, will still be represented —to define some other powers proposed to be vested in the general government, more carefully, and to establish a few principles to secure a proper exercise of the powers given it. It is not my object to multiply objections, or to contend about inconsiderable powers or amendments; I wish the system adopted with a few alterations; but those, in my mind, are essential ones; if adopted without, every good citizen will acquiesce though I shall consider the duration of our governments, and the liberties of this people, very much dependent on the administration, of the general government. A wise and honest administration, may make the people happy under any government; but necessity only can justify even our leaving open

SOURCE: First published, as a pamphlet containing the first five of Lee's essays, in New York in 1787.

avenues to the abuse of power, by wicked, unthinking, or ambitious men. I will examine, first, the organization of the proposed government, in order to judge; 2nd, with propriety, what powers are improperly, at least prematurely lodged in it. I shall examine, 3rd, the undefined powers; and 4th, those powers, the exercise of which is not secured on safe and proper ground.

First. As to the organization—the house of representatives, the democratic branch, as it is called, is to consist of 65 members: that is, about one representative for fifty thousand inhabitants, to be chosen biennially—the federal legislature may increase this number to one for each thirty thousand inhabitants, abating fractional numbers in each state.—Thirty-three representatives will make a quorum for doing business, and a majority of those present determine the sense of the house.—I have no idea that the interests, feelings, and opinions of three or four millions of people, especially touching internal taxation, can be collected in such a house.—In the nature of things, nine times in ten, men of the elevated classes in the community only can be chosen—Connecticut, for instance, will have five representatives—not one man in a hundred of those who form the democratic branch in the state legislature, will, on a fair computation, be one of the five—The people of this country, in one sense, may all be democratic; but if we make the proper distinction between the few men of wealth and abilities, and consider them, as we ought, as the natural aristocracy of the country, and the great body of the people, the middle and lower classes, as the democracy, this federal representative branch will have but very little democracy in it, even this small representation is not secured on proper principles. . . .

In considering the practicability of having a full and equal representation of the people from all parts of the union, not only distances and different opinions, customs, and views, common in extensive tracts of country, are to be taken into view, but many differences peculiar to Eastern, Middle and Southern states. These differences are not so perceivable among the members of congress, and men of general information in the states, as among the men who would properly form the democratic branch. The Eastern states are very democratic, and composed chiefly of moderate freeholders: they have but few rich men and no slaves; the Southern states are composed chiefly of rich planters and slaves; they have but few moderate freeholders, and the prevailing influence, in them, is geny a dissipated aristocracy: The Middle states partake partly of Eastern, and partly of the Southern character.

Perhaps, nothing could be more disjointed, unwieldly and incompetent to doing business with harmony and dispatch, than a federal house of representatives properly numerous for the great objects of taxation, etc. collected from the several states; whether such men would ever act in concert; whether they would not worry along a few years, and then be the means of separating the parts of the union, is very problematical?—View this system in whatever form we can, propriety brings us still to this point, a federal government possessed of general and complete powers, as to those national objects which cannot well come under the cognizance of the internal laws of the respective states, and this federal government, accordingly, consisting of branches not very numerous.

The house of representatives is on the plan of consolidation, but the senate is entirely on the federal plan; and Delaware will have as much constitutional influence in the senate, as the largest state in the union: and in this senate are lodged legislative, executive and judicial powers: Ten states in this union urge that they are small states, nine of which were present in the convention. . . . The senate will consist of two members from each state, chosen by the state legislatures, every sixth year. The clause referred to, respecting the elections of representatives, empowers the general legislature to regulate the elections of senators also, "except as to the places of choosing senators."—There is, therefore, but little more security in the elections than in those of representatives: Fourteen senators make a quorum for business, and a majority of the senators present give the vote of the senate, except in giving judgment upon an impeachment, or in making treaties, or in expelling a member, when two-thirds of the senators present must agree—The members of the legislature are not excluded from being elected to any military offices, or any civil offices, except those created, or the emoluments of which shall be increased by themselves: two-thirds of the members present, of either house, may expel a member at pleasure. The senate is an independent branch of the legislature, a court for trying impeachments, and also a part of the executive, having a negative in the making of all treaties, and in appointing almost all officers.

The vice-president is not a very important, if not an unnecessary part of the system—he may be a part of the senate at one period, and act as the supreme executive magistrate at another—The election of this officer, as well as of the president of the United States seems to be properly secured; but when we examine the powers of the president, and the forms of the executive, we shall perceive that the general government, in this part, will have a strong tendency to aristocracy, or the government of the few. The executive is, in fact, the president and senate in all transactions of any importance; the president is connected with, or tied to the senate; he may always act with the senate, but never can effectually counteract its views: The president can appoint no officer, civil or military, who shall not be agreeable to the senate; and the presumption is, that the will of so important a body will not be very easily controlled, and that it will exercise its powers with great address.

In the judicial department, powers ever kept distinct in well-balanced governments, are not less improperly blended in the hands of the same men—in the judges of the supreme court is lodged, the law, the equity and the fact. It is not necessary to pursue the minute organical parts of the general government proposed.—There were various interests in the convention to be reconciled, especially of large and small states; of carrying and non-carrying states; and of states more and states less democratic—vast labor and attention were by the convention bestowed on the organization of the parts of the constitution offered; still it is acknowledged there are many things radically wrong in the essential parts of this constitution but it is said that these are the result of our situation: On a full examination of the subject, I believe it; but what do the laborious inquiries and determinations of the convention prove? If they prove anything, they prove that we cannot consolidate the states on proper principles: The organization of the government presented proves, that we cannot form a general government in which all power can be safely lodged; and a little attention to the parts of the one proposed will make it appear very evident, that all the powers proposed to be lodged in it, will not be then well deposited, either for the purposes of government, or the preservation of liberty. I will suppose no abuse of powers in those cases, in which the abuse of it is not well guarded against—I will suppose the words authorizing the general government to regulate the elections of its own members struck out of the plan, or free district elections, in each state, amply secured.—That the small representation provided for shall be as fair and equal as it is capable of being made—I will suppose the judicial department regulated on pure principles, by future laws, as far as it can be by the constitution, and consist with the situation of the country—still there will be an unreasonable accumulation of powers in the general government, if all be granted, enumerated in the plan proposed. The plan does not present a well-balanced government. The senatorial branch of the legislative and the executive are substantially united, and the present, or the first executive magistrate, may aid the senatorial interest when weakest, but never can effectually support the democratic, however it may be oppressed;— the excellency, in my mind, of a well-balanced government is that it consists of distinct branches, each sufficiently strong and independent to keep its own station, and to aid either of the other branches which may occasionally want aid. . . .

Impressed, as I am, with a sense of the difficulties there are in the way of forming the parts of a federal government on proper principles, and seeing a government so unsubstantially organized, after so arduous an attempt has been made, I am led to believe, that powers ought to be given to it with great care and caution.

In the second place it is necessary, therefore, to examine the extent, and the probable operations of some of those extensive powers proposed to be vested in this government. These powers, legislative, executive, and judicial, respect internal as well as external objects. Those respecting external objects, as all foreign concerns, commerce, imposts, all causes arising on the seas, peace and war, and Indian affairs, can be lodged nowhere else, with any propriety, but in this government. Many powers that respect internal objects ought clearly to be lodged in it; as those to regulate trade between the states, weights and measures, the coin or current monies, post offices, naturalization, etc. These powers may be exercised without essentially effecting the internal policy of the respective states: But powers to levy and collect internal taxes, to form the militia, to make bankrupt laws, and to decide on appeals, questions arising on the internal laws of the respective states, are of a very serious nature, and carry with them almost all other powers. These taken in connection with the others, and powers to raise armies and build navies, proposed to be lodged in this government, appear to me to comprehend all the essential powers in the community, and those which will be left to the states will be of no great importance.

A power to lay and collect taxes at discretion, is, in itself, of very great importance. By means of taxes, the government may command the whole or any part of the subject's property. Taxes may be

of various kinds; but there is a strong distinction between external
and internal taxes. External taxes are impost duties, which are laid
on imported goods; they may usually be collected in a few seaport
towns, and of a few individuals, though ultimately paid by the con-
sumer; a few officers can collect them, and they can be carried no
higher than trade will bear, or smuggling permit—that in the very
nature of commerce, bounds are set to them. But internal taxes, as
poll and land taxes, excises, duties on all written instruments, etc.
may fix themselves on every person and species of property in the
community; they may be carried to any lengths, and in proportion
as they are extended, numerous officers must be employed to assess
them, and to enforce the collection of them. In the United Nether-
lands the general government has complete powers as to external
taxation; but as to internal taxes, it makes requisitions on the provinces. Internal taxation in this country is more important, as the
country is so very extensive. As many assessors and collectors of
federal taxes will be above three hundred miles from the seat of the
federal government as will be less. Besides, to lay and collect internal taxes, in this extensive country, must require a great number
of congressional ordinances, immediately operating upon the body
of the people; these must continually interfere with the state laws,
and thereby produce disorder and general dissatisfaction, till the one
system of laws or the other, operating upon the same subjects, shall
be abolished. These ordinances alone, to say nothing of those respecting the militia, coin, commerce, federal judiciary, etc. etc. will
probably soon defeat the operations of the state laws and governments.

Should the general government think it politic, as some administrations (if not all) probably will, to look for a support in a system
of influence, the government will take every occasion to multiply
laws, and officers to execute them, considering these as so many
necessary props for its own support. Should this system of policy
be adopted, taxes more productive than the impost duties will,
probably, be wanted to support the government, and to discharge
foreign demands, without leaving anything for the domestic creditors. The internal sources of taxation then must be called into operation, and internal tax laws and federal assessors and collectors
spread over this immense country. All these circumstances considered, is it wise, prudent, or safe, to vest the powers of laying and
collecting internal taxes in the general government, while imper-

fectly organized and inadequate; and to trust to amending it here-after, and making it adequate to this purpose? Is it not only unsafe but absurd to lodge power in a government before it is fitted to receive it? It is confessed that this power and representation ought to go together. Why give the power first? Why give the power to the few, who, when possessed of it, may have address enough to prevent the increase of representation? Why not keep the power, and, when necessary, amend the constitution, and add to its other parts this power, and a proper increase of representation at the same time? Then men who may want the power will be under strong induce-ments to let in the people, by their representatives, into the govern-ment, to hold their due proportion of this power. If a proper repre-sentation be impracticable, then we shall see this power resting in the states, where it at present ought to be, and not inconsiderately given up.

When I recollect how lately congress, conventions, legislatures, and people contended in the cause of liberty, and carefully weighed the importance of taxation, I can scarcely believe we are serious in proposing to vest the powers of laying and collecting internal taxes in a government so imperfectly organized for such purposes. Should the United States be taxed by a house of representatives of two hun-dred members, which would be about fifteen members for Connect-icut, twenty-five for Massachusetts, etc. still the middle and lower classes of people could have no great share, in fact, in taxation. I am aware it is said, that the representation proposed by the new con-stitution is sufficiently numerous; it may be for many purposes; but to suppose that this branch is sufficiently numerous to guard the rights of the people in the administration of the government, in which the purse and sword is placed, seems to argue that we have forgotten what the true meaning of representation is. I am sensible also, that it is said that congress will not attempt to lay and collect internal taxes; that it is necessary for them to have the power, though it cannot probably be exercised. I admit that it is not prob-able that any prudent congress will attempt to lay and collect in-ternal taxes, especially direct taxes: but this only proves that the power would be improperly lodged in congress, and that it might be abused by imprudent and designing men. . . . The power in the general government to lay and collect internal taxes, will render its powers respecting armies, navies and the militia, the more exception-able. By the constitution it is proposed that congress shall have power "to raise and support armies," but no appropriation of money to that use shall be for a longer term than two years; to provide and maintain a navy; to provide for calling forth the militia to execute the laws of the union; suppress insurrections, and repel invasions: to provide for organizing, arming, and disciplining the militia: reserving to the states the right to appoint the officers, and to train the militia according to the discipline prescribed by congress; congress will have unlimited power to raise armies, and to engage officers and men for any number of years; but a legislative act applying money for their support can have operation for not longer term than two years, and if a subsequent congress do not within the two years renew the appropriation, or further appropriate monies for the use of the army, the army will be left to take care of itself. When an army shall once be raised for a number of years, it is not probable that it will find much difficulty in getting congress to pass laws for applying monies to its support. I see so many men in America fond of a standing army, and especially among those who probably will have a large share in administering the federal system; it is very evident to me, that we shall have a large standing army as soon as the monies to support them can be possibly found. An army is a very agreeable place of employment for the young gentlemen of many families. A power to raise armies must be lodged some where; still this will not justify the lodging this power in a bare majority of so few men without any checks; or in the government in which the great body of the people, in the nature of things, will be only nominally represented. In the state governments the great body of the people, the yeomanry, etc. of the country, are represented: It is true they will choose the members of congress, and may now and then choose a man of their own way of thinking; but it is impossible for forty, or thirty thousand people in this country, one time in ten to find a man who can possess similar feelings, views, and interests with themselves: Powers to lay and collect taxes and to raise armies are of the greatest moment; for carrying them into effect, laws need not be frequently made, and the yeomanry, etc. of the country ought substantially to have a check upon the passing of these laws; this check ought to be placed in the legislatures, or at least, in the few men the common people of the country, will, probably, have in congress, in the true sense of the word, "from among themselves." It is true, the yeomanry of the country possess the lands, the weight of property, possess arms, and are too strong a body of men to be openly offended—and, therefore, it is urged, they will take care of themselves, that men who shall govern will not dare pay any disrespect to their opinions. It is easily perceived, that if they have not their proper negative upon passing laws in congress, or on the passage of laws relative to taxes and armies, they may in twenty or thirty years be by means imperceptible to them, totally deprived of that boasted weight and strength. . . .

There are some powers proposed to be lodged in the general government in the judicial department, I think very unnecessarily. I mean powers respecting questions arising upon the internal laws of the respective states. It is proper the federal judiciary should have powers co-extensive with the federal legislature—that is, the power of deciding finally on the laws of the union. By Art. 3 Sect. 2 the powers of the federal judiciary are extended (among other things) to all cases between a state and citizens of another state—between citizens of different states—between a state or the citizens thereof, and foreign states, citizens or subjects. Actions in all these cases, except against a state government, are now brought and finally determined in the law courts of the states respectively; and as there are no words to exclude these courts of their jurisdiction in these cases, they will have concurrent jurisdiction with the inferior federal courts in them; and, therefore, if the new constitution be adopted without any amendment in this respect, all those numerous actions, now brought in the state courts between our citizens and foreigners, between citizens of different states, by state governments against foreigners, and by state governments against citizens of other states, may also be brought in the federal courts; and an appeal will lay in them from the state courts, to the supreme judicial court of the union. In almost all these cases, either party may have the trial by jury in the state courts; excepting paper money and tender laws, which are wisely guarded against in the proposed constitution, justice may be obtained in these courts on reasonable terms; they must be more competent to proper decisions on the laws of their respective states, than the federal courts can possibly be. I do not, in any point of view, see the need of opening a new jurisdiction to these causes—of opening a new scene of expensive law suits—of suffering foreigners, and citizens of different states, to drag each other many hundred miles into the federal courts. It is true, those courts may be so organized by a wise and prudent legislature, as to make the obtaining of justice in them tolerably easy; they may in general be organized on the common law principles of the country: But this benefit is by no means secured by the constitution. The trial by jury is secured only in those few criminal cases, to which the federal laws will extend—as crimes committed on the seas, against the laws of nations, treason, and counterfeiting the federal securities and coin: But even in these cases, the jury trial of the vicinage is not secured—particularly in the large states, a citizen may be tried for a crime committed in the state, and yet tried in some states 500 miles from the place where it was committed; but the jury trial is not secured at all in civil causes. Though the convention have not established this trial, it is to be hoped that congress, in putting the new system into execution, will do it by a legislative act, in all cases in which it can be done with propriety. Whether the jury trial is not excluded the supreme judicial court, is an important question. By Art. 3 Sect. 2 all cases affecting ambassadors, other public ministers, and consuls, and in those cases in which a state shall be party, the supreme court shall have jurisdiction. In all the other cases beforementioned, the supreme court shall have appellate jurisdiction, both as to *law and fact* with such exception, and under such regulations, as the congress shall make. By court is understood a court consisting of judges; and the idea of a jury is excluded. This court, or the judges, are to have jurisdiction on appeals, in all the cases enumerated, as to law and fact; the judges are to decide the law and try the fact, and the trial of the fact being assigned to the judges by the constitution, a jury for trying the fact is excluded; however, under the exceptions and powers to make regulations, congress may, perhaps, introduce the jury, to try the fact in most necessary cases.

There can be but one supreme court in which the final jurisdiction will center in all federal causes—except in cases where appeals by law shall not be allowed: The judicial powers of the federal courts extend in law and equity to certain cases: and, therefore, the powers to determine on the law, in equity, and as to the fact, all will concenter in the supreme court:—These powers, which by this constitution are blended in the same hands, the same judges, are in Great Britain deposited in different hands—to wit, the decision of the law in the law judges, the decision in equity in the chancellor, and the trial of the fact in the jury. It is a very dangerous thing to vest in the same judge power to decide on the law, and also general powers in equity; for if the law restrain him, he is only to step into his shoes of equity, and give what judgment his reason or opinions may dictate; we have no precedents in this country, as yet, to regulate the divisions in equity as in Great Britain; equity, therefore, in the supreme court for many years, will be mere discretion. I confess in the constitution of this supreme court, as left by the constitution, I do not see a spark of freedom or a shadow of our own or the British common law. . . .

40. James Madison: *The Federalist,* Number 10, November 23, 1787 (favoring ratification)

Among the numerous advantages promised by a well-constructed Union, none deserves to be more accurately developed than its tendency to break and control the violence of faction. The friend of popular governments never finds himself so much alarmed for their character and fate as when he contemplates their propensity to this dangerous vice. He will not fail, therefore, to set a due value on any plan which, without violating the principles to which he is attached, provides a proper cure for it. The instability, injustice, and confusion introduced into the public councils have, in truth, been the mortal diseases under which popular governments have everywhere perished; as they continue to be the favorite and fruitful topics from which the adversaries to liberty derive their most specious declamations. The valuable improvements made by the American constitutions on the popular models, both ancient and modern, cannot certainly be too much admired; but it would be an unwarrantable partiality, to contend that they have as effectually obviated the danger on this side as was wished and expected. Complaints are every where heard from our most considerate and virtuous citizens, equally the friends of public and private faith, and of public and personal liberty; that our governments are too unstable; that the public good is disregarded in the conflicts of rival parties; and that measures are too often decided, not according to the rules of justice, and the rights of the minor party; but by the superior force of an interested and over-bearing majority. However anxiously we may wish that

SOURCE: *The New-York Packet,* November 23, 1787. The collected *Federalist* essays have been published in many editions.

these complaints had no foundation, the evidence of known facts will not permit us to deny that they are in some degree true. It will be found indeed, on a candid review of our situation, that some of the distresses under which we labor, have been erroneously charged on the operation of our governments; but it will be found, at the same time, that other causes will not alone account for many of our heaviest misfortunes; and particularly, for that prevailing and increasing distrust of public engagements, and alarm for private rights, which are echoed from one end of the continent to the other. These must be chiefly, if not wholly, effects of the unsteadiness and injustice, with which a factious spirit has tainted our public administrations.

By a faction I understand a number of citizens, whether amounting to a majority or minority of the whole, who are united and actuated by some common impulse of passion, or of interest, adverse to the rights of other citizens, or to the permanent and aggregate interests of the community.

There are two methods of curing the mischiefs of faction: the one, by removing its causes; the other, by controling its effects.

There are again two methods of removing the causes of faction: the one by destroying the liberty which is essential to its existence; the other, by giving to every citizen the same opinions, the same passions, and the same interests.

It could never be more truly said than of the first remedy, that it is worse than the disease. Liberty is to faction, what air is to fire, an element without which it instantly expires. But it could not be a less folly to abolish liberty, which is essential to political life, because it nourishes faction, than it would be to wish the annihilation of air, which is essential to animal life, because it imparts to fire its destructive agency.

The second expedient is as impracticable, as the first would be unwise. As long as the reason of man continues fallible, and he is at liberty to exercise it, different opinions will be formed. As long as the connection subsists between his reason and his self-love, his opinions and his passions will have a reciprocal influence on each other; and the former will be objects to which the latter will attach themselves. The diversity in the faculties of men, from which the rights of property originate, is not less an insuperable obstacle to a uniformity of interests. The protection of these faculties is the first object of government. From the protection of different and unequal faculties of acquiring property, the possession of different degrees and kinds of property immediately results; and from the influence of these on the sentiments and views of the respective proprietors ensues a division of the society into different interests and parties.

The latent causes of faction are thus sown in the nature of man; and we see them everywhere brought into different degrees of activity, according to the different circumstances of civil society. A zeal for different opinions concerning religion, concerning government, and many other points, as well of speculation as of practice; an attachment to different leaders ambitiously contending for preeminence and power; or to persons of other descriptions whose fortunes have been interesting to the human passions, have, in turn, divided mankind into parties, inflamed them with mutual animosity, and rendered them much more disposed to vex and oppress each other than to cooperate for their common good. So strong is this propensity of mankind to fall into mutual animosities that, where no substantial occasion presents itself, the most frivolous and fanciful distinctions have been sufficient to kindle their unfriendly passions and excite their most violent conflicts. But the most common and durable source of factions has been the various and unequal distribution of property. Those who hold and those who are without property have ever formed distinct interests in society. Those who are creditors and those who are debtors fall under a like discrimination. A landed interest, a manufacturing interest, a mercantile interest, a moneyed interest, with many lesser interests, grow up of necessity in civilized nations and divide them into different classes, actuated by different sentiments and views. The regulation of these various and interfering interests forms the principal task of modern legislation and involves the spirit of party and faction in the necessary and ordinary operations of the government.

No man is allowed to be a judge in his own cause, because his interest would certainly bias his judgment, and, not improbably, corrupt his integrity. With equal, nay with greater reason, a body of men, are unfit to be both judges and parties, at the same time; yet, what are many of the most important acts of legislation, but so many judicial determinations, not indeed concerning the rights of single persons, but concerning the rights of large bodies of citizens; and what are the different classes of legislators, but advocates and parties to the causes which they determine? Is a law proposed concerning private debts? It is a question to which the creditors are parties on one side, and the debtors on the other. Justice ought to hold the balance between them. Yet the parties are and must be themselves the judges; and the most numerous party, or, in other words, the most powerful faction must be expected to prevail. Shall domestic manufactures be encouraged, and in what degree, by restrictions on foreign manufactures? are questions which would be differently decided by the landed and the manufacturing classes; and probably by neither, with a sole regard to justice and the public good. The apportionment of taxes on the various descriptions of property, is an act which seems to require the most exact impartiality; yet, there is perhaps no legislative act in which greater opportunity and temptation are given to a predominant party, to trample on the rules of justice. Every shilling with which they over-burden the inferior number, is a shilling saved to their own pockets.

It is in vain to say, that enlightened statesmen will be able to adjust these clashing interests, and render them all subservient to the public good. Enlightened statesmen will not always be at the helm: Nor, in many cases, can such an adjustment be made at all, without taking into view indirect and remote considerations, which will rarely prevail over the immediate interest which one party may find in disregarding the rights of another, or the good of the whole.

The inference to which we are brought, is, that the causes of faction cannot be removed; and that relief is only to be sought in the means of controling its effects.

If a faction consists of less than a majority, relief is supplied by the republican principle, which enables the majority to defeat its sinister views by regular vote: It may clog the administration, it may convulse the society; but it will be unable to execute and mask its violence under the forms of the Constitution. When a majority is included in a faction, the form of popular government on the other hand enables it to sacrifice to its ruling passion or interest, both the public good and the rights of other citizens. To secure the public good, and private rights, against the danger of such a faction, and at the same time to preserve the spirit and the form of popular government, is then the great object to which our enquiries are directed: Let me add that it is the great desideratum, by which alone this form of government can be rescued from the opprobrium under which it has so long labored, and be recommended to the esteem and adoption of mankind.

By what means is this object attainable? Evidently by one of two only. Either the existence of the same passion or interest in a majority at the same time, must be prevented; or the majority, having such co-existent passion or interest, must be rendered, by their number and local situation, unable to concert and carry into effect schemes of oppression. If the impulse and the opportunity be suffered to coincide, we well know that neither moral nor religious motives can be relied on as an adequate control. They are not found to be such on the injustice and violence of individuals, and lose their efficacy in proportion to the number combined together; that is, in proportion as their efficacy becomes needful.

From this view of the subject, it may be concluded, that a pure Democracy, by which I mean, a Society, consisting of a small number of citizens, who assemble and administer the Government in person, can admit of no cure for the mischiefs of faction. A common passion or interest will, in almost every case, be felt by a majority of the whole; a communication and concert results from the form of Government itself; and there is nothing to check the inducements to sacrifice the weaker party, or an obnoxious individual. Hence it is, that such Democracies have ever been spectacles of turbulence and contention; have ever been found incompatible with personal security, or the rights of property; and have in general been as short in their lives, as they have been violent in their deaths. Theoretic politicians, who have patronized this species of Government, have erroneously supposed, that by reducing mankind to a perfect equality in their political rights, they would, at the same time, be perfectly equalized and assimilated in their possessions, their opinions, and their passions.

A Republic, by which I mean a Government in which the scheme of representation takes place, opens a different prospect, and promises the cure for which we are seeking. Let us examine the points in which it varies from pure Democracy, and we shall comprehend both the nature of the cure and the efficacy which it must derive from the Union.

The two great points of difference between a democracy and a republic are: first, the delegation of the government, in the latter, to a small number of citizens elected by the rest; secondly, the greater number of citizens, and greater sphere of country, over which the latter may be extended.

The effect of the first difference is, on the one hand, to refine and enlarge the public views, by passing them through the medium of a chosen body of citizens, whose wisdom may best discern the true interest of their country, and whose patriotism and love of justice will be least likely to sacrifice it to temporary or partial considerations. Under such a regulation, it may well happen that the public voice, pronounced by the representatives of the people, will be more consonant to the public good than if pronounced by the people themselves, convened for the purpose. On the other hand, the effect may be inverted. Men of factious tempers, of local prejudices, or of sinister designs may, by intrigue, by corruption, or by other means, first obtain the suffrages, and then betray the interests, of the people. The question resulting is, whether small or extensive republics are more favorable to the election of proper guardians of the public weal; and it is clearly decided in favor of the latter by two obvious considerations:

In the first place, it is to be remarked that, however small the republic may be, the representatives must be raised to a certain number, in order to guard against the cabals of a few; and that, however large it may be, they must be limited to a certain number, in order to guard against the confusion of a multitude. Hence, the number of representatives in the two cases not being in proportion to that of the two constituents, and being proportionally greater in the small republic, it follows that, if the proportion of fit characters be not less in the large than in the small republic, the former will present a greater option, and consequently a greater probability of a fit choice.

In the next place, as each representative will be chosen by a greater number of citizens in the large than in the small republic, it will be more difficult for unworthy candidates to practice with success the vicious arts by which elections are too often carried and, the suffrages of the people being more free, will be more likely to center in men who possess the most attractive merit and the most diffusive and established characters.

It must be confessed that in this, as in most other cases, there is a mean, on both sides of which inconveniencies will be found to lie. By enlarging too much the number of electors, you render the representative too little acquainted with all their local circumstances and lesser interests; as by reducing it too much, you render him unduly attached to these, and too little fit to comprehend and pursue great and national objects. The Federal Constitution forms a happy combination in this respect; the great and aggregate interests being re-

ferred to the national, the local and particular, to the state legislatures.

The other point of difference is, the greater number of citizens
and extent of territory which may be brought within the compass
of Republican, than of Democratic Government; and it is this circumstance principally which renders factious combinations less to
be dreaded in the former, than in the latter. The smaller the society,
the fewer probably will be the distinct parties and interests composing it; the fewer the distinct parties and interests, the more frequently will a majority be found of the same party; and the smaller
the number of individuals composing a majority, and the smaller
the compass within which they are placed, the more easily will they
concert and execute their plans of oppression. Extend the sphere,
and you take in a greater variety of parties and interests; you make it
less probable that a majority of the whole will have a common motive to invade the rights of other citizens; or if such a common
motive exists, it will be more difficult for all who feel it to discover
their own strength, and to act in unison with each other. Besides
other impediments, it may be remarked, that where there is a con-
sciousness of unjust or dishonorable purposes, communication is
always checked by distrust, in proportion to the number whose concurrence is necessary.

Hence it clearly appears, that the same advantage, which a Republic has over a Democracy, in controling the effects of faction, is
enjoyed by a large over a small Republic—is enjoyed by the Union
over the States composing it. Does this advantage consist in the
substitution of Representatives, whose enlightened views and virtuous sentiments render them superior to local prejudices, and to
schemes of injustice? It will not be denied, that the Representation
of the Union will be most likely to possess these requisite endowments. Does it consist in the greater security afforded by a greater
variety of parties, against the event of any one party being able to
outnumber and oppress the rest? In an equal degree does the en-
creased variety of parties, comprised within the Union, encrease this
security. Does it, in fine, consist in the greater obstacles opposed to
the concert and accomplishment of the secret wishes of an unjust
and interested majority? Here, again, the extent of the Union gives
it the most palpable advantage.

The influence of factious leaders may kindle a flame within their
particular States, but will be unable to spread a general conflagration

through the other States: a religious sect, may degenerate into a political faction in a part of the Confederacy; but the variety of sects dispersed over the entire face of it, must secure the national Councils against any danger from that source: a rage for paper money, for an abolition of debts, for an equal division of property, or for any other improper or wicked project, will be less apt to pervade the whole body of the Union, than a particular member of it; in the same proportion as such a malady is more likely to taint a particular county or district, than an entire state.

In the extent and proper structure of the Union, therefore, we behold a Republican remedy for the diseases most incident to Republican Government. And according to the degree of pleasure and pride, we feel in being Republicans, ought to be our zeal in cherishing the spirit, and supporting the character of Federalists.

41. Reasons for the Dissent of the Anti-Federalist Minority in Pennsylvania, December 18, 1787 (opposing ratification)

. . . We dissent, first, because it is the opinion of the most celebrated writers on government, and confirmed by uniform experience, that a very extensive territory cannot be governed on the principles of freedom, otherwise than by a confederation of republics, possessing all the powers of internal government, but united in the management of their general and foreign concerns. . . .

We dissent, secondly, because the powers vested in Congress by this constitution, must necessarily annihilate and absorb the legislative, executive, and judicial powers of the several States, and produce from their ruins one consolidated government, which from the nature of things will be an *iron handed despotism*, as nothing short of the supremacy of despotic sway could connect and govern these United States under one government.

As the truth of this position is of such decisive importance, it ought to be fully investigated, and if it is founded to be clearly as-

SOURCE: McMaster and Stone, *Pennsylvania and the Federal Constitution*, pp. 464–483.

certained; for, should it be demonstrated that the powers vested by this constitution in Congress will have such an effect as necessarily to produce one consolidated government, the question then will be reduced to this short issue, viz.: whether satiated with the blessings of liberty, whether repenting of the folly of so recently asserting their unalienable rights against foreign despots at the expense of so much blood and treasure, and such painful and arduous struggles, the people of America are now willing to resign every privilege of freemen, and submit to the dominion of an absolute government that will embrace all America in one chain of despotism; or whether they will, with virtuous indignation, spurn at the shackles prepared for them, and confirm their liberties by a conduct becoming freemen.

That the new government will not be a confederacy of States, as it ought, but one consolidated government, founded upon the destruction of the several governments of the States, we shall now show.

The powers of Congress under the new constitution are complete and unlimited over the *purse* and the *sword*, and are perfectly independent of and supreme over the State governments, whose intervention in these great points is entirely destroyed. By virtue of their power of taxation, Congress may command the whole or any part of the property of the people. They may impose what imposts upon commerce, they may impose what land taxes, poll taxes, excises, duties on all written instruments and duties on every other article, that they may judge proper; in short, every species of taxation, whether of an external or internal nature, is comprised in section the eighth of article the first, viz.:

"The Congress shall have power to lay and collect taxes, duties, imposts, and excises, to pay the debts, and provide for the common defence and general welfare of the United States."

As there is no one article of taxation reserved to the State governments, the Congress may monopolize every source of revenue, and thus indirectly demolish the State governments, for without funds they could not exist; the taxes, duties and excises imposed by Congress may be so high as to render it impracticable to levy farther sums on the same articles; but whether this should be the case or not, if the State governments should presume to impose taxes, duties or excises on the same articles with Congress, the latter may abrogate and repeal the laws whereby they are imposed, upon the allegation that they interfere with the due collection of their taxes, duties or excises, by virtue of the following clause, part of section eighth, article first, viz.:

"To make all laws which shall be necessary and proper for carrying into execution the foregoing powers, and all other powers vested by this constitution in the government of the United States, or in any department or officer thereof."

The Congress might gloss over this conduct by construing every purpose for which the State legislatures now lay taxes, to be for the "*general welfare*," and therefore as of their jurisdiction.

And the supremacy of the laws of the United States is established by article sixth, viz.: "That this constitution and the laws of the United States which shall be made in pursuance thereof, and *all treaties* made, or which shall be made under the authority of the United States, shall be the *supreme law* of the *land; and the judges in every State shall be bound thereby; anything in the constitution or laws of any State to the contrary notwithstanding*." It has been alleged that the words "pursuant to the constitution," are a restriction upon the authority of Congress; but when it is considered that by other sections they are invested with every efficient power of government, and which may be exercised to the absolute destruction of the State governments, without any violation of even the forms of the constitution, this seeming restriction, as well as every other restriction in it, appears to us to be nugatory and delusive; and only introduced as a blind upon the real nature of the government. In our opinion, "pursuant to the constitution" will be co-extensive with the *will* and *pleasure* of Congress, which, indeed, will be the only limitation of their powers.

We apprehend that two co-ordinate sovereignties would be a solecism in politics; that, therefore, as there is no line of distinction drawn between the general and State governments, as the sphere of their jurisdiction is undefined, it would be contrary to the nature of things that both should exist together—one or the other would necessarily triumph in the fulness of dominion. However, the contest could not be of long continuance, as the State governments are divested of every means of defence, and will be obliged by "the supreme law of the land" *to yield at discretion*.

It has been objected to this total destruction of the State governments that the existence of their legislatures is made essential to the organization of Congress; that they must assemble for the appointment of the senators and President-general of the United States. True, the State legislatures may be continued for some years, as boards of appointment merely, after they are divested of every other function; but the framers of the constitution, foreseeing that the people will soon become disgusted with this solemn mockery of a government without power and usefulness, have made a provision for relieving them from the imposition in section fourth of article first, viz.: "The times, places and manner of holding elections for senators and representatives shall be prescribed in each State by the legislature thereof; but the Congress may at any time by law make or alter such regulations, except as to the place of choosing senators."

As Congress have the control over the time of the appointment of the President-general, of the senators and of the representatives of the United States, they may prolong their existence in office for life by postponing the time of their election and appointment from period to period under various pretences, such as an apprehension of invasion, the factious disposition of the people, or any other plausible pretence that the occasion may suggest; and having thus obtained life-estates in the government, they may fill up the vacancies themselves by their control over the mode of appointment; with this exception in regard to the senators that as the place of appointment for them must, by the constitution, be in the particular State, they may depute some body in the respective States, to fill up the vacancies in the senate, occasioned by death, until they can venture to assume it themselves. . . .

The new Constitution, consistently with the plan of consolidation, contains no reservation of the rights and privileges of the State governments, which was made in the confederation of the year 1778, by article the 2d, viz.: "That each State retains its sovereignty, freedom and independence, and every power, jurisdiction and right which is not by this confederation expressly delegated to the United States in Congress assembled."

The legislative power vested in Congress by the foregoing recited sections, is so unlimited in its nature, may be so comprehensive and boundless in its exercise, that this alone would be amply sufficient to annihilate the State governments, and swallow them up in the grand vortex of general empire.

The judicial powers vested in Congress are also so various and extensive, that by legal ingenuity they may be extended to every

case, and thus absorb the State judiciaries; and when we consider
the decisive influence that a general judiciary would have over the
civil polity of the several States, we do not hesitate to pronounce
that this power, unaided by the legislative, would effect a consolidation of the States under one government. . . .

In short, consolidation pervades the whole constitution. It begins
with an annunciation that such was the intention. The main pillars
of the fabric correspond with it, and the concluding paragraph is a
confirmation of it. The preamble begins with the words, "We the
people of the United States," which is the style of a compact between individuals entering into a state of society, and not that of a
confederation of States. . . .

We dissent, thirdly, because if it were practicable to govern so
extensive a territory as these United States include, on the plan of
a consolidated government, consistent with the principles of liberty
and the happiness of the people, yet the construction of this Constitution is not calculated to attain the object; for independent of
the nature of the case, it would of itself necessarily produce a despotism, and that not by the usual gradations, but with the celerity
that has hitherto only attended revolutions effected by the sword.

To establish the truth of this position, a cursory investigation of
the principles and form of this constitution will suffice.

The first consideration that this review suggests, is the omission
of a BILL OF RIGHTS ascertaining and fundamentally establishing
those unalienable and personal rights of men, without the full, free
and secure enjoyment of which there can be no liberty, and over
which it is not necessary for a good government to have the control
—the principal of which are the rights of conscience, personal liberty by the clear and unequivocal establishment of the writ of *habeas corpus*, jury trial in criminal and civil cases, by an impartial
jury of the vicinage or county, with the common law proceedings
for the safety of the accused in criminal prosecutions; and the liberty of the press, that scourge of tyrants, and the grand bulwark of
every other liberty and privilege. The stipulations heretofore made
in favor of them in the State constitutions, are entirely superseded
by this Constitution.

The legislature of a free country should be so formed as to have a
competent knowledge of its constituents, and enjoy their confidence. To produce these essential requisites, the representation
ought to be fair, equal and sufficiently numerous to possess the

same interests, feelings, opinions and views which the people themselves would possess, were they all assembled; and so numerous as to prevent bribery and undue influence, and so responsible to the people, by frequent and fair elections, as to prevent their neglecting or sacrificing the views and interests of their constituents to their own pursuits.

We will now bring the legislature under this Constitution to the test of the foregoing principles, which will demonstrate that it is deficient in every essential quality of a just and safe representation.

The House of Representatives is to consist of sixty-five members; that is one for about every 50,000 inhabitants, to be chosen every two years. Thirty-three members will form a quorum for doing business, and seventeen of these, being the majority, determine the sense of the house.

The Senate, the other constituent branch of the legislature, consists of twenty-six members, being two from each State, appointed by their legislatures every six years; fourteen senators make a quorum —the majority of whom, eight, determines the sense of that body, except in judging on impeachments, or in making treaties, or in expelling a member, when two-thirds of the senators present must concur.

The president is to have the control over the enacting of laws, so far as to make the concurrence of two-thirds of the representatives and senators present necessary, if he should object to the laws. . . .

The representation is moreover inadequate and unsafe, because of the long terms for which it is appointed, and the mode of its appointment, by which Congress may not only control the choice of the people, but may so manage as to divest the people of this fundamental right, and become self-elected. . . .

The next consideration that the constitution presents, is the undue and dangerous mixture of the powers of government; the same body possessing legislative, executive and judicial powers. The Senate is a constituent branch of the legislature, it has judicial power in judging on impeachments, and in this case unites in some measure the characters of judge and party, as all the principal officers are appointed by the president-general, with the concurrence of the Senate, and therefore they derive their offices in part from the Senate. This may bias the judgments of the senators, and tend to screen great delinquents from punishment. And the Senate has, moreover, various and great executive powers, viz., in concurrence with the president-general, they form treaties with foreign nations, that may control and abrogate the constitutions and laws of the several States. Indeed, there is no power, privilege or liberty of the State governments, or of the people, but what may be affected by virtue of this power. For all treaties, made by them, are to be the "supreme law of the land; anything in the constitution or laws of any State, to the contrary notwithstanding. . . ."

We have before considered internal taxation as it would effect the destruction of the State governments, and produce one consolidated government. We will now consider that subject as it affects the personal concerns of the people.

The power of direct taxation applies to every individual, as Congress, under this government, is expressly vested with the authority of laying a capitation or poll tax upon every person to any amount. This is a tax that, however oppressive in its nature, and unequal in its operation, is certain as to its produce and simple in its collection; it cannot be evaded like the objects of imposts or excise, and will be paid, because all that a man hath will he give for his head. This tax is so congenial to the nature of despotism, that it has ever been a favorite under such governments. Some of those who were in the late general convention from this State, have labored to introduce a poll tax among us.

The power of direct taxation will further apply to every individual, as Congress may tax land, cattle, trades, occupations, etc., to any amount, and every object of internal taxation is of that nature that however oppressive, the people will have but this alternative, either to pay the tax or let their property be taken, for all resistance will be vain. The standing army and select militia would enforce the collection.

For the moderate exercise of this power, there is no control left in the State governments, whose intervention is destroyed. No relief, or redress of grievances, can be extended as heretofore by them. There is not even a declaration of RIGHTS to which the people may appeal for the vindication of their wrongs in the court of justice. They must therefore, implicitly obey the most arbitrary laws, as the most of them will be pursuant to the principles and form of the constitution, and that strongest of all checks upon the conduct of administration, *responsibility to the people*, will not exist in this government. The permanency of the appointments of senators and representatives, and the control the congress have over their election, will place them independent of the sentiments and resentment of the people, and the administration having a greater interest in the government than in the community, there will be no consideration to restrain them from oppression and tyranny. In the government of this State, under the old confederation, the members of the legislature are taken from among the people, and their interests and welfare are so inseparably connected with those of their constituents, that they can derive no advantage from oppressive laws and taxes; for they would suffer in common with their fellow-citizens, would participate in the burthens they impose on the community, as they must return to the common level, after a short period; and notwithstanding every exertion of influence, every means of corruption, a necessary rotation excludes them from permanency in the legislature. . . .

A standing army in the hands of a government placed so independent of the people, may be made a fatal instrument to overturn the public liberties; it may be employed to enforce the collection of the most oppressive taxes, and to carry into execution the most arbitrary measures. An ambitious man who may have the army at his devotion, may step up into the throne, and seize upon absolute power.

The absolute unqualified command that Congress have over the militia may be made instrumental to the destruction of all liberty, both public and private; whether of a personal, civil or religious nature.

First, the personal liberty of every man, probably from sixteen to sixty years of age, may be destroyed by the power Congress have in organizing and governing of the militia. As militia they may be subjected to fines to any amount, levied in a military manner; they may be subjected to corporal punishments of the most disgraceful and humiliating kind; and to death itself, by the sentence of a court martial. To this our young men will be more immediately subjected, as a select militia, composed of them, will best answer the purposes of government.

Secondly, the rights of conscience may be violated, as there is no exemption of those persons who are conscientiously scrupulous of bearing arms. These compose a respectable proportion of the community in the State. This is the more remarkable, because even when the distresses of the late war, and the evident disaffection of many citizens of that description, inflamed our passions, and when every person who was obliged to risk his own life, must have been exasperated against such as on any account kept back from the common danger, yet even then, when outrage and violence might have been expected, the rights of conscience were held sacred.

At this momentous crisis, the framers of our State Constitution made the most express and decided declaration and stipulations in favor of the rights of conscience; but now, when no necessity exists, those dearest rights of men are left insecure.

Thirdly, the absolute command of Congress over the militia may be destructive of public liberty; for under the guidance of an arbitrary government, they may be made the unwilling instruments of tyranny. The militia of Pennsylvania may be marched to New England or Virginia to quell an insurrection occasioned by the most galling oppression, and aided by the standing army, they will no doubt be successful in subduing their liberty and independency; but in so doing, although the magnanimity of their minds will be extinguished, yet the meaner passions of resentment and revenge will be increased, and these in turn will be the ready and obedient instruments of despotism to enslave the others; and that with an irritated vengeance. Thus may the militia be made the instruments of crushing the last efforts of expiring liberty, of riveting the chains of despotism on their fellow-citizens, and on one another. This power can be exercised not only without violating the Constitution, but in strict conformity with it; it is calculated for this express purpose, and will doubtless be executed accordingly. . . .

We have not noticed the smaller, nor many of the considerable blemishes, but have confined our objections to the great and essential defects, the main pillars of the constitution; which we have shown to be inconsistent with the liberty and happiness of the people, as its establishment will annihilate the State governments, and produce one consolidated government that will eventually and speedily issue in the supremacy of despotism. . . .

42. The Bill of Rights, 1789–1791

Because of widespread demands made during the contest over ratification, friends of the Constitution, led by James Madison, moved swiftly to draft a bill of rights. In September 1789 Congress approved twelve proposed amendments and submitted them to the states for ratification. The first two were never ratified; the other ten, known as the Bill of Rights, became part of the Constitution on December 15, 1791.

A. Rejected Proposals

Article the first . . . After the first enumeration required by the first Article of the Constitution, there shall be one Representative for every thirty thousand, until the number shall amount to one hundred, after which, the proportion shall be so regulated by Congress, that there shall be not less than one hundred Representatives, nor less than one Representative for every forty thousand persons, until the number of Representatives shall amount to two hundred, after which the proportion shall be so regulated by Congress, that there shall not be less than two hundred Representatives, nor more than one Representative for every fifty thousand persons.

Article the second . . . No law, varying the compensation for the services of the Senators and Representatives, shall take effect, until an election of Representatives shall have intervened.

B. The Bill of Rights

ARTICLE I

Congress shall make no law respecting an establishment of religion, or prohibiting the free exercise thereof; or abridging the freedom of speech, or of the press; or the right of the people peaceably to assemble, and to petition the Government for a redress of grievances.

ARTICLE II

A well regulated Militia, being necessary to the security of a free State, the right of the people to keep and bear Arms, shall not be infringed.

SOURCE: Winton U. Solberg, ed., *The Federal Convention and the Formation of the Union of the American States* (New York, 1958), 376ff.

Article III

No Soldier shall, in time of peace be quartered in any house, without the consent of the Owner, nor in time of war, but in a manner to be prescribed by law.

Article IV

The right of the people to be secure in their persons, houses, papers, and effects, against unreasonable searches and seizures, shall not be violated, and no Warrants shall issue, but upon probable cause, supported by Oath or affirmation, and particularly describing the place to be searched, and the persons or things to be seized.

Article V

No person shall be held to answer for a capital, or otherwise infamous crime, unless on a presentment or indictment of a Grand Jury, except in cases arising in the land or naval forces, or in the Militia, when in actual service in time of War or public danger; nor shall any person be subject for the same offence to be twice put in jeopardy of life or limb; nor shall be compelled in any criminal case to be a witness against himself, nor be deprived of life, liberty, or property, without due process of law; nor shall private property be taken for public use, without just compensation.

Article VI

In all criminal prosecutions, the accused shall enjoy the right to a speedy and public trial, by an impartial jury of the State and district wherein the crime shall have been committed, which district shall have been previously ascertained by law, and to be informed of the nature and cause of the accusation; to be confronted with the witnesses against him; to have compulsory process for obtaining witnesses in his favor, and to have the Assistance of Counsel for his defence.

Article VII

In Suits at common law, where the value in controversy shall exceed twenty dollars, the right of trial by jury shall be preserved, and no fact tried by a jury, shall be otherwise re-examined in any Court of the United States, than according to the rules of the common law.

Article VIII

Excessive bail shall not be required, nor excessive fines imposed, nor cruel and unusual punishments inflicted.

Article IX

The enumeration in the Constitution, of certain rights, shall not be construed to deny or disparage others retained by the people.

Article X

The powers not delegated to the United States by the Constitution, nor prohibited by it to the States, are reserved to the States respectively, or to the people.

University of Tulsa
McFarlin Library
Tulsa, Okla.